Collins

Cambridge Lower Secondary
Science

STAGE 9: STUDENT'S BOOK

Mark Levesley, Aidan Gill, Gemma Young,
Sheila Tarpey, Beverly Rickwood, Nigel Saunders

Collins

William Collins' dream of knowledge for all began with the publication of his first book in 1819. A self-educated mill worker, he not only enriched millions of lives, but also founded a flourishing publishing house. Today, staying true to this spirit, Collins books are packed with inspiration, innovation and practical expertise. They place you at the centre of a world of possibility and give you exactly what you need to explore it.

Collins. Freedom to teach.

Published by Collins
An imprint of HarperCollins*Publishers*
The News Building
1 London Bridge Street
London
SE1 9GF

HarperCollins*Publishers*
Macken House, 39/40 Mayor Street Upper,
Dublin 1, D01 C9W8, Ireland

Browse the complete Collins catalogue at
www.collins.co.uk

© HarperCollins*Publishers* Limited 2021

10 9 8 7 6 5 4

ISBN 978-0-00-836427-4

MIX
Paper | Supporting responsible forestry
FSC™ C007454

This book is produced from independently certified FSC™ paper to ensure responsible forest management.

For more information visit:
www.harpercollins.co.uk/green

All rights reserved. No part of this publication may be reproduced, stored in a retrieval system, or transmitted in any form by any means, electronic, mechanical, photocopying, recording or otherwise, without the prior written permission of the Publisher or a licence permitting restricted copying in the United Kingdom issued by the Copyright Licensing Agency Ltd, 5th Floor, Shackleton House, 4 Battle Bridge Lane, London SE1 2HX.

British Library Cataloguing-in-Publication Data
A catalogue record for this publication is available from the British Library.

Updating authors: Mark Levesley, Aidan Gill, Gemma Young, Sheila Tarpey, Beverly Rickwood, Nigel Saunders
Contributing authors: Lucy Hawkins, Fran Eardley, Chris Meunier
Development editors: Anna Clark, Julie Thornton, Rose Parkin, Gillian Lindsey, Tony Wayte, Fiona McDonald, Sarah Binns
Product manager: Joanna Ramsay
Content editor: Tina Pietron
Project manager: Amanda Harman
Copyeditor: Debbie Oliver
Proofreader: Jan Schubert
Safety checker: Joe Jefferies
Indexer: Jackie Butterley
Illustrator: Jouve India Private Limited
Cover designer: Gordon MacGilp
Cover artwork: Maria Herbert-Liew
Internal designer: Jouve India Private Limited
Typesetter: Jouve India Private Limited
Production controller: Lyndsey Rogers
Printed and bound in India by Replika Press Pvt. Ltd.

The publishers gratefully acknowledge the permission granted to reproduce the copyright material in this book. Every effort has been made to trace copyright holders and to obtain their permission for the use of copyright material. The publishers will gladly receive any information enabling them to rectify any error or omission at the first opportunity.

Cambridge International copyright material in this publication is reproduced under licence and remains the intellectual property of Cambridge Assessment International Education.

End of chapter questions and sample answers have been written by the authors. These may not fully reflect the approach of Cambridge Assessment International Education.

Contents

How to use this book   v

Chapter 1 • Photosynthesis and plant growth

1.1 Photosynthesis   3
1.2 Transport of water and mineral salts in plants   12
End of chapter review   21

Chapter 2 • The excretory system

2.1 Producing urine   26
End of chapter review   31

Chapter 3 • Variation and inheritance

3.1 Variation within a species   34
3.2 Chromosomes, genes and DNA   41
3.3 Fertilisation and inheritance   44
3.4 Fetal growth and development   50
3.5 Natural selection   55
End of chapter review   62

Chapter 4 • Population change

4.1 Populations and extinction   67
End of chapter review   75
End of stage review   77

Chapter 5 • The Periodic Table

5.1 Atomic structure and the Periodic Table   82
5.2 Trends in the Periodic Table   87
End of chapter review   90

Chapter 6 • Structure, bonding and the properties of matter

6.1 Chemical bonds   93
6.2 Simple and giant structures   98
6.3 Density   103
End of chapter review   107

Chapter 7 • Chemical changes

7.1 Changes in chemical reactions   109
7.2 Word and symbol equations   114
7.3 Methods for making salts   118
7.4 Displacement reactions   124
7.5 Rates of reaction   128
End of chapter review   135
End of stage review   138

Chapter 8 • Energy

8.1 Energy conservation   142
8.2 Heating and cooling   148
8.3 Conduction, convection, radiation and evaporation   152
End of chapter review   161

Chapter 9 • Forces

9.1 Floating and sinking	165	End of chapter review ... 173

Chapter 10 • Electricity

10.1 Voltage and resistance 176 End of chapter review 190
10.2 Measuring current and voltage in series and parallel circuits 184

Chapter 11 • Sound

11.1 Loudness and pitch 193 End of chapter review 205
11.2 Interference 200 End of stage review 207

Chapter 12 • Plate tectonics

12.1 Evidence for plate tectonics 211 End of chapter review 228
12.2 Explaining plate movement 224

Chapter 13 • Climate change

13.1 The carbon cycle 232 End of chapter review 248
13.2 Impacts of climate change 240

Chapter 14 • Astronomy

14.1 Collisions 252 End of chapter review 266
14.2 Observing the Universe 262 End of stage review 270

Periodic Table 272
Glossary 273
Index 280
Acknowledgements 284

How to use this book

This book is designed to challenge you to go beyond the content you need to learn on your course. Have a go at the questions in dark green, blue, orange and purple to challenge yourself, and read more about the scientific world in the discovering sections.

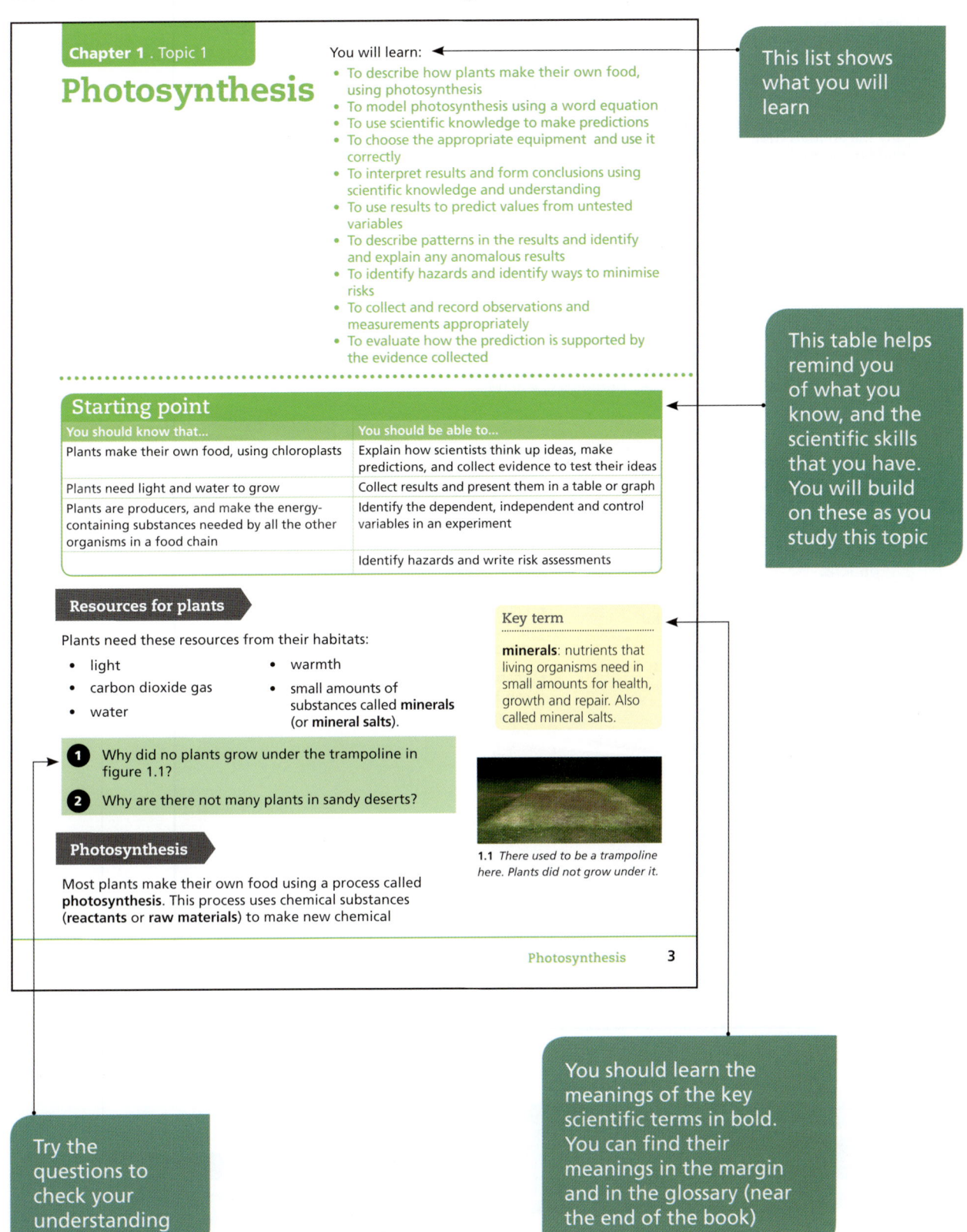

Chapter 1 . Topic 1

Photosynthesis

You will learn:
- To describe how plants make their own food, using photosynthesis
- To model photosynthesis using a word equation
- To use scientific knowledge to make predictions
- To choose the appropriate equipment and use it correctly
- To interpret results and form conclusions using scientific knowledge and understanding
- To use results to predict values from untested variables
- To describe patterns in the results and identify and explain any anomalous results
- To identify hazards and identify ways to minimise risks
- To collect and record observations and measurements appropriately
- To evaluate how the prediction is supported by the evidence collected

This list shows what you will learn

Starting point

You should know that...	You should be able to...
Plants make their own food, using chloroplasts	Explain how scientists think up ideas, make predictions, and collect evidence to test their ideas
Plants need light and water to grow	Collect results and present them in a table or graph
Plants are producers, and make the energy-containing substances needed by all the other organisms in a food chain	Identify the dependent, independent and control variables in an experiment
	Identify hazards and write risk assessments

This table helps remind you of what you know, and the scientific skills that you have. You will build on these as you study this topic

Resources for plants

Plants need these resources from their habitats:
- light
- carbon dioxide gas
- water
- warmth
- small amounts of substances called **minerals** (or **mineral salts**).

Key term

minerals: nutrients that living organisms need in small amounts for health, growth and repair. Also called mineral salts.

1. Why did no plants grow under the trampoline in figure 1.1?
2. Why are there not many plants in sandy deserts?

Try the questions to check your understanding

1.1 There used to be a trampoline here. Plants did not grow under it.

Photosynthesis

Most plants make their own food using a process called **photosynthesis**. This process uses chemical substances (**reactants** or **raw materials**) to make new chemical

You should learn the meanings of the key scientific terms in bold. You can find their meanings in the margin and in the glossary (near the end of the book)

Photosynthesis 3

v

Science in context: Coral reef bleaching

Some types of environmental variation are used to monitor changes in the conditions in habitats. For example, coral reefs are made by tiny sea animals that build hard structures in which they live. Corals come in many different colours. However, if the sea becomes warmer, more of the corals become white rather than coloured. Global warming is making some areas of sea warmer than usual.

3.11 *Warmer temperatures have caused this coral to turn white (or 'bleach').*

Making links

In Stage 7 Topic 4.2 Chemistry you may have learned about indicators. In what way are the hydrangeas in figure 3.9 similar to litmus, and in what way are they different?

14 Discuss how observing the coral for any colour changes can help scientists with their research into the global environmental impact of global warming.

Key facts:

✔ Data that shows continuous variation may have any value (within a range).
✔ Data that shows discontinuous variation has a limited number of options.
✔ Variation that is caused by environmental factors is environmental variation.
✔ Variation that an organism gets from its parents is inherited variation.

Check your skills progress:

- I can identify the range of a set of data.
- I can divide data into smaller groups of equal size.
- I can design and use a tally chart to help count items.
- I can select and draw the correct type of bar chart to show my continuous and discontinuous data.
- I can suggest further investigations that can be done based on conclusions from an investigation.

Variation and inheritance

Discover more about where scientific ideas have come from and how they are used around the world now

Try the link questions to strengthen your understanding across topics.

3.2

4 Look at the box about discovering DNA.
  a) Which scientists were involved in the discovery of the structure of DNA?
  b) What was their main research question?
  c) Describe *one* piece of evidence that Watson and Crick used.
  d) Why is it important to collect plenty of evidence when conducting an investigation?
  e) Along with other scientists' results, what did Watson and Crick use to help them develop their structure for DNA?

5 Draw or make a model to explain where genes are found in a cell nucleus.

Making links

In Chemistry you may have met many different types of molecules. Name one molecule you have met and explain why it is a molecule. Give *one* way in which your chosen molecule is the same as DNA, and *one* way in which it differs.

Challenge yourself with these questions in dark green, blue, orange and purple

Activity 3.3: Researching work on genes

Extension For this activity, use secondary sources to research your answers. First identify some suitable sources of information. Then extract the relevant information needed to answer the questions. Try to put your answers in your own words, and avoid copying out large chunks of information that is not relevant.

The Human Genome Project ran from 1990 to 2003 and involved scientists from all over the world.

A1 What did the project want to discover about genes?
A2 The Human Genome Project involved many different people. How was it possible to use so many different people, and why is this an advantage?
A3 What were the findings of the Human Genome Project?
A4 What are some benefits of having this information?

Try out the science for yourself with step-by-step activities

Key facts:
- ✓ DNA is the genetic material that carries information determining how individual plants and animals develop.
- ✓ Chromosomes are found in the nucleus of the cell and contain DNA.
- ✓ Genes are sections of DNA that control the development of a specific characteristic and so control an organism's inherited variation.

Check your skills progress:
- I can explain the use of models.
- I can extract relevant and precise information from secondary sources.

Chromosomes, genes and DNA

Check your mastery of key ideas and skills with this list

> This section helps you check that you understand the scientific ideas and can apply them to new situations

End of chapter review

Quick questions

1. The loss of water through the stomata of the leaves on a plant, is called:
   a translocation
   b transport
   c transpiration
   d transcription

2. Which *two* substances in the list below does a plant need for photosynthesis?
   a oxygen
   b carbon dioxide
   c water
   d glucose

3. What gas does a plant make as a product of photosynthesis?

4. Where in the plant in figure 1.20 does most photosynthesis take place? Choose *one* letter.

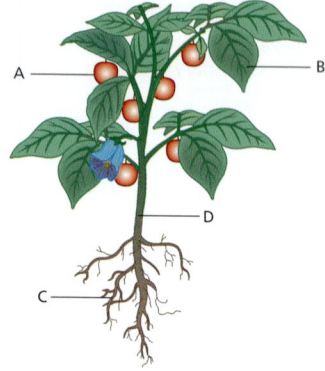

1.20

5. Why do plants need nitrogen?
   a to make sugars
   b to make proteins
   c to make fats
   d for respiration

End of stage review

1. (a) A student measured the lengths of some leaves on one type of plant. The student measured the leaves in centimetres (cm) using a ruler.

   10.8 11.0 10.5 12.6 11.7

   12.7 10.2 12.9 12.5 12.0

   12.2 11.9 10.1 11.2 12.6

   11.0 11.7 11.9 12.8 12.1

   11.7 10.8 11.4 11.3 12.0

   (i) Name the type of variation shown by this data.

   (ii) Copy and complete this tally chart for the data.

Grouped lengths of leaves (cm)	Tally	Total
10.1 – 10.5		
10.6 – 11.0		
11.1 – 11.5		
11.6 – 12.0		
12.1 – 12.5		
12.6 – 13.0		

   (iii) Suggest what type of chart or graph you would use to present the data from your tally chart.

   (b) (i) Plants use leaves for photosynthesis. Copy and complete this word equation for photosynthesis.

   carbon dioxide + water → glucose + _____

   (ii) Which *one* of the following words best describes what type of substance glucose is?

   amino acid   carbohydrate   fat   protein

   (iii) Photosynthesis requires chlorophyll. Give the name of the element gained from mineral salts that plants need to make chlorophyll.

At the end of the stage, try the end of stage review! This contains questions on all the chapters.

Glossary

absorb: to take in or soak up; to take in energy.

adaptation: characteristic of an organism that helps it to survive in a certain ecosystem.

aerobic respiration: respiration that requires oxygen to release energy from glucose.

alkali: a base that is soluble.

alkaline solution: a solution formed when a base dissolves in water.

amplitude: the maximum height of the wave, from the centre to the top or bottom.

anomalous: result that is very different from what you expect based on other results, perhaps because you made a mistake while recording it or something unexpected happened.

balanced forces: when the resultant force is zero.

basalt: a type of rock that contains quantities of minerals that can be magnetised.

base: a compound that can react with an acid and neutralise it.

bladder: organ that stores urine.

blood vessels: tube-shaped organs that carry blood around the body.

capture hypothesis: the idea that the Moon is a large asteroid that has been pulled into orbit around the Earth.

carbohydrate: nutrient needed for energy. Examples include starch and sugars (such as glucose).

chemical property: a property that is seen when a substance takes part in a chemical change.

chemical reaction: change in which new substances are produced.

chlorophyll: green substance that absorbs light, to get energy for photosynthesis.

chloroplast: green part of a cell that contains chlorophyll.

chromosome: structure containing a molecule of DNA, which carries genetic information in genes.

coastline: outside edge of a continent, where rock meets the ocean.

co-formation hypothesis: the idea that the Moon and Earth formed together, close to each other, at the same time.

collision hypothesis: the idea that a large object roughly the same size and mass as the planet Mars collided with the Earth, releasing rocks that were pulled together to form the Moon.

combustion: chemical reaction between a substance and oxygen, which transfers energy as heat and light.

compound: substance made from elements.

concentration: a measurement of how many particles of a certain type there are in a volume of liquid or gas.

conduction: form of heat transfer in which thermal energy passes through a substance from particle to particle. Conduction occurs mainly in solids.

conservation of energy: energy cannot be created or destroyed. The total amount of energy is constant.

constructive interference: this happens when two or more waves are added together to make a bigger wave.

continuous variation: variation that can have any value within a range.

convection: form of thermal transfer in which thermal energy causes a substance to expand and rise. This then cools and sinks. Convection only occurs in gases and liquids.

convection current: the movement of particles in a fluid due to convection.

covalent bond: a bond made when a pair of electrons is shared by two atoms.

You can look up definitions for key terms in the glossary

Biology

Chapter 1: Photosynthesis and plant growth
1.1: Photosynthesis — 3
1.2: Transport of water and mineral salts in plants — 12
End of chapter review — 21

Chapter 2: The excretory system
2.1: Producing urine — 26
End of chapter review — 31

Chapter 3: Variation and inheritance
3.1: Variation within a species — 34
3.2: Chromosomes, genes and DNA — 41
3.3: Fertilisation and inheritance — 44
3.4: Fetal growth and development — 50
3.5: Natural selection — 55
End of chapter review — 62

Chapter 4: Population change
4.1: Populations and extinction — 67
End of chapter review — 75
End of stage review — 77

Chapter 1
Photosynthesis and plant growth

What's it all about?

There are approximately 391 000 different species of plants. The forests that they create cover over 30% of our planet.

Plants come in all shapes and sizes – from giant *Sequoia* trees (pictured here) that reach over 80 m high, to tiny *Wolffia* plants that are less than 2 mm tall.

You will learn about:
- What plants need, in order to photosynthesise
- What happens to the products of photosynthesis
- How plants take in and use water and minerals
- How water and mineral salts flow through a plant

You will build your skills in:
- Developing testable hypotheses
- Planning investigations based on previous knowledge and research
- Collecting reliable results
- Identifying and explaining anomalous results
- Deciding whether to use your own results or those of others
- Describing the use of science in society, industry and research
- Evaluating issues using scientific understanding
- Describing the use of scientific understanding by individuals and groups working together
- Discussing the global environmental impacts of some uses of science

Chapter 1 . Topic 1

Photosynthesis

You will learn:
- To describe how plants make their own food, using photosynthesis
- To model photosynthesis using a word equation
- To use scientific knowledge to make predictions
- To choose the appropriate equipment and use it correctly
- To interpret results and form conclusions using scientific knowledge and understanding
- To use results to predict values from untested variables
- To describe patterns in the results and identify and explain any anomalous results
- To identify hazards and identify ways to minimise risks
- To collect and record observations and measurements appropriately
- To evaluate how the prediction is supported by the evidence collected

Starting point

You should know that...	You should be able to...
Plants make their own food, using chloroplasts	Explain how scientists think up ideas, make predictions, and collect evidence to test their ideas
Plants need light and water to grow	Collect results and present them in a table or graph
Plants are producers, and make the energy-containing substances needed by all the other organisms in a food chain	Identify the dependent, independent and control variables in an experiment
	Identify hazards and write risk assessments

Resources for plants

Plants need these resources from their habitats:
- light
- carbon dioxide gas
- water
- warmth
- small amounts of substances called **minerals** (or **mineral salts**).

> **Key term**
>
> **minerals**: nutrients that living organisms need in small amounts for health, growth and repair. Also called mineral salts.

1. Why did no plants grow under the trampoline in figure 1.1?
2. Why are there not many plants in sandy deserts?

1.1 There used to be a trampoline here. Plants did not grow under it.

Photosynthesis

Most plants make their own food using a process called **photosynthesis**. This process uses chemical substances (**reactants** or **raw materials**) to make new chemical

Photosynthesis 3

substances (**products**). A process in which reactants form products is a **chemical reaction**.

Photosynthesis is a process involving a series of chemical reactions by which carbon dioxide and water are converted into glucose and oxygen.

1.2 There are not many plants in the Rub al Khali desert (which is in Oman, Saudi Arabia, the United Arab Emirates and Yemen).

> **3** a) What are the raw materials for photosynthesis?
> b) What are the products of photosynthesis?

Many cells in leaves contain **chloroplasts**, which contain a green substance called **chlorophyll**. This substance absorbs energy from light. This energy is used to power photosynthesis. A lot of the energy is then stored in the glucose that is produced.

The oxygen made in photosynthesis is released by the plant into the air (or water) and is used by the plant in the process of respiration.

We can summarise the changes that happen during the series of reactions in photosynthesis using a word equation:

carbon dioxide + water → glucose + oxygen

The words 'light' and 'chlorophyll' are sometimes written in small letters above and below the arrow to show that they are both needed for the reaction to happen.

> **4** a) What makes chloroplasts green?
> b) What is the function of this green substance?
>
> **5** a) What process in plants produces oxygen?
> b) What process do humans need this gas for?
>
> **6** All organisms carry out seven life processes. Which of these do plants need carbon dioxide for?
>
> **7** Write out a summary word equation for photosynthesis, including the words 'light' and 'chlorophyll'.
>
> **8** Why is light *not* a raw material for photosynthesis?

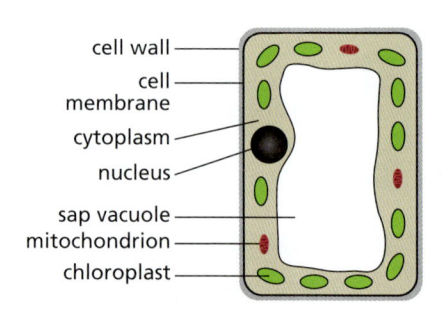

Key terms

chemical reaction: change in which new substances are produced.

glucose: sugar made by digesting carbohydrates (in animals) and by photosynthesis (in plants).

photosynthesis: a series of chemical reactions in which carbon dioxide and water are converted to glucose and oxygen.

product: substance made during a chemical reaction.

raw material: another term for reactant.

reactant: substance that changes in a chemical reaction to form products.

1.3 A diagram of a leaf cell, magnified about × 800.

Activity 1.1: Investigating photosynthesis in pondweed

How do we show that photosynthesis produces oxygen?

If you light a wooden splint and blow it out, it glows. If you put the glowing splint into pure oxygen, it relights.

Photosynthesis and plant growth

1.1

This is the test for oxygen. You will have met this test in Chemistry.

A1 The diagram shows how to collect the gas made by pondweed. Plan a way of showing that the gas is oxygen and not carbon dioxide.

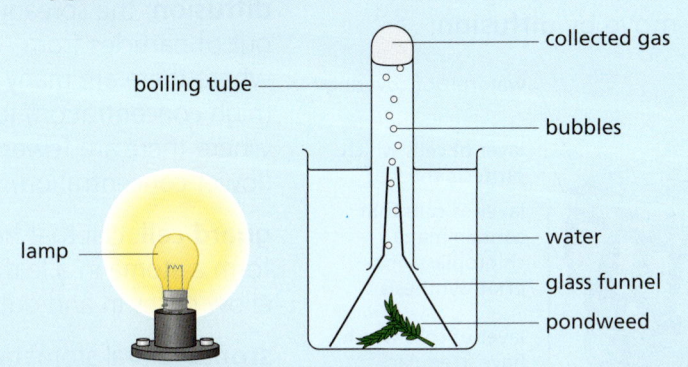

1.4 Collecting the gas made by pondweed.

A2 Make a prediction. Explain why you think this will happen.

A3 Why do you need a lamp?

A4 Why do we use a glass funnel in the experiment and not a white plastic one?

A5 Write a risk assessment for this experiment. Think about the lamp and the glass.

Key terms

chlorophyll: green substance that absorbs light, to get energy for photosynthesis.

chloroplast: green part of a cell that contains chlorophyll.

Science in context: Artificial photosynthesis

Working in Italy 100 years ago, Giacomo Ciamician had an idea to use artificial photosynthesis to make fuels in countries that did not have oil or coal.

In 2016, American scientists made an 'artificial leaf', to produce oxygen and hydrogen gas using water and the power of sunlight. The hydrogen can then be mixed with carbon dioxide, and bacteria convert the mixture into a liquid fuel. These scientists are now working with others from all over the world, setting up a Global Project on Artificial Photosynthesis. They want to produce cheap fuels that do not add carbon dioxide to the atmosphere.

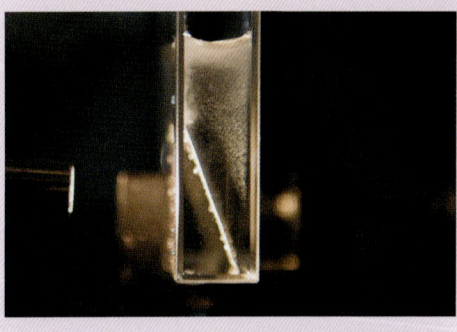

1.5 This artificial leaf makes bubbles of oxygen and hydrogen gases. Hydrogen gas can be used directly as a fuel but scientists are working on ways to combine it with carbon dioxide to make liquid fuels.

Carbon dioxide causes the greenhouse effect, which keeps the Earth warm. However, the burning of fossil fuels has released too much carbon dioxide, and this is now causing global warming. It is hoped that this new fuel will be almost 'carbon neutral', which means that its manufacture and use will not add more carbon dioxide to the atmosphere.

1. Discuss why it is important that the American scientists work with other scientists from around the world on this Global Project.
2. Discuss the potential global environmental impact of this project.

Adaptations of a leaf

Leaves are adapted for photosynthesis by containing different specialised cells. For example, palisade cells are adapted for photosynthesis and guard cells are adapted to form a hole through which gases can move by **diffusion**.

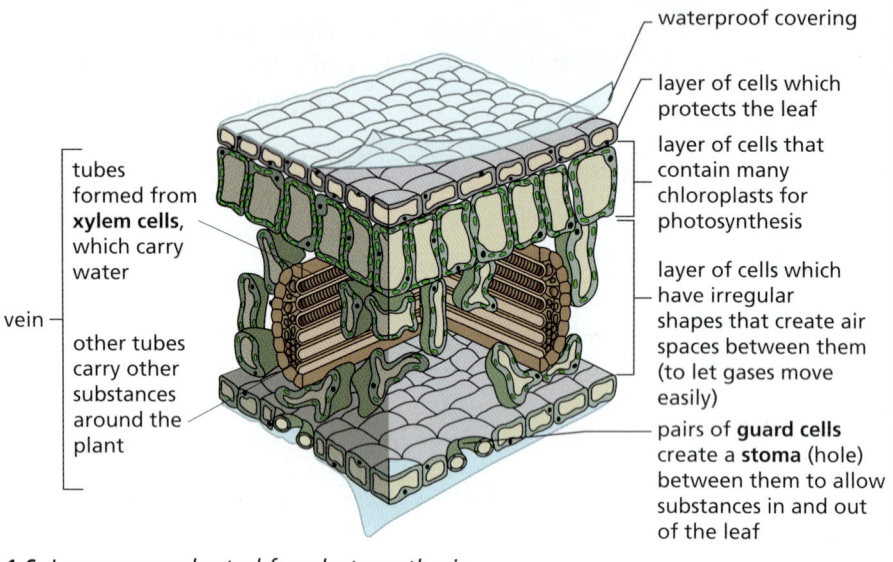

Key terms

diffusion: the spreading out of particles from where there are many (high concentration) to where there are fewer (lower concentration).

guard cell: cell that helps form a stoma in a leaf, to allow gases in and out.

stoma (plural stomata): hole in a leaf, formed between two guard cells.

xylem cell: plant cell that is adapted to form hollow tubes to transport water.

Labels on diagram:
- waterproof covering
- layer of cells which protects the leaf
- layer of cells that contain many chloroplasts for photosynthesis
- layer of cells which have irregular shapes that create air spaces between them (to let gases move easily)
- pairs of **guard cells** create a **stoma** (hole) between them to allow substances in and out of the leaf
- vein
  - tubes formed from **xylem cells**, which carry water
  - other tubes carry other substances around the plant

1.6 *Leaves are adapted for photosynthesis.*

---

9 What gas from the air needs to enter leaves through a stoma, for photosynthesis?

10 Which cells bring the liquid raw material for photosynthesis into a leaf?

11 Describe how oxygen gets into the air from inside a leaf.

Plant veins contain tubes that carry substances to and from a leaf. Xylem cells in a vein carry water into a leaf and to its cells. Some of the water evaporates from the cells and becomes a gas. This water vapour diffuses out of the leaves through small holes. One hole is called a stoma and the plural is **stomata**. Plants need a constant supply of water because they lose water through their stomata.

---

12 What do we call water when it is a gas?

13 Describe how a cell gets the reactants for photosynthesis.

14 How do plants lose water from their leaves?

Photosynthesis and plant growth

> **15** Pairs of guard cells open and close the stomata between them. In some plants, stomata close if it gets very hot. Explain how this helps the plant.

Plant carbohydrates

A **compound** is a substance made from simpler substances called **elements**. Carbon, hydrogen and oxygen are all elements.

Carbohydrates are a group of compounds made from carbon, hydrogen and oxygen. Some carbohydrates are small and we call them sugars. Glucose is a **sugar**.

All plant cells use glucose for **aerobic respiration**, which occurs all the time. Plants also make all their compounds using glucose. Some compounds also require small amounts of minerals.

> **16** a) Carbon dioxide is a compound. What does this mean?
> b) What process in a plant cell *produces* carbon dioxide?
>
> **17** a) Which elements does glucose contain?
> b) By what process does a plant produce glucose?

An important compound that plants make is a large carbohydrate, called **starch**. Plants use starch as a store of energy. Plants use glucose to make starch in chloroplasts, as they photosynthesise. At night, when photosynthesis stops, the plant uses the starch to make other compounds, which it transports out of the leaves.

> **18** Why does photosynthesis stop at night?
>
> **19** a) At which of these times would you find most starch in a leaf?
> - At the start of a day
> - In the middle of a day
> - At the end of a day
>
> b) Explain your choice in part a).

We test for starch using **iodine solution**. When we add iodine solution to starch, it changes from orange to a blue-black colour. Before we test a leaf, we remove the chlorophyll (by heating in a liquid called ethanol). Removing the green colour shows up the colour of the iodine better.

Key terms

aerobic respiration: respiration that requires oxygen to release energy from glucose.

carbohydrate: nutrient needed for energy. Examples include starch and sugars (such as glucose).

compound: substance made from elements.

element: substance that contains only one type of atom.

starch: large, insoluble carbohydrate made by plants to store energy and an important energy source in human diets.

sugar: soluble carbohydrate, which exists as small molecules. Glucose is an example.

Key term

iodine solution: liquid that turns from orange to blue-black when added to starch.

Photosynthesis

We boil the leaves in water (to make them soft).

We then put them in hot ethanol (to remove the green colour).

We wash the leaves in water.

We add iodine solution to the leaves.

1.7 *Testing leaves for starch.*

20 Look at figure 1.7.
  a) Which leaf on the white tile contains starch?
  b) Explain your answer to part a).

21 A scientist puts a plant in a dark place for two days. The scientist then tests the leaves for starch.
  a) Describe how the scientist would do the test.
  b) Predict what will happen.
  c) Explain your prediction.

Hazards and risks

The table shows how to control the **risks** from different **hazards** when using iodine solution and ethanol.

	Hazards	Controlling the risks
Iodine solution	Stains skin and clothing	Do not touch iodine solution
		Keep clothes away from iodine solution
	Stings if it gets in your eyes	Wear eye protection
Ethanol	Catches fire very easily	Do not use near flames
	Irritates your eyes	Wear eye protection

Key terms

hazard: harm that something may cause.

risk: chance of a hazard causing harm.

Photosynthesis and plant growth

22 Describe how to stop iodine solution getting in your eyes.

23 Describe how to control the risks of using ethanol.

24 When a gas burner heats things, it gets very hot.
   a) Describe the hazard of using a gas burner.
   b) Suggest *one* way of controlling the risk.

Activity 1.2: Investigating photosynthesis in leaves 1

Does photosynthesis require light?

A hypothesis is an idea about how or why something happens. In science, we must make sure that a hypothesis is testable. This means that we must be able to do experiments that give results that either support the idea or show that it is wrong. You can also use a testable hypothesis to make predictions about what will happen in an experiment.

Figure 1.8 shows some of the apparatus needed to investigate photosynthesis. Some of the leaves are covered with foil and the plant is put in a sunny place for two days.

A1 Write down what testable hypothesis is being investigated.
A2 Write a plan for this experiment.
A3 Write a risk assessment for this experiment.
A4 Make a prediction. Explain why you think this will happen.
A5 What is the *independent* variable in this experiment?

1.8 *Covering part of a leaf with foil.*

Activity 1.3: Investigating photosynthesis in leaves 2

Does photosynthesis require chlorophyll?

A 'variegated leaf' has white patches, in which there is no chlorophyll. You will use variegated leaves from a plant that has been in a sunny place for two days. You will test the leaves for starch.

A1 Write down a testable hypothesis that could be investigated using variegated leaves.
A2 Write a plan for your experiment.
A3 Write a risk assessment for this experiment.
A4 Make a prediction. Explain why you think this will happen.
A5 What is the *dependent* variable in this experiment?

1.9 *A variegated leaf.*

Photosynthesis

Activity 1.4: Investigating how light can affect the rate (speed) of photosynthesis

Does photosynthesis happen faster or slower in different conditions?

Scientists take time to carefully plan their experimental methods. However, sometimes scientists need to change a method as they are doing an experiment.

When planning an investigation, you usually choose the same interval between each value of the independent variable. You also choose an upper and a lower limit for your independent variable. Sometimes, when you are doing an experiment a pattern starts to appear but you can't see how or if the pattern continues and so you need to change your limits, to carry on collecting data. Sometimes, when you are doing an experiment, a pattern is unclear because your intervals are too close or too far apart. So they may also need to be changed.

In an experiment, we often measure the dependent variable several times for each value of the independent variable. If we always get the same value we can be more sure that the measurement is correct. We can rely on the measurement because it is **repeatable**. We say that repeatable measurements are **reliable**. Sometimes, we find that a repeated measurement does not match the others. It is **anomalous**. If this happens, it is a good idea to repeat the measurement a few more times to check it again and obtain reliable data.

The evidence collected during the experiment can be evaluated to see whether it supports the prediction (proves it to have been correct) or refutes the prediction (proves it to have been incorrect).

Use your scientific knowledge to plan an experiment to answer the question above. You have access to some pondweed, a beaker of water, a lamp, a metre rule and a stopwatch. You might choose other apparatus too. Your set-up might look similar to figure 1.10.

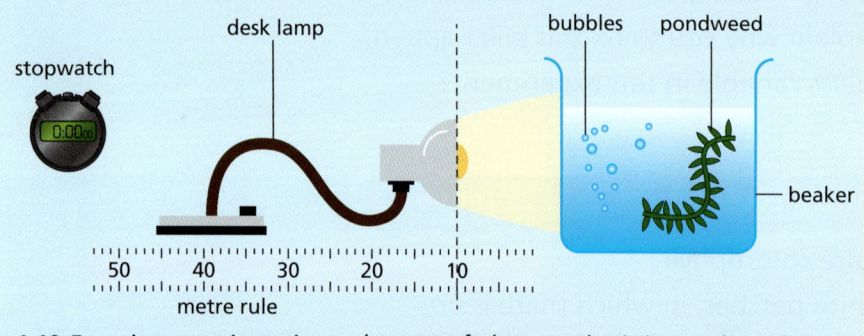

1.10 *Experiment to investigate the rate of photosynthesis in pondweed.*

A1 Write a plan for your investigation. Include your testable hypothesis, a step-by-step method and a prediction. (Note: When you make a change to your independent variable, it is best to wait a minute before you make readings of your dependent variable.)

A2 Write a risk assessment for this experiment.

A3 Carry out your planned investigation. Collect and record your results in a suitable table.

A4 Explain why you made repeated measurements for each change of your independent variable.

Key terms

anomalous: result that is very different from what you expect based on other results, perhaps because you made a mistake while recording it or something unexpected happened.

reliable: measurements are reliable when repeated measurements give results that are very similar.

repeatable: results that are the same each time they are taken, when the same method and equipment are used.

Photosynthesis and plant growth

A5 Did you change the number of repeated measurements you made? If you did, explain why.

A6 Did you have any anomalous readings? If you did, suggest a reason how they may have been caused.

A7 Did you change the upper or lower limits of your independent variable? If you did, explain why.

A8 Calculate the mean of the recordings for each distance. In your calculations, do not include any results that are anomalous.

A9 Draw a scatter graph of your mean results.

A10 Write a conclusion and explain whether your evidence is strong enough to support (or refute) your prediction.

A11 Look at your scatter graph again. Use it to predict some values of your dependent variable for *two* values of your independent variable that you did not test.

Key facts:

✔ Photosynthesis can be modelled using a word equation:

carbon dioxide + water → glucose + oxygen

✔ Inside chloroplasts, chlorophyll traps some energy from light, which is used to power photosynthesis.

✔ Glucose is a carbohydrate.

✔ Plants use glucose to make the other compounds that they need, including starch (another carbohydrate, which they use as a store of energy).

✔ Gases (such as carbon dioxide, oxygen and water vapour) diffuse in and out of open stomata.

Making links

In Stage 8 Chemistry, you may have learned about exothermic and endothermic reactions. Explain why photosynthesis is an endothermic reaction.

Check your skills progress:

- I can identify and design a testable hypothesis.
- I can decide on the dependent, independent and control variables in an investigation.
- I can write a risk assessment.
- I can make sufficient measurements to obtain reliable results.
- I can identify anomalous results and suggest how they have occurred.

Chapter 1 . Topic 2

Transport of water and mineral salts in plants

You will learn:

- To describe the importance of elements found in mineral salts (magnesium and nitrates) for the growth and development of plants
- To collect and record observations and measurements appropriately
- To interpret and present results appropriately
- To interpret results and form conclusions using scientific knowledge and understanding
- To evaluate experimental methods, explaining any improvements suggested
- To suggest a testable hypothesis and make predictions of likely outcomes
- To plan methods used to test hypotheses
- To decide whether evidence from first-hand experience should be used instead of secondary sources

Starting point

You should know that...	You should be able to...
Plants have organs, such as roots, stems and leaves	Identify and design a testable hypothesis.
Plants need water for photosynthesis	Plan investigations to test ideas
Plants have specialised cells, such as root hair cells and guard cells (that have stomata between them)	Make predictions and conclusions
	Present results in appropriate tables, charts and graphs

Roots are plant organs that hold a plant in the ground. Roots also take in water and minerals (or mineral salts).

Mineral salts are substances that plants need in very small amounts. Plants use them to make some of the substances they need.

A plant needs water to make its own food, using photosynthesis. It also needs water to give cells their shapes. Without enough water, plant cells start to collapse and the plant **wilts** (becomes floppy).

Key term

wilting: when a plant becomes floppy due to lack of water.

1.12 *A wilted plant.*

Photosynthesis and plant growth

1.2

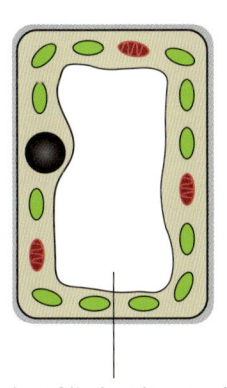

When filled with enough water, the sap vacuole pushes outwards on the cell. This keeps its shape.

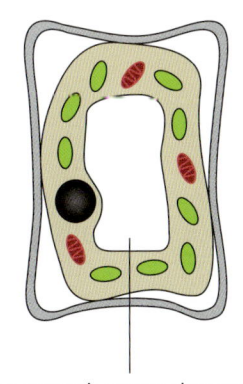

Without enough water, the sap vacuole shrinks. There is no longer enough force pushing outwards. The cell wall starts to bend and the cell loses its shape.

1.11 *Plant cells need water to keep their shapes.*

Key terms

absorb: to take in or soak up.

root hair cell: plant cell found in roots that is adapted for taking in water quickly.

xylem vessel: tube formed by the joining of many dead xylem cells.

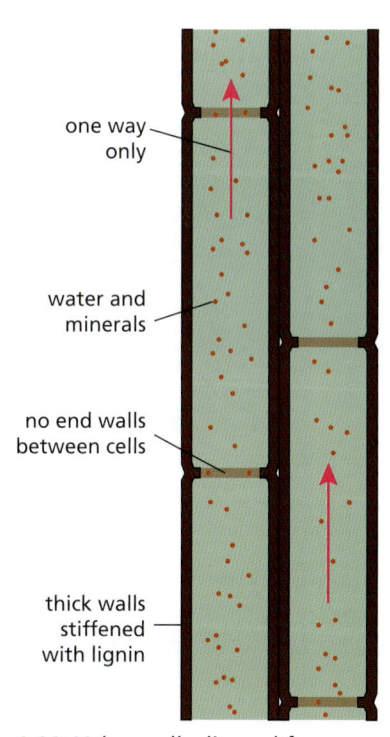

1 Describe *two* functions of roots.

2 Explain why a plant wilts when it lacks water.

Absorbing water

Roots use specialised **root hair cells** to **absorb** (take in) water. These cells have bits sticking out of them that look a bit like hairs. A 'root hair' gives a cell a lot of surface area, which helps it absorb water quickly. These cells also absorb mineral salts.

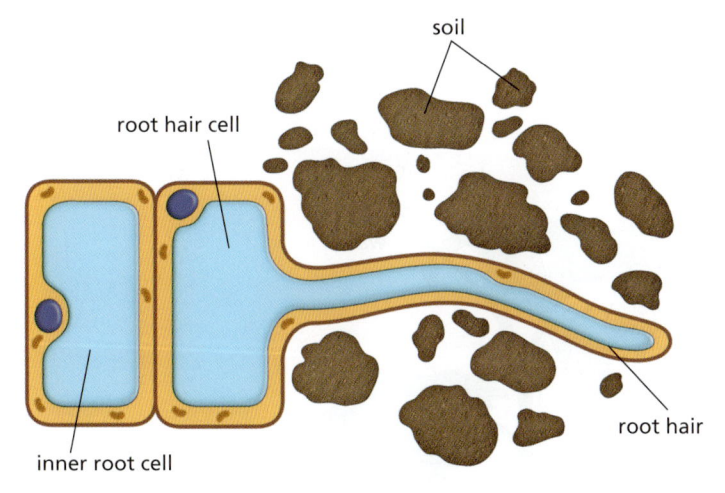

1.13 *A root hair cell.*

3 a) What do root hairs absorb?

b) Explain how 'root hairs' help cells to absorb substances quickly.

4 Make a labelled drawing of a root hair cell, showing all its parts.

1.14 *Xylem cells die and form hollow tubes.*

Transport of water and mineral salts in plants

Transporting water

A plant transports water and minerals salts in specialised xylem cells. These cells form chains and then die, to form hollow tubes (or vessels). The **xylem vessels** run continuously from the roots up to the leaves. They have thick cell walls, containing lignin. This substance makes the walls very strong and stops them collapsing.

> **5** How are xylem cells adapted to their function?

Transpiration

Water and mineral salts move from root hair cells though other root cells and into xylem vessels, which are found in the middle of roots. They then travel up to the leaves where they enter the cells. The water evaporates into the air spaces and the water vapour exits the leaves through stomata. As water is lost, it pulls more water up through the xylem and into the leaves. **Transpiration** is defined as the loss of water vapour through the stomata on the surface of the leaves.

The route taken by water through the plant into the roots, up the stem and out through the leaves can be described as the transpiration stream. This is shown in figure 1.15.

The speed of water loss from the plant depends on the conditions around the plant. If the weather is windy, dry and warm, transpiration happens quickly. On a still, damp, cold day, transpiration is very slow.

> **Key term**
>
> **transpiration**: the loss of water vapour through the stomata on the surface of the leaves.

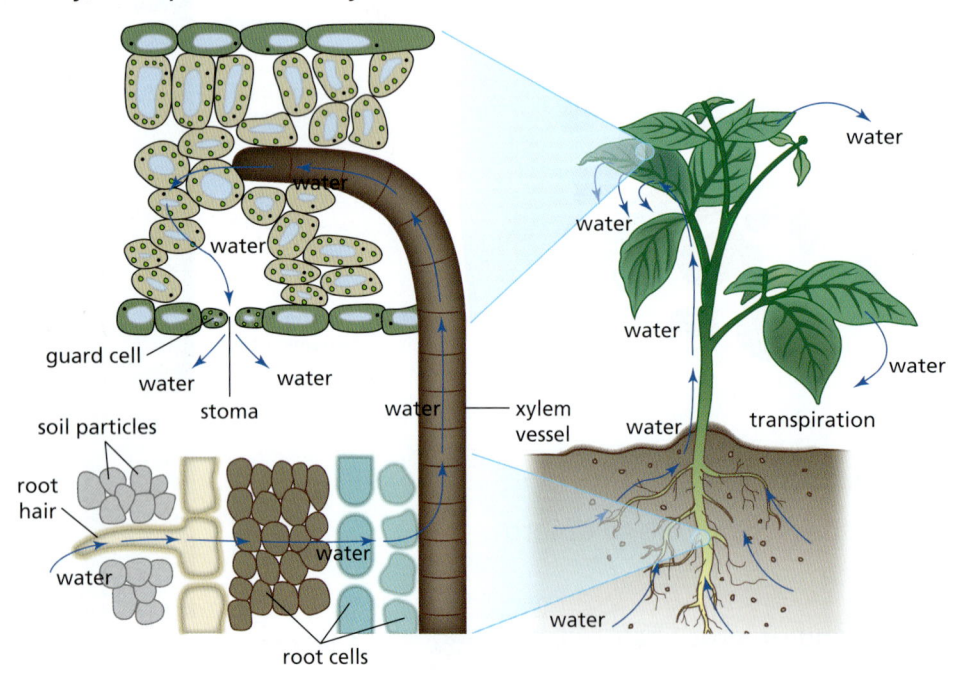

1.15 *Movement of water through a plant*

14 Photosynthesis and plant growth

6. How does water move into the plant's leaves from the soil?

7. Describe what happens in the process of transpiration.

8. Suggest what the structure labelled A in figure 1.16 is.

9. List the organs in a plant's 'water transport system'.

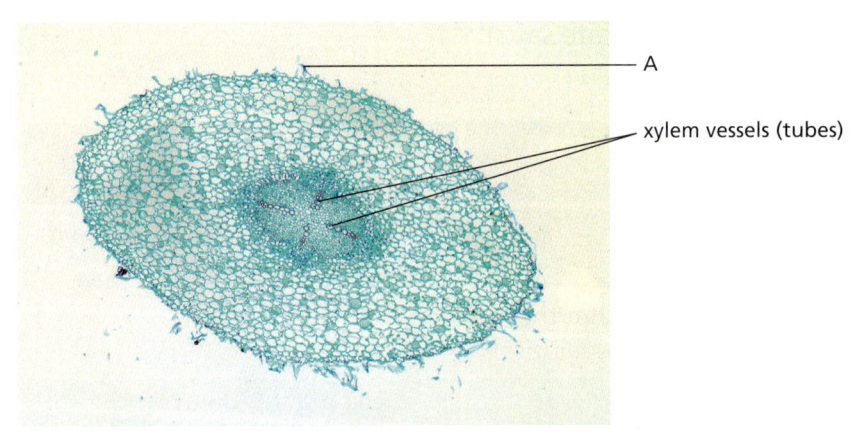

1.16 *Cross section through a bean root. Magnification x40.*

Activity 1.5: Investigating water transport in stems

What affects how far water moves in a stem in a certain time?

Water rises up some plant stems when placed in water. Colouring the water helps you to see this. You can find the level that the water reaches by cutting the stem.

A1 Think of a variable that might affect how quickly water flows up a stem. Write down a testable hypothesis and explain how you have used scientific understanding to develop your hypothesis.

A2 Plan an investigation method to answer your question. Make sure you include the independent variable (which you change), the dependent variable and any control variables.

A3 Predict what will happen and explain your prediction.

A4 Present your results neatly.

A5 Compare your prediction with your results, and make a conclusion.

A6 Look at your conclusion and use it to outline another investigation that you could do to test the same hypothesis.

Transport of water and mineral salts in plants

Mineral salts and healthy plant growth

Plants need small quantities of chemical elements found in different mineral salts to grow healthily, and to produce flowers, fruits and seeds. Mineral salts are dissolved in water in the soil and they enter a plant through its roots. Different plants need different elements in different quantities, but there are some that all plants need.

If plants do not get the elements that they need from mineral salts, they have deficiency symptoms. Some examples are shown in the table. The two that you need to remember are the uses of nitrogen (found in nitrate salts) and magnesium (found in magnesium salts).

Element (needed from mineral salts)	Why does the plant need this?	What happens if the plant does not get this?
Magnesium (from magnesium salts)	To make chlorophyll	The plant turns yellow because it cannot make chlorophyll
Nitrogen (from nitrate salts)	To make proteins so that the plant can grow and repair itself	Reduced plant growth
Phosphorus (from phosphate salts)	For respiration and growth	Reduced plant growth
Potassium (from potassium salts)	To help plants absorb and transport water	The edges of leaves turn brown

10 What *two* types of substance do plants absorb through their roots?

11 Explain why a plant that lacks nitrates does not grow very well.

12 Explain why a plant that lacks magnesium has yellow leaves.

Activity 1.6: Investigating minerals and plant growth

Do different mineral salts affect plant growth differently? Thema wanted to investigate how different minerals affect the growth of plants. She used duckweed plants, which grow on water.

Thema wanted to test how well plants grew in the absence of each of the following elements: nitrogen and magnesium. She set up four jars, half filling them with distilled or deionised water and then adding nutrients to each to form a culture solution.

Photosynthesis and plant growth

1.2

duckweed plants floating

culture solution

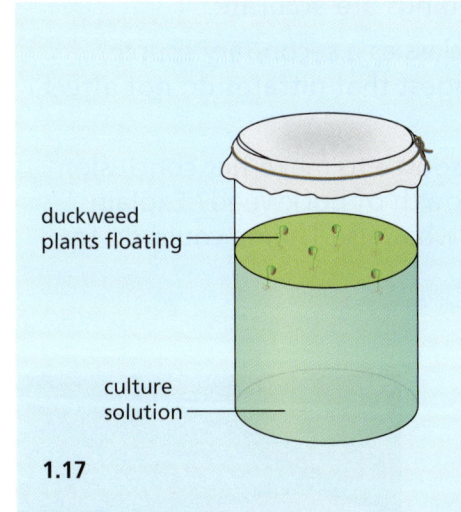

1.17

Jar 1: water only (a control, to see what happens to the plants when none of the minerals are present)

Jar 2: water and magnesium (no nitrogen)

Jar 3: water and nitrates (no magnesium)

Jar 4: water, nitrates and magnesium

It is important that the water used is distilled or deionised to make sure that it is pure, and does not contain any minerals other than those added by the students during the investigation.

The presence of any other minerals in the water could affect the growth of the plants, meaning that the water used in Jar 1 could not act as a control.

Thema put 10 duckweed plants in each jar and then left them for four weeks. Each week Thema collected evidence about the jars, including the area of the water surface covered by plants, root length and colour of the plants.

A1 Suggest a testable hypothesis for Thema's investigation.

A2 Suggest why Thema used 10 duckweed plants in each jar rather than just one.

Thema's final observations after 4 weeks are summarised in the table below:

Jar	Description of conditions used	Changes observed in duckweed plants after four weeks
1	Water only	No growth of plants or roots Some yellowing of the leaves seen
2	Water and magnesium	Small amount of growth of plants and roots with healthy green leaves
3	Water and nitrates	Growth of plants and roots but some leaves have turned yellow
4	Water, magnesium and nitrates	Lots of growth of plant and roots with healthy green leaves

A3 The evidence shown by Thema's observations after 4 weeks supported her initial prediction. Describe what Thema predicted about the effect of magnesium and nitrates on the growth of duckweed.

Thema decides to use secondary sources to check whether her findings are accurate. Secondary sources are those that are produced by other people who have not been directly involved in your work. Examples of secondary sources that Thema could use include science textbooks, the results from similar investigations done by other students or scientists, photographs, or internet search results.

Transport of water and mineral salts in plants

A4 Explain why it is important for Thema to check her findings are accurate.

Thema uses the findings from another group in the same class as a secondary source. Their findings do not agree with Thema's findings and suggest that nitrates do not affect the growth of duckweed plants.

A5 Should Thema use her own findings or the secondary source to make her conclusion about the effect of magnesium and nitrates on the growth of duckweed? Explain your answer in as much detail as you can and suggest what else Thema could do to improve her confidence in her conclusions.

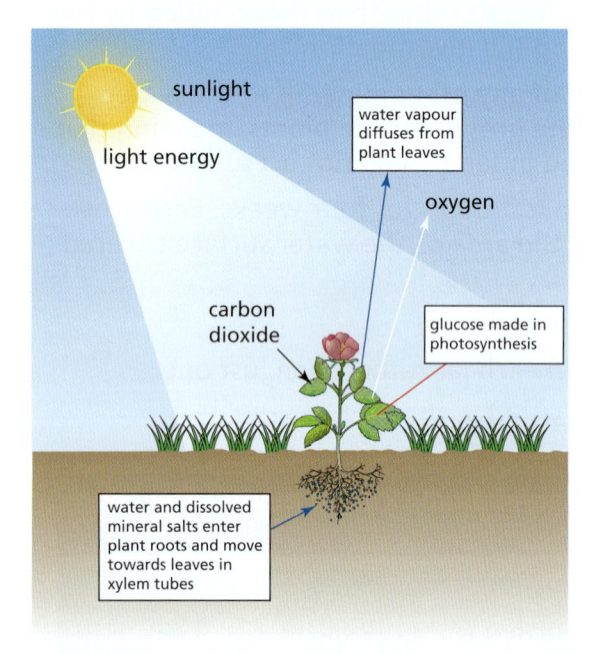

1.18 *A summary of how substances move around a plant.*

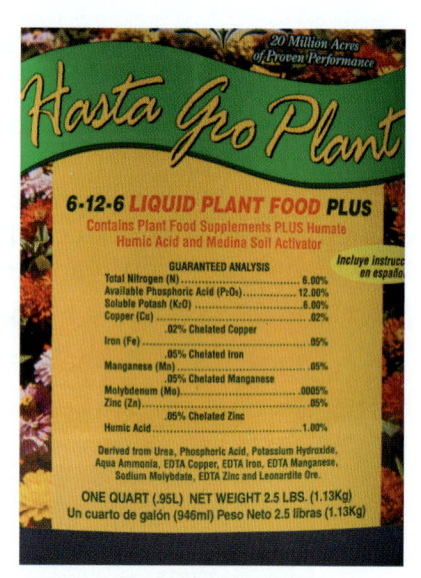

1.19 *Artificial fertilisers are used to provide plants with the elements they need for healthy growth.*

Sometimes soil does not contain enough mineral salts to support the healthy growth of all the plants rooted in it. To overcome this, farmers and gardeners often add fertilisers to the soil. These contain mineral salts such as nitrates. The elements in these mineral salts help the plants to grow and produce good-quality flowers, fruits and seeds.

13 What type of compound is often found in fertilisers to supply nitrogen to plants?

14 The mixture in figure 1.19 contains nitrates. Name the element that plants need from these.

15 What can gardeners add to their soil to help their plants to grow?

Photosynthesis and plant growth

16 Suggest *one* advantage and *one* disadvantage for farmers using fertilisers to grow crops.

Science in context: Mineral salts from natural fertiliser

Farmers in Hlokozi, South Africa, are spreading decomposing cow manure on their fields to help the crops to grow. Manure is a free resource for the farmers because they raise cows on their farms. It is a natural fertiliser and is rich in mineral salts containing important elements for plants, such as nitrogen. Manure also improves the soil and helps it to hold together better. However, manure can contain dangerous microorganisms and takes a long time to release its mineral salts.

An alternative is for farmers who don't have farm animals to buy artificial fertilisers. These provide mineral salts more quickly to plants but they can be dangerous to use (particularly if farmers breath in the dust).

Both natural and artificial fertilisers can cause problems for the environment if too much is used. The extra mineral salts wash into lakes and rivers, and cause plants and algae to grow very quickly. When these plants and algae die, the decomposer bacteria that break them down use up all the oxygen in the water and fish can die.

Use the information in the box above to answer Questions 17 and 18.

17 Draw a table to compare the benefits and drawbacks of natural and artificial fertilisers.

18 a) Suggest what type of fertiliser a farmer who only grows wheat should use. Explain your reasoning.

b) Describe *two* ways in which a farmer should be careful when using artificial fertilisers.

Making links

The mineral salts found in artificial fertilisers are made in big factories. In Chemistry you may have learned about how salts are made. State *two* reactants you would need to make magnesium chloride salt.

Key facts:

✔ Plants need water to make their own food (by photosynthesis) and for cells to keep their shape.

✔ A plant needs mineral salts to make certain substances.

✔ Plants need magnesium to make chlorophyll and nitrates to make protein.

✔ Water and mineral salts are absorbed by a plant using root hair cells.

✔ Water and mineral salts are transported in tubes formed by dead xylem cells.

✔ Transpiration is the loss of water vapour through the stomata on the surface of leaves.

✔ The movement of water through a plant is called the transpiration stream.

Check your skills progress:

- I can use scientific questions to develop testable hypotheses.
- I can evaluate the reliability of the data collected.
- I can use the data to make a conclusion, and explain my findings using my scientific knowledge and understanding.
- I can decide whether to use my own results or secondary sources.

End of chapter review

Quick questions

1. The loss of water through the stomata of the leaves on a plant, is called:

    a translocation

    b transport

    c transpiration

    d transcription

2. Which *two* substances in the list below does a plant need for photosynthesis?

    a oxygen

    b carbon dioxide

    c water

    d glucose

3. What gas does a plant make as a product of photosynthesis?

4. Where in the plant in figure 1.20 does most photosynthesis take place? Choose *one* letter.

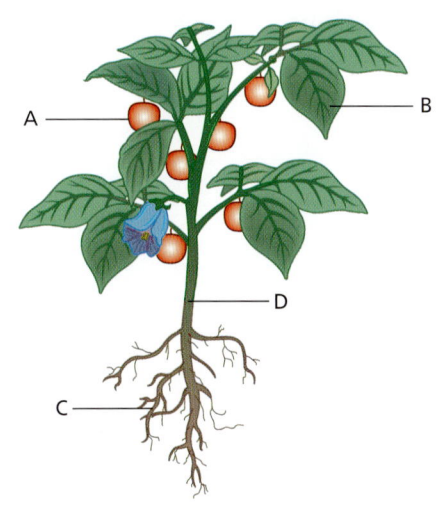

    1.20

5. Why do plants need nitrogen?

    a to make sugars

    b to make proteins

    c to make fats

    d for respiration

6. What chemical reaction happens continuously in plant cells to release energy?

7. A student is looking at some pondweed, in a large beaker of water. A lamp is shining on the plant and bubbles are rising from its leaves.

   (a) What gas do the bubbles contain?

   (b) Through which part of the leaf does the gas leave the plant?

   (c) Why is the plant making these bubbles?

   (d) What raw materials does the plant need for this process?

Connect your understanding

8. (a) Where in a plant cell would you find chlorophyll?

   (b) Describe the function of chlorophyll.

   (c) Name the element from mineral salts that a plant needs to make chlorophyll.

   (d) How would a plant appear if the element you named in part (c) were not present in the soil around its roots?

9. (a) Describe the movement of gases into and out of a plant during the daytime.

   (b) Give *two* ways in which a plant uses the glucose that it makes.

10. Use figure 1.21 to help you answer the following questions.

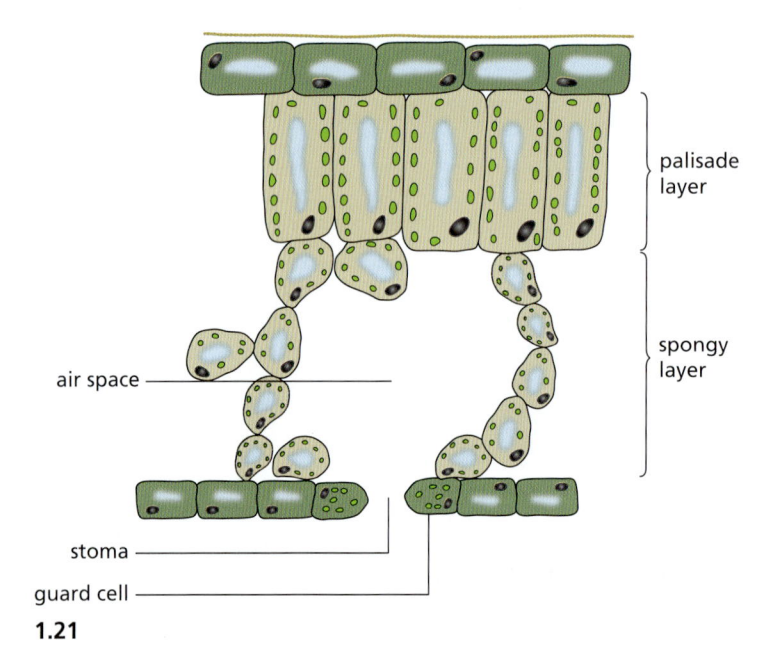

1.21

(a) Describe how cells in the palisade layer are adapted for photosynthesis.

(b) Explain the function of the guard cells.

(c) Where do plant cells store most of their water?

11. Figure 1.22 shows a plant leaf with some foil covering part of it. The plant grows under a bright light. A student tests the leaf to see if it contains glucose.

   (a) Suggest why the student thinks the leaf contains a lot of glucose.

   (b) Explain why the test will be negative (no glucose).

   (c) What substances should the student test for?

   (d) In which areas of the leaf will you find this substances? Choose one or more of A, B and C.

   (e) Explain your answer to part (d).

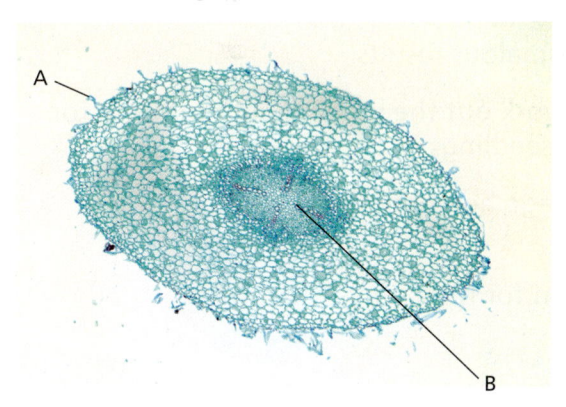

12. Figure 1.23 is a photo taken using a high-powered microscope. It shows a cross section through the root of a broad bean plant.

    1.23

    (a) Name structure A.

    (b) Describe how A is adapted for its function.

    (c) Suggest what structure B could be.

    (d) Describe the function of B.

13. Making sure that you include the keywords below, describe the journey that water makes from the soil through a plant.

    evaporate   root   stem   leaf   xylem   stomata   diffusion

End of chapter review

Challenge questions

14. Mira wanted to find out whether plants need water to grow. She numbered two dishes, 1 and 2, and put some cotton wool in the bottom of both of them. Then she put five seedlings on the cotton wool in each dish. Mira recorded the height of each seedling at the start of the investigation.

Mira put both dishes near a window and added some water to dish 1. She did not add water to dish 2. Mira continued to add water to dish 1 every day, but did not give dish 2 any water.

One week later, Mira recorded the height of each seedling again. Her results are shown in the tables below.

Dish 1

Seedling	Height at start (mm)	Height after 1 week (mm)
1	10	32
2	9	34
3	11	15
4	10	33
5	12	35

Dish 2

Seedling	Height at start (mm)	Height after 1 week (mm)
1	10	15
2	10	14
3	12	16
4	11	16
5	9	12

(a) Look at the tables. Identify any anomalous results.

(b) Removing any anomalous results, work out the mean height increase for the seedlings in dish 1, and for the seedlings in dish 2.

(c) Draw a bar graph to show the average height increase of the seedlings in dish 1 and dish 2.

(d) Using your graph, write a conclusion for Mira's investigation.

Chapter 2
The excretory system

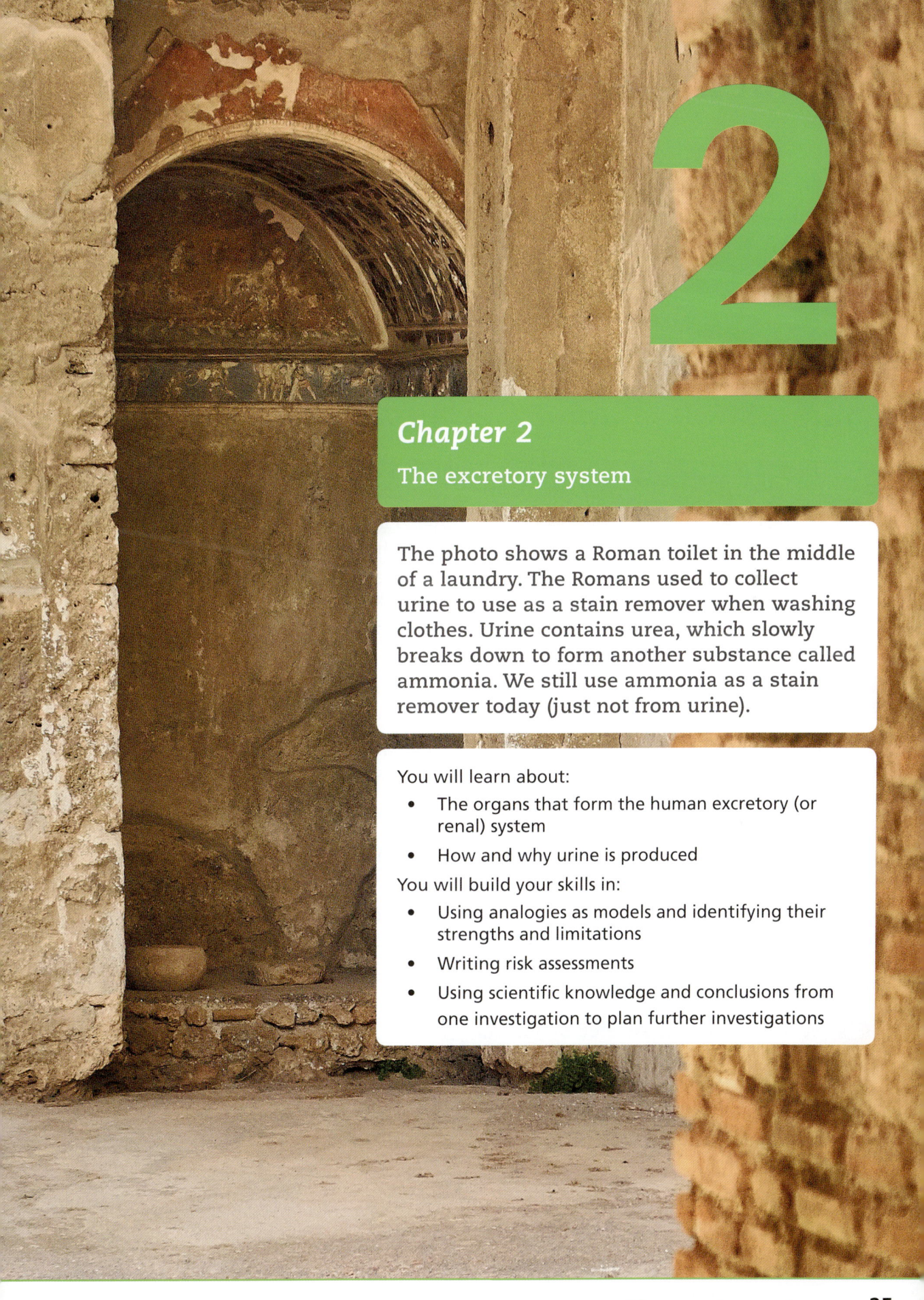

The photo shows a Roman toilet in the middle of a laundry. The Romans used to collect urine to use as a stain remover when washing clothes. Urine contains urea, which slowly breaks down to form another substance called ammonia. We still use ammonia as a stain remover today (just not from urine).

You will learn about:
- The organs that form the human excretory (or renal) system
- How and why urine is produced

You will build your skills in:
- Using analogies as models and identifying their strengths and limitations
- Writing risk assessments
- Using scientific knowledge and conclusions from one investigation to plan further investigations

Chapter 2
Producing urine

You will learn:
- To describe the structure of the human excretory (renal) system
- To describe how the kidneys filter blood to remove urea, which is excreted in urine
- To describe examples where scientific understanding has been improved by the unexpected outcomes of scientific enquiries
- To identify hazards and identify ways to minimise risks
- To carry out practical work in a safe manner to minimise risks
- To interpret results and form conclusions using scientific knowledge and understanding
- To describe the uses, strengths and limitations of models and analogies

Starting point

You should know that...	You should be able to...
Humans have organ systems	Identify the use of analogies as models
Organisms carry out seven life processes (including excretion)	Identify hazards and suggest ways to reduce risks
	Use results to make conclusions

Excretion

Excretion is when an organism gets rid of waste substances that it has made inside its cells. Excretion is one of the seven life processes that all living organisms do.

For example, plants excrete oxygen (which is produced by photosynthesis). Animals excrete carbon dioxide (which is produced by respiration).

Our lungs excrete carbon dioxide, but our **kidneys** excrete most of the other wastes that our bodies make.

Key terms

excretion: getting rid of wastes that are made inside an organism.

kidney: an organ that removes waste substances from the blood.

1. List the seven life processes.
2. What substance is excreted by your lungs?
3. Undigested food passes out of your digestive system as faeces. Explain why this process is not an example of excretion.

The excretory system

Blood vessels carry blood to the kidneys and take the cleaned blood away from the kidneys.

Each kidney cleans the blood by removing waste substances and producing urine.

The **ureters** are tubes that carry urine to the bladder.

The **bladder** stores urine. A muscle at the bottom of the bladder keeps the urine in until the person wants to **urinate**.

The **urethra** is a tube that carries urine out of the body.

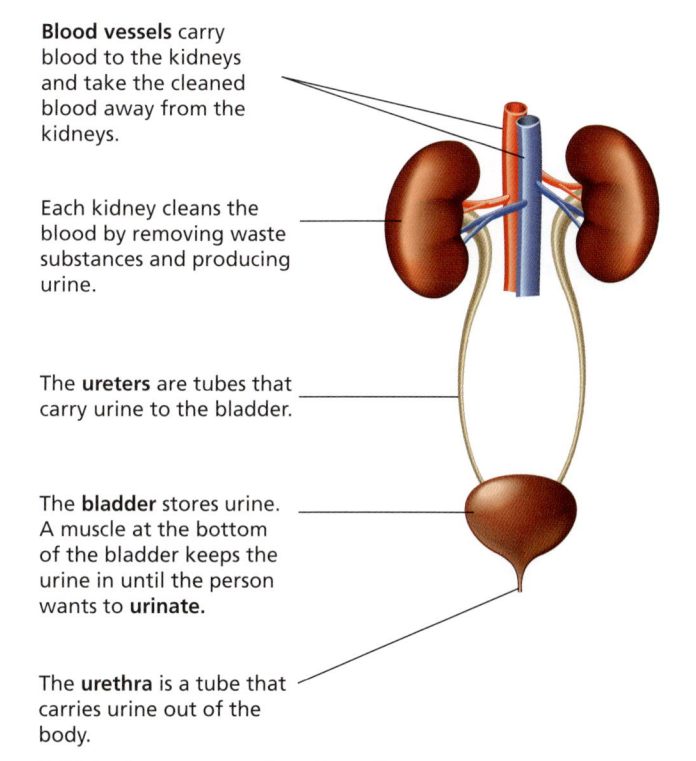

2.1 *The human excretory (renal) system.*

Key terms

bladder: organ that stores urine.

blood vessels: tube-shaped organs that carry blood around the body.

excretory system: organ system that removes wastes from the blood and produces urine.

organ system: group of organs working together.

renal system: another name for the excretory system.

ureter: tube-shaped organ that carries urine from a kidney to the bladder.

urethra: tube-shaped organ that carries urine from the bladder to outside of the body.

urinate: to release urine from the bladder.

urea: main waste substance removed from the blood by the kidneys.

urine: liquid containing urea and other wastes.

The excretory system

Your body contains many **organ systems**. One of these is the **excretory system**, which is also called the **renal system**. Its function is to remove wastes from your blood by making **urine**. The organs in the excretory system are shown in figure 2.1.

The main waste that the kidneys remove is **urea**. This substance is made when your body breaks down proteins. Having too much urea in your blood can damage other important organs in your body, such as your liver and heart.

All the blood in your body passes through your kidneys every 30–40 minutes. Inside the kidneys, the blood is filtered. The blood cells stay inside blood vessels but the urea and some water pass out of them and are collected. This forms **urine**, which then flows into the bladder along a tube called a ureter.

The bladder stores the urine. It expands as it fills, a bit like a party balloon filling with air. When a person decides to urinate, the urine passes out of the body along another tube called the urethra.

4 List all the organs in the human excretory system.

5 Give another term for the excretory system.

Producing urine 27

6 Explain why it is important that your kidneys filter your blood.

7 An analogy is used in the last paragraph above.
 a) Write down the analogy that has been used.
 b) Give *one* way in which the analogy is good and *one* way in which it is poor.

8 An analogy for a kidney is that it is like the filter in a fish aquarium. An aquarium filter is used to remove waste materials from the water to keep the water clean and the fish healthy.
 a) Describe how the kidney is like an aquarium filter.
 b) Give *one* way in which the analogy is good and one way in which it is poor.

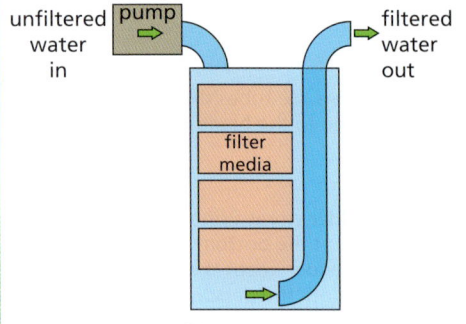

2.2 *Aquarium filter*

Kidney problems

The table shows the approximate concentrations of some substances in blood plasma and in urine.

Substance	In blood plasma (g/100 cm³)	In urine (g/100 cm³)
Protein	7	0
Urea	0.03	2
Other substances	1	0.5

Sometimes, a person's kidneys do not work very well because they have a disease. People with kidney disease often have proteins in their urine because the filters inside the kidney have been damaged. So, doctors test urine for protein if they suspect a patient has kidney disease.

9 Give the name of *one* substance that the kidneys:
 a) remove from the blood
 b) do not remove from the blood.

10 Calculate the mass of urea you would expect to find in 1 litre of urine.

11 Name the substance that gives urine most of its mass.

12 How many times more concentrated is the urea in urine than in blood plasma?

28   The excretory system

Activity 2.1: Detecting kidney disease

How could you test urine to identify people with kidney disease?

Plan an experiment to test urine to find out if a person has kidney disease. Think about what you learnt about food tests in Stage 8 Chapter 2.

A1 Write a plan for your experiment.

A2 Write a risk assessment for your experiment.

A3 After your plan has been checked by a teacher, carry out your plan using different samples of urine and record your results in a table.

A4 Make a conclusion about which urine sample was from someone with kidney disease.

A5 Think about what you have discovered in your investigation and suggest how your conclusion could be further investigated. Discuss your ideas with others in group and agree on one further investigation that you could do.

Science in context: Kidney dialysis

In the 1850s, Scottish scientist Thomas Graham was trying to invent a way of using a very thin sheet of material to act as a very fine filter. One of the things he tried to filter was urine, from which he was able to extract urea. Working with Richard Bright, an English doctor, the two men realised that this filtering method could be used to filter the blood of people whose kidneys were not working.

Today, around 2 million people worldwide receive this sort of treatment, which is called dialysis. People with kidneys that are not working usually have dialysis three times a week, for about four hours each time. Blood vessels in their arms are connected up to a dialysis machine, which pumps their blood through a fine set of filters and removes the urea.

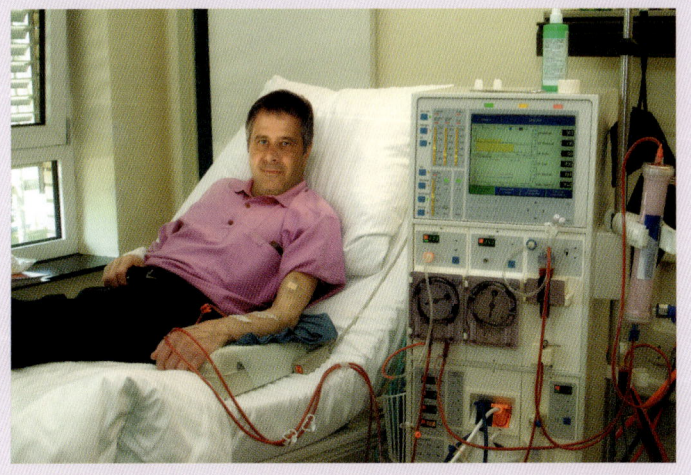

2.3 *Kidney dialysis.*

Making links

In Stage 7 you may have learned about pH. Urea dissolved in water forms a neutral solution but all the other substances in urine mean that the pH of urine varies from about pH 5 to pH 8. Describe how a doctor can find out the pH of a person's urine.

Producing urine

Key facts:

- ✔ The human excretory system contains the kidneys, ureters, bladder and urethra.
- ✔ The kidneys filter the blood and remove wastes, such as urea.
- ✔ The wastes are dissolved in water and form urine, which passes down the ureters to the bladder.
- ✔ The bladder stores urine until it can be emptied.

Check your skills progress:

- I can suggest strengths and weaknesses for analogy models.
- I can write risk assessments.
- I can suggest further investigations that can be done based on conclusions from an investigation.

End of chapter review

Quick questions

1. What is excretion?

    a getting rid of waste materials made inside cells

    b another term for aerobic respiration

    c taking in food

    d getting rid of undigested food

2. Another name for the human excretory system is the:

    a digestive system

    b circulatory system

    c kidney system

    d renal system

3. The main substance that kidneys remove from the blood is:

    a urine

    b urea

    c uranus

    d urinol

4. What substance do human lungs excrete?

    a oxygen

    b carbon dioxide

    c nitrogen

    d urinol

5. The kidneys remove waste substances from the blood. Which part of the blood carries these waste substances?

    a platelets

    b red blood cells

    c plasma

    d blood vessels

6. List *three* organs found in the human excretory system.

7. The excretory system is an example of an organ system. What is an organ system?

8. (a) Describe how the kidneys make urine.

   (b) Describe the route that urine takes from your kidneys and out of your body.

Connect your understanding

9. In an experiment, two groups of rats had diets that contained different amounts of protein. Samples of their blood were taken, and the concentrations of urea and protein were measured. The mean values are shown on the bar chart.

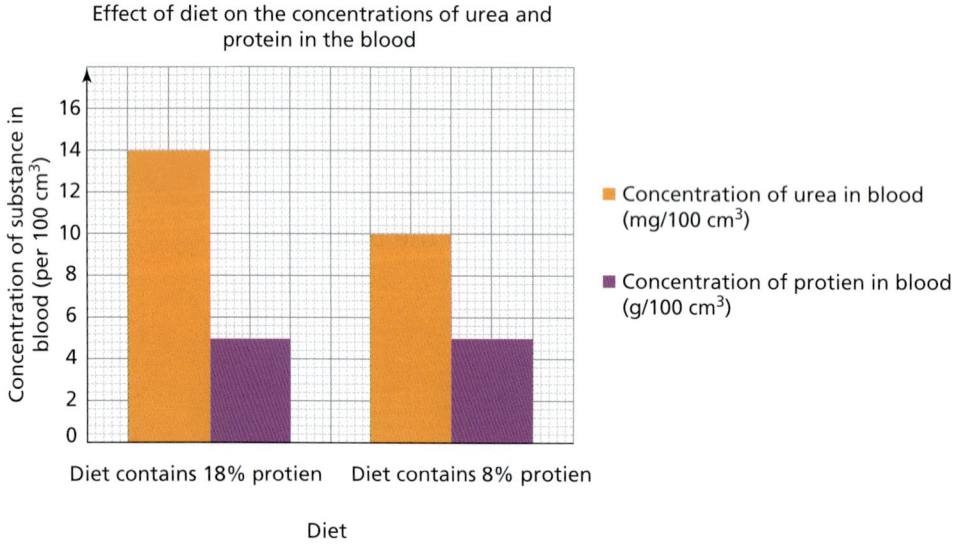

Effect of diet on the concentrations of urea and protein in the blood

- Concentration of urea in blood (mg/100 cm^3)
- Concentration of protien in blood (g/100 cm^3)

Diet contains 18% protien — Diet contains 8% protien

Diet

2.4

   (a) Describe how the amount of protein in the diet affects urea and protein concentrations in the blood.

   (b) Give the reason why the diet affects urea concentration.

10. Doctors often test the urine of people to try to find out what is wrong with them. Explain why *normal* urine does not contain protein or sugars.

Eohippus *Mesohippus* *Merychippus* *Pliohippus*

3

Chapter 3
Variation and inheritance

Modern horse

What's it all about?

Most scientists think that species of organisms change gradually over many millions of years. This gradual change is called evolution. The drawings show how scientists think horses have evolved from other animals over the last 50 million years. A scientist called Charles Darwin developed an idea that explained how evolution of species could occur. He called his idea 'natural selection'.

You will learn about:
- Different types of variation in organisms
- DNA, genes and chromosomes and their roles in inherited variation
- How chromosomes determine sex in humans
- How a fetus is protected as it develops, and how it can be harmed
- How organisms inherit characteristics
- The work of Darwin on natural selection
- How and why species may become extinct

You will build your skills in:
- Using models and thinking about their strengths and limitations
- Plotting and interpreting graphs (including rates of change)
- Identifying the range of a set of data
- Using tally charts and plotting bar charts of grouped data
- Identifying appropriate secondary sources of information and extracting relevant information
- Considering the importance of questions, experiments, evidence, explanations and creative thought
- Discussing the development of scientific knowledge
- Describing the use of science in society, industry and research
- Describing the use of scientific understanding by individuals and groups working together
- Discussing the global environmental impacts of some uses of science

Chapter 3 . Topic 1

Variation within a species

You will learn:
- To describe how genetic differences between organisms can lead to variation within the species
- To collect and record observations and measurements appropriately
- To interpret results and form conclusions using scientific knowledge and understanding
- To present results appropriately

Starting point

You should know that...	You should be able to...
Characteristics vary between one organism and another	Use tables, and bar charts
Scientists classify organisms by putting them into groups, based on their characteristics	Use results to make conclusions
A species is a group of organisms that share very similar characteristics	

Proboscis monkeys and orangutans live on the island of Borneo. They share many characteristics, such as having a nose and ears. However, there are big differences between those characteristics because they are different species. Differences in a characteristic are called **variation**.

There is much less variation in a characteristic between members of the same species. For example, all humans have the same type of skin but it varies in colour (see figure 3.5).

3.1 *A proboscis monkey.*

1 Look at figures 3.1 and 3.2.
  a) Both proboscis monkeys and orangutans have noses. Describe the variation in this characteristic between the two species.
  b) Choose *one* other characteristic of the animals. Describe how it varies.

2 Think of someone famous. Describe the variation in *two* characteristics that you and that person both have.

3.2 *An orangutan.*

Discontinuous variation

Variation with a distinct set of options is **discontinuous variation**. For example, some people are able to roll their tongues and others are not. There are only two possible options in the characteristic of tongue rolling – 'able to roll' and 'not able to roll'.

Another example is the number of peas in a pea pod (the casing in which the pea seeds grow), which is a **whole number**. Some peas are smaller than others, but fractions of peas do not grow.

Key terms

discontinuous variation: variation that has a distinct set of options or categories.

variation: differences between characteristics.

whole number: number without fractions or a decimal point.

34   Variation and inheritance

3.1

We show discontinuous variation on a bar chart, with gaps between the bars.

The number of pods containing different numbers of peas

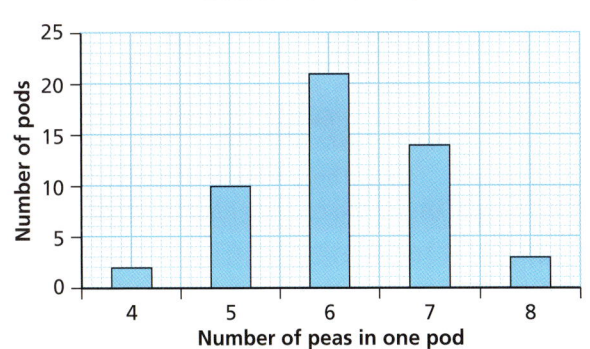

3.4 Scientists counted the number of peas in 50 different pea pods.

3.3 Can you roll your tongue?

3 Look at the bar chart in figure 3.4.
   a) How many pods contained six peas?
   b) What was the least common number of peas in one pod?

4 The table shows the number of nails on the front feet of elephant species.

Elephant species	Number of nails on front feet
African forest elephant	5
African savanna elephant	4
Asian elephant	5

   a) Explain why this data shows discontinuous variation.
   b) Present the data using a suitable chart or graph.

Activity 3.1: Investigating discontinuous variation

Find out if your friends or family have straight little fingers or bent little fingers.

A1 Draw a table to show the number of people who have attached bent little fingers and the number who have straight little fingers.
A2 Present your data using a suitable chart or graph.
A3 Make a conclusion.

Continuous variation

Some variation does not have a set of distinct options but varies gradually. This is called **continuous variation**. Examples include human skin colour and human height.

Key term

continuous variation: variation that can have any value within a range.

Variation within a species   35

Human height can be measured in numbers. Numerical **data** such as this has a **range**. To describe a range we find the highest and lowest values. In the tables below, the top value is 104 mm and the bottom value is 80 mm. We say that the range is 'from 80 to 104 mm'.

Very few people in your class have exactly the same height because height varies continuously. Someone's height may have any value within a range.

To show continuous variation on a bar chart, we put the data into groups of smaller ranges. These ranges must not overlap and must all be the same size. Here is an example using pea pod length.

3.5 *There is continuous variation in the colour of human skin.*

- *Group your data:* Look at the data showing pea pod lengths. Groups could be: 80–84 mm, 85–89 mm, 90–95 mm and so on. We do not include groups outside the range of the data.

Lengths of some pea pods (mm)
80 99 104 84 96 94 97 98 89 90 88 91 93 96 87 88 90

- *Draw a tally chart:* We write the groups into a table called a **tally chart**.

Grouped lengths of pea pods (mm)	Tally	Total
80–84		
85–89		
90–94		
95–99		
100–104		

> **Key terms**
>
> **data**: numbers and words that can be organised to give information.
>
> **range**: the highest and lowest values in a set of data.
>
> **tally chart**: a table used to help count things.

- *Complete the tally:* One by one, we cross out each value and put a mark in the 'tally column' to show its group.

Lengths of some pea pods (mm)
80 91 104 84 93 92 94 91 89 90 88 91 98 96 87 88 96 86 90 99

Grouped lengths of pea pods (mm)	Tally	Total
80–84	//	
85–89		
90–94	ℋℋ	
95–99		
100–104	/	

When you have four tally marks and add a fifth, you draw it through the other four. So ℋℋ means '5'.

Variation and inheritance

- *Complete the totals:* We add up each tally and write in the totals.

Grouped lengths of pea pods (mm)	Tally	Total
80–84	//	2
85–89	////	5
90–94	//// ///	8
95–99	////	4
100–104	/	1

> **Key terms**
>
> **frequency**: the number of times an event occurs.
>
> **frequency diagram**: any diagram showing the frequency of something.

- *Draw a bar chart without gaps:* We show the grouped data on a bar chart. The data is continuous so we do not have gaps between the bars.
- The number of pea pods in each group is their **frequency**. So, this bar chart is also a **frequency diagram**.

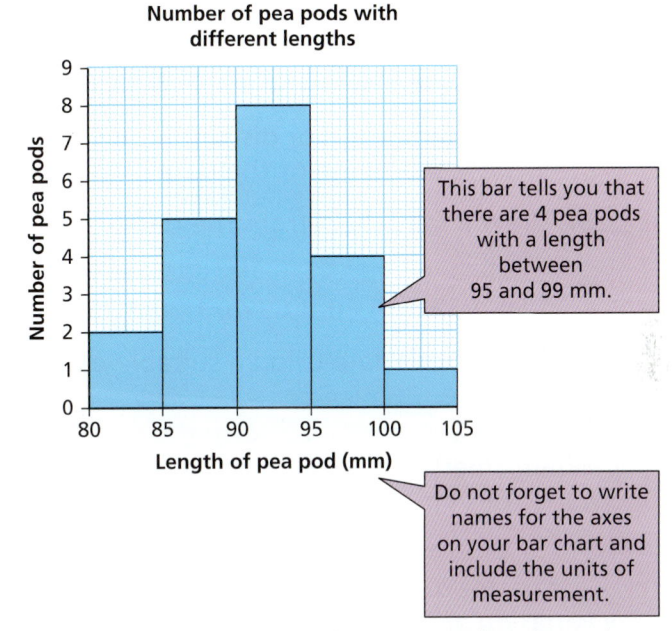

This bar tells you that there are 4 pea pods with a length between 95 and 99 mm.

Do not forget to write names for the axes on your bar chart and include the units of measurement.

3.6 Bar charts with grouped continuous data do not have gaps between the bars.

Activity 3.2: Investigating continuous variation

- Take off your shoes and stand against a wall or a board.
- Ask someone to put a pencil on top of your head and make a mark.
- Use a tape measure to measure the height of the mark. This is your height.
  - A1 Collect height measurements from others in your class.
  - A2 State the range of the measurements.
  - A3 Design groups for the measurements.
  - A4 Draw a tally chart for your data.
  - A5 Present your data using a bar chart.
  - A6 Make a conclusion about which heights are most common.
  - A7 Does your conclusion work for everyone in your school? Explain your reasoning.
  - A8 Describe how you could investigate your answer to A7 further.

3.7

Variation within a species 37

5 State whether each of the following describes continuous or discontinuous variation:

a) heights of trees

b) lengths of leaves

c) having an earring

d) number of times your heart beats in 10 seconds

e) the sizes of cakes

6 Look at the data in the table below, which shows some human heights.

| 1.76 m | 1.70 m | 1.56 m | 1.87 m | 1.60 m | 1.67 m | 1.75 m |
| 1.83 m | 1.61 m | 1.84 m | 1.82 m | 1.77 m | 1.72 m | 1.57 m |

a) Is this continuous or discontinuous variation? What is the range of the data?

b) Draw a tally chart from the data. Use these groups:

1.50–1.59 m, 1.60–1.69 m, 1.70–1.79 m, 1.80–1.89 m

c) Present this data using a suitable chart or graph.

7 Some ID cards contain information about variation. When a person uses the card, a computer checks the variations in the real person with the information stored in the card.

Is it better to use continuous or discontinuous variation about humans for ID cards?
Explain your reasoning.

Key term

environmental variation: variation in characteristics caused by an organism's surroundings.

Causes of variation

Variation in a characteristic can be caused by two factors:

- the environment
- an organism's parents

Variation caused by the environment is called **environmental variation**. It happens when things in the surroundings cause changes to an organism. For example, trees growing on a windy coast are often shaped by the wind (see figure 3.8). Plants may grow tall or short or may have different flower colours caused by the soil they are growing in (see figure 3.9).

3.8 This tree's shape has been altered by the wind.

38 Variation and inheritance

In humans, having a scar caused by an accident, the languages you speak, and the length of your hair are all examples of environmental variation.

Variation caused by parents is called **inherited variation**. For example, in humans you inherit your natural eye and hair colours. These are variations that you are born with.

Some variation is both inherited and environmental. For example, you inherit a certain skin colour but this can be changed by sunlight. Some songbirds inherit a basic song pattern, which then alters when the bird hears the songs of other birds.

3.9 *Hydrangeas have pink flowers in alkaline soils and blue flowers in acidic soils.*

8 State whether each of these human characteristics is an example of inherited or environmental variation:
   a) natural hair colour
   b) hair length
   c) language
   d) natural eye colour

9 Give the reason why the tree's shape in figure 3.8 is not an example of inherited variation.

10 a) What type of soil are the hydrangeas in figure 3.9 growing in?
   b) Give a reason for your answer to part **a)**.

11 Look at figure 3.10.
   a) Give *two* examples of inherited variation that you can see in the girl.
   b) Give *two* examples of environmental variation that you can see in the girl.

12 Explain why human weight is caused by both inherited and environmental factors.

13 Describe the following human variations as inherited or environmental and continuous or discontinuous.
   a) hair length
   b) eye colour
   c) scars

3.10 *Human characteristics include both inherited and environmental variation.*

Key term

inherited variation: variation in characteristics caused by an organism's parents.

Variation within a species 39

Science in context: Coral reef bleaching

Some types of environmental variation are used to monitor changes in the conditions in habitats. For example, coral reefs are made by tiny sea animals that build hard structures in which they live. Corals come in many different colours. However, if the sea becomes warmer, more of the corals become white rather than coloured. Global warming is making some areas of sea warmer than usual.

3.11 *Warmer temperatures have caused this coral to turn white (or 'bleach').*

Making links

In Stage 7 Topic 4.2 Chemistry you may have learned about indicators. In what way are the hydrangeas in figure 3.9 similar to litmus, and in what way are they different?

14 Discuss how observing the coral for any colour changes can help scientists with their research into the global environmental impact of global warming.

Key facts:

- ✔ Data that shows continuous variation may have any value (within a range).
- ✔ Data that shows discontinuous variation has a limited number of options.
- ✔ Variation that is caused by environmental factors is environmental variation.
- ✔ Variation that an organism gets from its parents is inherited variation.

Check your skills progress:

- I can identify the range of a set of data.
- I can divide data into smaller groups of equal size.
- I can design and use a tally chart to help count items.
- I can select and draw the correct type of bar chart to show my continuous and discontinuous data.
- I can suggest further investigations that can be done based on conclusions from an investigation.

Chapter 3 . Topic 2

Chromosomes, genes and DNA

You will learn:
- To describe how a chromosome contains a molecule of DNA, some sections of which are genes
- To describe the role of genes in inherited variation
- To understand that models and analogies can change according to scientific evidence

Starting point

You should know that...	You should be able to...
The nucleus of a cell contains instructions that control what a cell does	Identify and use appropriate secondary sources to collect information
Inherited variation is caused by an organism's parents	Use models to explain scientific ideas

DNA

DNA is a substance found in the nucleus of every cell in an organism. It carries information about how the organism develops and functions. It is DNA that causes inherited variation and we say that DNA is the organism's **genetic material**.

DNA has a special structure. It is one molecule made of two 'backbone strand' spirals, twisting around one another in a 'double-helix' shape (figure 3.13).

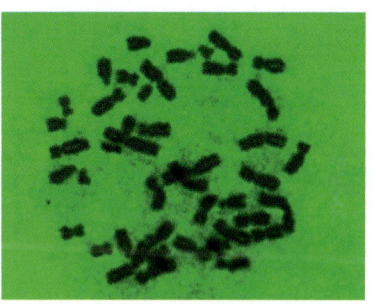

3.12 *Human chromosomes from the nucleus of one cell.*

Chromosomes

One extremely long DNA molecule is folded up together with some proteins to form a structure called a **chromosome**. Different species have different numbers of chromosomes in their nuclei. For example, there are 46 chromosomes inside the nucleus of almost every cell in humans.

Genes

Certain sections of a DNA molecule in a chromosome contain instructions for a characteristic. These sections are called **genes**. Genes control characteristics such as fur colour, eye colour, height or tail length. Sometimes a single gene controls how a characteristic develops, but usually many genes act together to determine the characteristic.

Every individual in a species has the same number of chromosomes. However, the genes on those chromosomes have slight differences between them in each individual.

Key terms

chromosome: structure containing a molecule of DNA, which carries genetic information in genes.

DNA: the substance that carries genetic information.

gene: section of DNA that controls the development of a specific characteristic.

genetic material: substance found in a cell that controls how the cell develops and what it does. The genetic material of most organisms is DNA.

For example, two mice each have 40 chromosomes in their cell nuclei, and the chromosomes in both mice contain genes that make them grow fur. However, one mouse may have genes for white fur, while the other mouse may have genes for brown fur.

The chromosomes in each human cell nucleus contain about 20 000 different genes. And each of these genes can come in slightly different forms. That is why humans all look so different. It is an organism's genes that are responsible for its inherited variation.

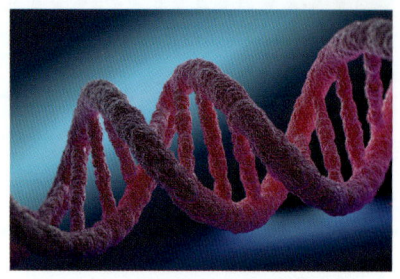

3.13 *DNA inside a chromosome has a double-helix shape, in which two strands coil around each other with crosslinks between them. The overall structure is a bit like a twisted ladder.*

1. a) What is the substance that makes up genetic material in plants and animals?
   b) Where in a human cell would you find the genetic material?

2. a) What is a gene?
   b) Suggest *three* examples of characteristics controlled by genes in humans.

3. If you took a cell from your cheek and counted the chromosomes inside it, how many would you expect to find?

Science in context: Discovering DNA

James Watson and Francis Crick were the first scientists to discover the structure of DNA, in 1953. They were working together in a laboratory in Cambridge, UK, trying to answer the research question 'What is the structure of DNA?' They realised that understanding the structure of DNA would help to explain how genes work and how genes are passed on from parents to offspring.

To be able to answer their research question Watson and Crick needed a lot of evidence. Some of this evidence came from special X-ray photographs of DNA taken by Rosalind Franklin and Maurice Wilkins. Using this evidence, along with work from other scientists and their own scientific knowledge and understanding, they built a 3D model of DNA showing its structure. Their structure is still accepted today.

3.14 *James Watson (right) and Francis Crick (left), in 1953, with their model of the structure of DNA.*

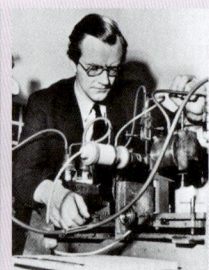

3.15 *Rosalind Franklin (left) and Maurice Wilkins (right) used special X-ray machines to take photographs of DNA.*

Variation and inheritance

3.2

4 Look at the box about discovering DNA.

   a) Which scientists were involved in the discovery of the structure of DNA?

   b) What was their main research question?

   c) Describe *one* piece of evidence that Watson and Crick used.

   d) Why is it important to collect plenty of evidence when conducting an investigation?

   e) Along with other scientists' results, what did Watson and Crick use to help them develop their structure for DNA?

5 Draw or make a model to explain where genes are found in a cell nucleus.

Making links

In Chemistry you may have met many different types of molecules. Name one molecule you have met and explain why it is a molecule. Give *one* way in which your chosen molecule is the same as DNA, and *one* way in which it differs.

Activity 3.3: Researching work on genes

Extension For this activity, use secondary sources to research your answers. First identify some suitable sources of information. Then extract the relevant information needed to answer the questions. Try to put your answers in your own words, and avoid copying out large chunks of information that is not relevant.

The Human Genome Project ran from 1990 to 2003 and involved scientists from all over the world.

A1 What did the project want to discover about genes?

A2 The Human Genome Project involved many different people. How was it possible to use so many different people, and why is this an advantage?

A3 What were the findings of the Human Genome Project?

A4 What are some benefits of having this information?

Key facts:

✔ DNA is the genetic material that carries information determining how individual plants and animals develop.

✔ Chromosomes are found in the nucleus of the cell and contain DNA.

✔ Genes are sections of DNA that control the development of a specific characteristic and so control an organism's inherited variation.

Check your skills progress:

- I can explain the use of models.
- I can extract relevant and precise information from secondary sources.

Chromosomes, genes and DNA

Chapter 3 . Topic 3

Fertilisation and inheritance

You will learn:

- To describe how fertilisation in humans occurs
- To explain why organisms inherit features from both their parents
- To describe the role of the XX and XY chromosomes in human sex determination
- To describe the uses, strengths and limitations of models and analogies
- To decide whether evidence from first-hand experience or secondary sources should be used

Starting point

You should know that...	You should be able to...
Reproduction is one of the seven life processes	
Males and females are involved in human reproduction	Understand how and why models are used
Genes are found in the DNA of chromosomes and control inherited characteristics	

Sexual reproduction

Most larger organisms reproduce using **sexual reproduction**, which means that males and females are needed to produce offspring. Plants and animals both use sexual reproduction.

For sexual reproduction to occur, an organism needs to produce **gametes** (or **sex cells**). These are specialised cells and their nuclei only contain half the normal number of chromosomes. For example, most human body cells contain 46 chromosomes but human gametes contain 23 chromosomes.

The male gametes in animals (including humans) are **sperm cells** and the female gametes are **egg cells**. Figures 3.16 and 3.17 show some features of egg cells and sperm cells.

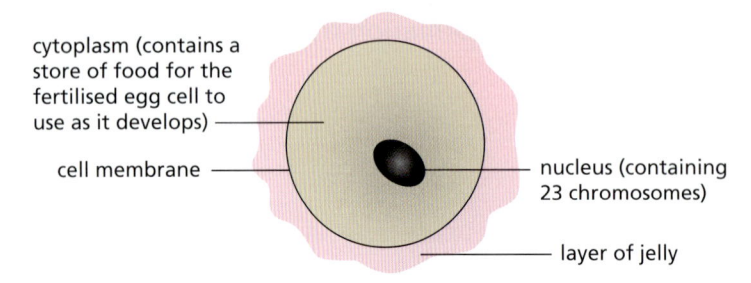

Key terms

egg cell: female gamete.

gamete: specialised cell needed for sexual reproduction.

sex cell: another term for a gamete.

sexual reproduction: the type of reproduction involving male and female gametes coming together.

sperm cell: male gamete.

3.16 *A human egg cell.*

44   Variation and inheritance

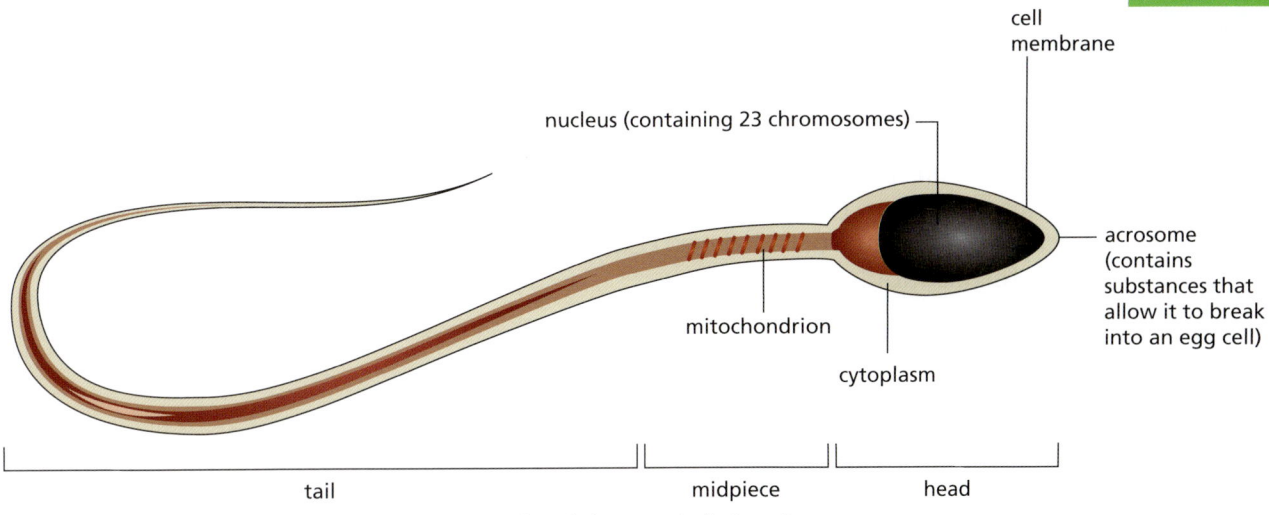

3.3

3.17 *A human sperm cell has a tail and a streamlined shape to help it swim.*

For sexual reproduction to occur, a male gamete and a female gamete need to join together, so that their two nuclei can become one. This process is called **fertilisation** and forms a **fertilised egg cell**. The nucleus of the fertilised egg cell contains the full number of chromosomes.

> **Key terms**
>
> **fertilisation**: when an egg cell nucleus and a sperm cell nucleus fuse (join) and form a fertilised egg cell.
>
> **fertilised egg cell**: cell produced when a sperm and egg cell fuse

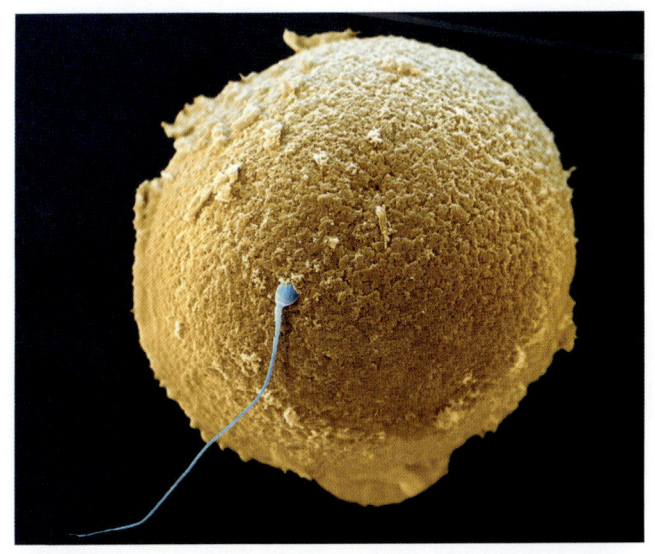

3.18 *A human sperm cell entering an egg cell to fertilise it (×700).*

1. What happens during sexual reproduction?
2. What are the *two* human gametes?
3. Give *three* adaptations of a sperm cell that make it good at its job.
4. Explain why it is important for the egg cell to have only half of the instructions to make a new human.

Fertilisation and inheritance 45

Fertilisation in humans

The tip of a sperm cell contains substances that allow it to break through the jelly layer and cell membrane of the egg cell. Only one sperm cell can break through the jelly coat of the egg cell. Once the sperm cell has broken through the layers, the nuclei of the sperm cell and egg cell fuse (join) together. This is fertilisation.

The sperm cell nucleus and egg cell nucleus each have only half the number of chromosomes needed to make a new human. When they fuse, the new cell has a full set of chromosomes. This cell contains a new combination of DNA, half from the mother and half from the father. This means children have features from both their parents, but they do not look exactly like either parent.

The fertilised egg cell forms a ball of cells, then an **embryo**, and eventually a new baby.

Key term

embryo: small ball of cells that develops from a fertilised egg cell. It becomes attached to the uterus lining and develops into a fetus.

3.19 *Human fertilisation.*

46   Variation and inheritance

5 What happens during fertilisation?

6 Where does fertilisation usually happen?

7 How does a fertilised egg cell turn into an embryo?

8 Why is it important that the nucleus from the egg cell and the sperm 'fuse' during fertilisation?

Human chromosomes

The chromosomes in figures 3.19 and 3.21 have been arranged in pairs. They do not look like this in a nucleus, but it is easier to see the pairs if we use a diagram as a model.

There are 23 different types of chromosome in humans. Each type is a different size, and in diagrams they are arranged in size order. A fertilised egg cell gets two copies of *each* type of chromosome – one copy from the father and one copy from the mother. That is why all your body cells contain 46 chromosomes.

The genes in the genetic material in each chromosome control your inherited variation. So, you get half of your inherited variation from your mother and half from your father. That is why your characteristics look like a combination of your parents' characteristics. We say that you inherit features from your parents. This can be called **inheritance**.

3.20 *Children inherit features from both their parents.*

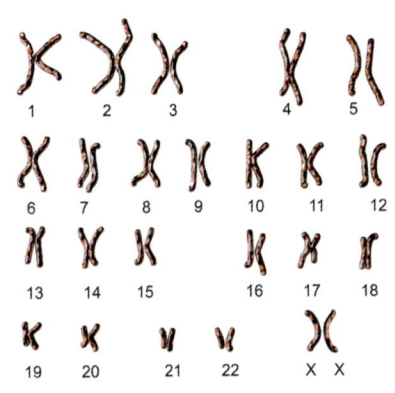

3.21 *Diagrams show human chromosomes arranged in pairs and in size order.*

Sex determination

If you look carefully at the chromosomes in figures 3.19 and 3.21, you will notice that the last two chromosomes are slightly different. These are the **sex chromosomes** – X and Y. They control whether someone is male or female. Females have two X sex chromosomes (XX) and males have an X and a Y (XY).

When a gamete is made, it gets one copy of each chromosome, including one sex chromosome. Female egg cells always contain one X chromosome. Half of a man's sperm cells will contain an X and half will contain a Y chromosome. If a sperm cell carrying an X sex chromosome fertilises an egg cell, the baby will be female. If a sperm cell carrying a Y sex chromosome fertilises an egg cell, the baby will be male. Sex chromosomes are used for **sex determination** (they determine a person's sex).

Key terms

inheritance: passing of features from parents to children.

sex chromosome: chromosome that comes in two types, X and Y. Sex chromosomes control whether someone is male (XY) or female (XX).

sex determination: how a person's sex (whether they are male or female) is controlled.

Fertilisation and inheritance

Brothers, sisters and twins

The chromosome that a gamete gets from each pair of chromosomes is random. So, each gamete that is made has a different combination of chromosomes. That is why brothers and sisters do not look exactly the same as one another. The gametes that made them contained different combinations of chromosomes. The only exception are identical twins, which are formed when a fertilised egg cell splits into two cells, and each cell then develops into an embryo.

Activity 3.4: Modelling chromosomes

How could you make a model to explain why you get half your chromosomes from your mother and half from your father?

Your teacher may give you some ideas or equipment to use.

A1 Write a short description of your model.

A2 Get together with a few others and discuss your models. Think about the strengths and weaknesses of each model.

A3 Work together to plan the model you would like to make.

A4 Show your plan to your teacher before you start making your model.

9 State the number of chromosomes in the nucleus of a human:
   a) fertilised egg cell
   b) egg cell
   c) liver cell

10 A fruit fly body cell contains 8 chromosomes. How many chromosomes will be in a fruit fly sperm cell?

11 Look at figure 3.19. Explain whether the fertilised egg cell will grow into a boy or a girl.

12 Look at figure 3.21. Explain whether these chromosomes are from a female or a male.

13 Your teacher has asked you to find out the length of the longest human chromosome. Would you look this up (using a secondary source) or find out for yourself using a microscope? Explain your choice.

Making links

In Stage 8 Physics you may have learned about pressure. Explain why the needle use to inject a sperm cell into an egg cell in IVF treatment must have a very sharp point.

Variation and inheritance

14 Explain why about half of all babies born are male and half are female.

15 Why is the total number of chromosomes in an animal's body cells always an even number?

Key facts:
- Male gametes are sperm cells and female gametes are egg cells.
- Gametes carry only one copy of each type of chromosome.
- When a sperm cell nucleus and an egg cell nucleus fuse, a fertilised egg cell is made. This develops into an embryo, which develops into a baby.
- A fertilised egg cell contains two copies of each type of chromosome (one from the mother and one from the father).
- In humans, males have XY sex chromosomes and females have XX.

Check your skills progress:
- I can design a model to explain a complex process.

Chapter 3 . Topic 4

Fetal growth and development

You will learn:

- To describe the development of the fetus
- To explain how the fetus is protected and nourished
- To discuss the ways in which a mother's health and lifestyle choices (diet, smoking and drugs) can affect the development of a fetus.
- To interpret results and form conclusions using scientific knowledge and understanding

Starting point

You should know that...	You should be able to...
A fertilised egg cell grows and develops into a baby, inside a mother	Collect and use information from secondary sources
	Plot and interpret graphs
People need to eat balanced diets in order to stay healthy	
Microorganisms (such as viruses) can cause diseases	

An embryo becomes a fetus

After the embryo has implanted in the uterus lining, cell division continues. During this time, cells also begin to become specialised to form different parts of the body. Between 8 and 10 weeks after fertilisation, the embryo's organs have formed and its heart has started to beat. The arms and legs also begin to form and the embryo begins to resemble a baby. After this time, the developing baby is called a fetus.

Science in context: Fetal scanning

The gestation period is the length of time it takes for a baby to grow and be ready to be born. In humans, this takes 40 weeks (nine months) but it is different in different animals. For example, the gestation period for rabbits is 31 days and for elephants it is 22 months.

Many women have ultrasound scans to check on the health and development of a fetus. Ultrasound was first developed in the early 20th century, so that ships could detect icebergs. A sound wave is emitted from a device, which then listens for an echo (when the sound wave bounces back off an object).

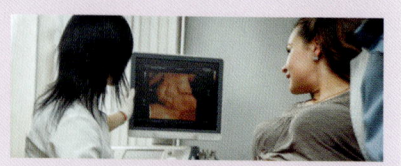

3.22 A fetus' face appears on a modern 3D ultrasound scanner.

In the 1960s, scientists and doctors realised that this idea could be used to 'see' inside people's bodies. Modern ultrasound scanners can produce very clear pictures of a fetus, some of which are in 3D.

50 Variation and inheritance

1 Describe how fetal scanning can be used to improve scientists' understanding of fetal development and improve the care given to women during their pregnancy.

Diet during pregnancy

It is important that a pregnant woman has a healthy, balanced diet. This ensures that the fetus gets all the nutrients it needs, so it has energy and the raw materials for growth and development.

2 Give the name of the nutrient in the diet that is the most important for providing energy.

3 Give the name of the nutrient that is important for growth.

There are some things that women are advised not to eat during pregnancy. This is because they may contain bacteria that could harm a fetus. For example, soft blue cheeses can contain listeria bacteria. Infection with this bacterium is very rare, but if it does occur it can harm the fetus (or even cause it to die).

Pregnant women are also often told to eat leafy green vegetables and brown rice, because these foods contain a lot of a vitamin called folic acid. This vitamin is needed to help the fetus' spinal cord to form properly. A lack of it may cause spina bifida, which may cause a child to have difficulty in walking.

3.23 Many women avoid foods that may contain harmful bacteria during pregnancy, such as blue cheese.

3.24 Many women take folic acid supplements during pregnancy.

4 Give *one* reason why women may need to be more careful about what they eat when pregnant.

5 Give the reason why a pregnant woman may take folic acid supplement tablets.

Activity 3.5 Healthy eating during pregnancy

How would you help pregnant women to eat healthily?

Use your scientific knowledge about healthy diets to design a poster to display in a doctor's office with advice for pregnant women. Make sure you explain the reasons behind your advice.

Fetal growth and development

Drugs and pregnancy

A **drug** is a substance that changes the way your body works. Drugs can be used for many different purposes. Some drugs help to fight disease, some reduce pain and others are decongestants (drugs that can provide relief from a blocked nose). Drugs that are used for medical purposes are **medicines**. Other drugs are used for enjoyment and many of these recreational drugs are illegal.

Because drugs affect how a person's body works, they may also change how it grows and develops. Many drugs can pass into a fetus' blood through the placenta and some can harm the fetus (even if they don't have an effect on the mother). So, pregnant women need to be particularly careful about taking medicines. Doctors also need to be careful about medicines they give pregnant women.

In the 1950s, many pregnant women were given a medicine called thalidomide. This stopped them feeling sick. Very sadly, it caused tens of thousands of babies to be born with very short arms and legs.

3.25 *Doctors need to be careful about the medicines they give pregnant woman.*

> **Key term**
>
> **drug**: any substance that changes something about the way your body works.

3.26 *Victims of thalidomide.*

> **6** What is a drug?
>
> **7** In many countries it is the law to have an information leaflet with any medicine to say whether a woman can take the medicine if pregnant. Evaluate this idea.

Tobacco smoke and pregnancy

When smoking tobacco, a person inhales over 4000 substances, most of which have harmful effects on the body. Smoking as an adult causes problems for many different organ systems, including the respiratory system. Inhaling other people's smoke can also cause harm.

Variation and inheritance

3.4

If a woman smokes while she is pregnant, or lives in a place where a lot of people smoke the substances in the smoke move into the blood of the developing fetus through the placenta. Two of these substances are carbon monoxide and nicotine (the drug in tobacco). They can reduce the amount of oxygen that the fetus gets, which can have damaging effects.

Babies born to mothers who smoke during pregnancy may have a low mass, reduced growth, underdeveloped lungs, heart defects and delayed brain development. Smoking during pregnancy also increases the chances of a **stillborn** baby (a baby that is dead when it is born).

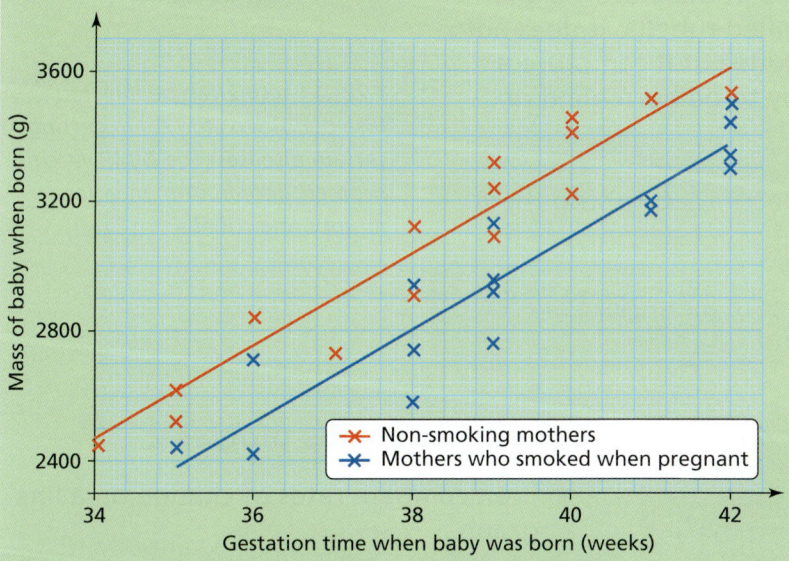

Key term

stillborn: the term used to describe a baby that is dead when it is born.

8 Name *two* substances that are inhaled when a person smokes.

9 Give *three* ways in which a woman who smokes may damage her developing fetus.

3.27 A graph showing how the mass of babies is affected by smoking during pregnancy.

10 Look at the scatter graph in figure 3.27.

  a) Make a conclusion from the graph.

  b) Explain why the line of best fit for 'non-smokers' is above that of 'smokers'.

Fetal growth and development

Activity 3.6: Researching the effects of drugs on a fetus' development

How can you inform people about the harmful effects of drugs in pregnancy?

Imagine that you are doctor. One of your jobs is to advise women who are trying to get pregnant about the risks of taking drugs.

A1 Research the impact of *four* different drugs on the development of a fetus.

A2 Create a leaflet or poster to give information to women about the dangers of taking drugs while they are pregnant.

A3 Sometimes a doctor may give a pregnant woman a medicine even though there is some risk that it will cause harm. Suggest why a doctor may sometimes do this.

Diseases and pregnancy

A fetus' growth and development can also be affected by diseases. For example, some viruses can cross from the mother's blood into the fetus' blood in the placenta and harm the fetus. One such virus is called rubella. It does not usually cause a serious illness in adults but it can cause a fetus to be stillborn or cause a baby to be born blind or deaf.

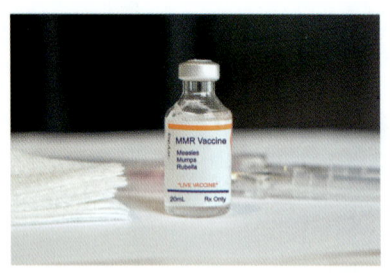

3.28 *A vaccine can be injected into people to stop them getting certain diseases. The MMR vaccine protects people from measles, mumps and rubella.*

11 Explain why girls are often vaccinated to stop them getting rubella.

12 Explain why only some viruses in a mother's blood will reach the fetus.

Key facts:

✔ A fertilised egg cell develops into an embryo, which implants into the uterus lining and grows into a fetus.

✔ Substances diffuse between the mother's blood and the fetus' blood in the placenta.

✔ The lack of mixing of the fetus' blood with the mother's blood protects the fetus.

✔ The fetus' development can be slowed or harmed by poor diet (e.g. lack of folic acid), drugs (including medicines), smoking and diseases.

Check your skills progress:

- I can compare rates of change on a line graph.
- I can use information from secondary sources to explain scientific ideas to others.

Making links

You may have studied diffusion in Stage 8. Explain how urea molecules (a waste produced by the fetus) move by diffusion from the fetus' blood into the mother's blood.

Chapter 3 . Topic 5
Natural selection

You will learn:
- To describe how organisms are adapted to where they live
- To state what is meant by 'evolution'
- To describe how genetic differences between organisms can lead to variation within the species
- To describe how genetic changes over time result in natural selection
- To understand that models and analogies can change according to scientific evidence
- To collect and record observations and measurements appropriately
- To interpret results and form conclusions using scientific knowledge and understanding
- To present results appropriately

Starting point

You should know that...	You should be able to...
Organisms live in different ecosystems and have different characteristics to survive in their ecosystems	Understand the importance of evidence collection to support a hypothesis.
Genetic information is found on genes and passes from parents to offspring during reproduction	Use tables to record results.

Adaptation

Organisms have **adaptations** so that they can survive in the places where they live. For example, polar bears live in the cold, snowy Arctic **ecosystem**. Their adaptations include:

- thick fur (so that they do not lose too much heat)
- white fur (so that they are camouflaged and can creep up on their prey)
- feet with a large surface area (for swimming and to stop them sinking into snow)

3.29 *Polar bears are adapted to live in the Arctic ecosystem.*

There is inherited variation in the adaptations of a species. For example, the average length of hair on individual polar bears is slightly different. This variation is caused by each polar bear's slightly different genes, which they have inherited from their parents.

> **1** Give a reason why polar bears have white fur.
>
> **2** Explain why it is important that polar bears have thick fur.
>
> **3** Suggest a reason why polar bears have small ears.

Key terms

adaptation: characteristic of an organism that helps it to survive in a certain ecosystem.

ecosystem: all the organisms and the physical factors in an area.

Natural selection 55

Activity 3.7: Imaginative adaptations

What sort of adaptations are useful for an animal that lives in a sandy desert?

Use your imagination to design an animal that would be adapted to live in a sandy desert.

A1 Draw your animal (without any labels).

A2 On a separate sheet of paper, list the adaptations of your animal.

A3 Now swap your drawing with a partner. See how many adaptations your partner can spot without seeing your list.

A4 Working with your partner, add labels to your drawing to explain its adaptations.

Bird adaptations

Figure 3.30 shows ten different species of finches that live in the Galápagos Islands, in the Pacific Ocean. They all have beaks (or bills) that are adapted for the food they eat. Birds that crush up large seeds have big strong beaks. Birds that dig small insects out of small cracks have thinner beaks to push into the cracks.

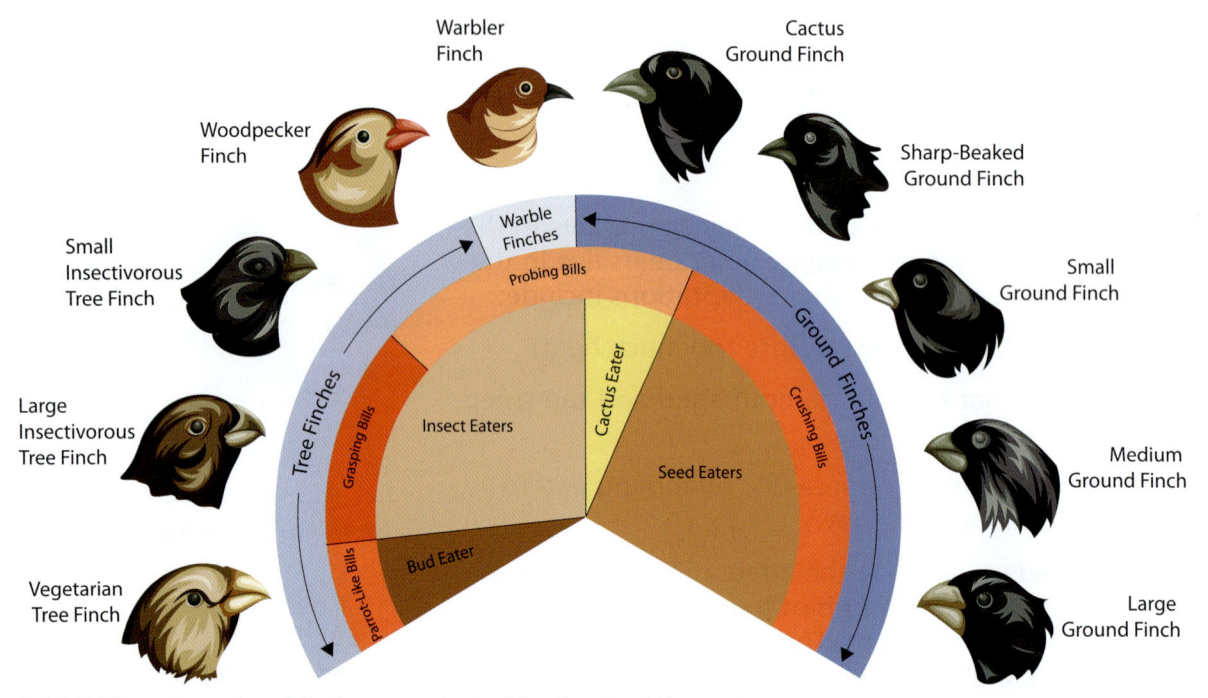

3.30 *Different species of finches are adapted for the food they eat.*

4 Look at figure 3.30.

a) Explain which finch eats the largest seeds.

b) Explain which finch eats very small insects found in cracks.

56 Variation and inheritance

Natural selection

There is also variation in the sizes of beaks in each species of finch. For example, in figure 3.30 the Large Insectivorous Tree Finch has a big beak with a slight hook for grabbing big insects. In any **population** of this species, some birds have slightly bigger beaks than average, and some have slightly smaller beaks than average. This sort of variation occurs in all animal characteristics.

Now, imagine that a disease kills many of the smaller species of insect, leaving the much bigger insects. The birds that naturally have a slightly bigger beak are better adapted to catch the bigger insects. The birds that have a smaller than average beak will not be able to catch so many of these bigger insects. So, many of the birds with the smaller beaks may not survive.

This bird population now contains more birds with bigger beaks. When these birds breed, more of the offspring will have bigger beaks (because more of the parents had bigger beaks). If this process happens over and over again, this population of birds will soon all have bigger beaks.

This process is called **natural selection**. It means that the environment of a **population** causes some of the organisms to survive and not others. This is due to slight differences in their characteristics.

> **5** What does the term 'natural selection' mean?
>
> **6** On one island in the Galápagos, finches collect insects from trees. The temperature in this area rises and the insects move deeper into the cracks in the tree bark. This makes them more difficult to catch. Explain what may happen to the number of finches with slightly longer beaks.

Key terms

evolution: a gradual change in something over time.

natural selection: the process by which organisms have (by chance) better adaptations for new environmental conditions, making them more likely to survive and reproduce than other individuals of that species.

population: the total number of individual organisms of one species living in a certain area.

3.31 Gomphotherium.

Evolution

A change in something over time is called **evolution**. In biology, the word means the gradual change in the characteristics of a population of organisms. It happens over thousands or millions of years. For example, scientists think that woolly mammoths evolved from an animal called *Gomphotherium*, which lived 23 million years ago.

Many scientists have invented hypotheses to try to explain how evolution happens. Today, the most widely accepted is Charles Darwin's theory, which says that evolution is caused by natural selection.

3.32 *Woolly mammoths lived in very cold ecosystems.*

The finches in figure 3.30 are some of the species that Darwin studied when he was collecting evidence to support his idea. He came to the conclusion that all of these different species evolved from a population of one species of finch, which arrived on the Galápagos islands over 2 million years ago.

These birds were probably blown in on a storm from South America. Although the population of finches that arrived were all one species, there was variation between the individuals, including small differences in beak shapes and sizes, feather colouring and bird size.

The conditions on the different islands in the Galápagos varied, with different habitats and food resources. These different environments led to natural selection. For example, on one island there may have been a good supply of large nuts with hard shells. In this case, those finches with slightly bigger, more powerful beaks would find it easier to get the food they required and therefore would be more likely to survive and reproduce. After many generations, many more of the finches on this island had the bigger, more powerful beaks.

7. What does the term 'evolution' mean?

8. Explain *one* way in which a woolly mammoth is adapted for its ecosystem.

9. A population of *Gomphotheria* moved into a much colder area to look for food. Use the idea of natural selection to explain how this population may have evolved into woolly mammoths.

Science in context: Charles Darwin

Charles Darwin was born in Shrewsbury in England in 1809. Many of his family before him were scientists – his father was a doctor – and he studied various aspects of science at two universities in England and Scotland from the age of 16, becoming increasingly interested in plants and the natural world through his studies.

In 1831, Darwin was invited to travel as a naturalist (a scientist who studies nature) aboard a ship called *HMS Beagle* during its five-year voyage around the world. Throughout the journey Darwin kept notes about the living things he encountered and collected samples of animals, plants and fossils wherever possible.

Some of the most famous samples that Darwin collected were birds from the Galápagos Islands. Darwin noticed

3.33 *Charles Robert Darwin (1809–1882).*

Variation and inheritance

that the mockingbirds from different islands had slight variations in certain characteristics. He also noticed that the islands had slightly different habitats.

At that time, most people believed that all living things appeared on the Earth just as we now find them. His observations of the mockingbirds made Darwin question this idea. He started to consider the idea – already suggested by scientists such as Lamarck – that a species might evolve over time.

Darwin continued his investigations when he arrived home in England. Other scientists helped him to classify some of the organisms that he had collected. Among these were some of the finches shown in figure 3.30. Once these had been classified, Darwin realised that they were like the mockingbirds he had seen – the finches from different islands had different characteristics.

He carried on collecting evidence until he thought he had enough to support his idea that natural selection can cause a group of organisms to change over time. In 1859, he published his ideas in a book for people (including other scientists) to read. His book was called *On the Origin of Species*. Many scientists thought that Darwin was correct. Others did not and there was a lot of scientific debate on the issue.

10 Look at the box about Charles Darwin.
  a) What did Darwin do while travelling on *HMS Beagle*?
  b) In Darwin's time what was the view held by most people about the evolution of living things?
  c) Suggest a research question that Darwin formed from his travels on the Beagle.
  d) Why was it important for Darwin to make careful notes about all the observations he made?
  e) Why was it important for Darwin to continue his investigations, and for him to work in collaboration with other scientists, when he got home?

Natural selection and genetics

Darwin had no idea why there is inherited variation in a characteristic between members of the same species. Today we know that this is caused by genes.

By chance, a gene may change slightly. If this change happens in a cell that is making gametes, that changed gene may be inherited by the offspring. The changed gene may then cause a slight difference in a characteristic. If this change helps the offspring to survive better than other individuals, that gene is more likely to be passed down to the next generation.

The peppered moth – natural selection in action

In the United Kingdom, there are two different colours of peppered moth – light and speckled, or dark (figure 3.34). The light-coloured moths used to be the most common form throughout Britain. However, during the 19th century, there was a large increase in the number of factories within cities, which were producing large amounts of smoke and soot. This black soot stuck to the walls of buildings and trees, giving them a much darker appearance. Due to the black soot on trees and buildings, the number of dark moths increased in the cities. In the countryside, there were still large numbers of light-coloured moths.

3.34 *Peppered moths may be light and speckled, or dark.*

11 What is the most obvious variation between the two moths in figure 3.34?

12 Which moth do you think would be best camouflaged on sooty buildings? Explain your idea.

13 Look at figure 3.34. Thinking about predators (bats and small birds) and using Darwin's idea of natural selection, explain why the number of dark moths increased in cities in the United Kingdom during the 19th century.

14 Giraffes are native to Africa and one of their main food sources is the umbrella thorn tree, which stands a couple of metres tall with leaves a long way from the ground. Explain how giraffes may have evolved their long necks, using Darwin's theory of natural selection.

Activity 3.8: Investigating natural selection

In this activity you will work with a partner to create a model to show natural selection.

You will need:

- rice grains
- dried peas or lentils
- beans of a larger type (e.g. haricot beans)
- forceps
- a small blunt knife
- tongs
- a large tray or piece of white paper
- stop clock or stopwatch

A Before you start, design a table in which to record your data.

B Spread out 20 rice grains, 20 dried peas and 20 haricot beans on your tray. These represent 'prey' of different sizes.

C Taking it in turns, see how many of the 'prey' you and your partner can pick up in 30 seconds using the tweezers to represent the beak of a bird.

Variation and inheritance

D After 30 seconds stop collecting and record how many of each type of 'prey' you have.

E Leave the remaining 'prey' on the tray and add copies of each one. For example, if you are left with 5 grains of rice and 3 peas, leave them on the tray and add another 5 grains of rice and 3 peas.

F Repeat the collection using tweezers, recording and the replacement at least three times – representing three generations.

   A1 Which type of 'prey' was easiest to collect with the forceps? Why do you think this was the case?

   A2 Which type of 'prey' were there most of at the end of your investigation?

   A3 Explain which 'prey' was most likely to survive and how this caused natural selection over several generations.

G As an extension, repeat steps A–F using first the tongs and then a blunt knife to represent the beaks of different birds. Record your results.

   A4 Describe your results.

   A5 Explain what your results show.
   - Is one type of 'beak' better at collecting a certain type of 'prey'?
   - Why do you think this is? Can you think up an hypothesis?

   A6 What would you need to do to test your hypothesis?

Key facts:

- Organisms have adaptations that help them to survive in their ecosystems.
- Evolution is a gradual change over time.
- Charles Darwin proposed the theory of evolution of organisms by natural selection.
- Natural selection happens when there is variation in a species, with some organisms being (by chance) better adapted than others.
- Natural selection means that those who are better adapted to their environment tend to be more likely to survive and have more offspring.
- Slight differences and natural changes to genes are what cause inherited variation.
- Genes that help an organism to survive better than others of the same species are more likely to be passed down to the next generation.

Check your skills progress:

- I can discuss the way that scientists worked in the past, including reference to collection of evidence.
- I can design a table to collect data, and analyse the data in it to explain what it is showing.

End of chapter review

Quick questions

1. Variation that has a limited range of options is:

    a characteristic
    b continuous
    c discounted
    d discontinuous

2. Which sex chromosomes do the cells of a male human have?

    a XY
    b XX
    c YY
    d YZ

3. What is the genetic material found in most organisms?

    a ribonucleic acid
    b proteins
    c DNA
    d chromosomes

4. If a pregnant woman lacks folic acid, her baby may suffer from a problem with its spinal cord. What is folic acid?

    a a mineral
    b a vitamin
    c a protein
    d a supplement

5. Evolution is:

    a a theory by Charles Darwin
    b a change in something over time
    c when an organism ceases to exist
    d when something turns around

6. Which letter is labelling the nucleus of the egg cell?

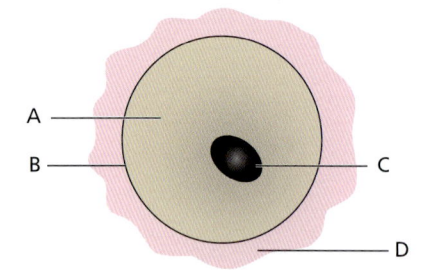

3.35

7. State whether each of the following describes continuous or discontinuous variation in humans:

   (a) length of hair

   (b) wearing glasses

   (c) having a scar

   (d) weight

   (e) height

   (f) arm length

8. Why does an egg cell contain a food store in its cytoplasm?

   a It protects the egg.

   b It contains nutrients for the developing embryo.

   c It contains the information for making a new animal.

   d It is a water reserve for the developing embryo.

9. What is the name given to the ball of cells formed when a fertilised egg cell divides?

10. Name *two* drugs that females should avoid using while pregnant.

Connect your understanding

11. Scientists classify human blood into four different 'blood groups'. These are: A, B, AB and O. Scientists in Saudi Arabia looked at the blood groups of 100 people. The table shows their results.

Blood group	Number of people
A	26
B	18
AB	4
O	52

    (a) Is variation in blood group continuous or discontinuous? Explain your choice.

    (b) Present the data using a suitable chart or graph.

12. The bar chart in figure 3.36 shows the results of the men's discus competition at the Rio Olympics in Brazil. The competition involves throwing a disc as far as possible.

    (a) Is variation in the bar chart continuous or discontinuous?
    Explain your choice.

    (b) How many men threw a distance between 55 and 59 m?

    (c) What was the most common range of distances thrown?

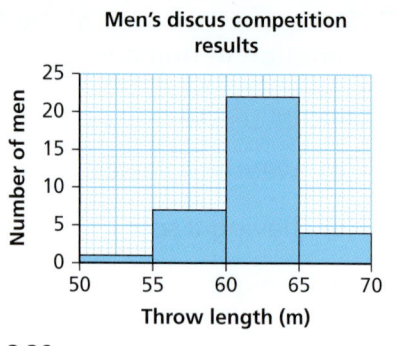

    3.36

13. The tally chart shows some lengths of beans. Some parts of it are missing.

Grouped lengths of beans (mm)	Tally	Total
70–74	//	
75–79		5
80–84	//// /	
	////	
90–94	///	

    Copy and complete the chart.

14. (a) A 'normal' human body cell contains 46 chromosomes in the nucleus. However, a sperm cell contains only 23. Explain why this is the case.

    (b) Explain how a person could inherit a variation in a *characteristic*, such as 'a dimpled chin', from their mother.

    3.37

Challenge questions

15. A student measured the widths of some leaves from a large garden plant. Their results are shown below.

6.8	7.0	5.5	5.6	7.7
6.7	7.2	5.9	5.5	5.8
6.2	5.9	6.1	6.2	7.6
6.0	6.7	6.9	5.8	7.1
5.7	6.8	6.4	6.3	7.0

    (a) The student forgot to write down the units for measuring the leaves. Suggest what the units are.

    (b) What is the range of the data?

64   Variation and inheritance

(c) Draw a tally chart to display this data.

(d) Use the data from your tally chart to draw a bar chart.

16. Suggest why Darwin's theory of natural selection was opposed when he announced it?

3.38

17. Look at figure 3.38. Use your knowledge of natural selection to explain each of the following possible situations.

   (a) The number of red frogs (like the one in the middle of the picture) decreases in subsequent generations, to the point that there are none remaining in 50 years' time.

   (b) The number of red frogs increases over the years and in 50 years' time there are more red-coloured frogs than brown frogs.

Chapter 4
Population change

What's it all about?

Loggerhead turtles live in many different places, including the Mediterranean Sea. Here, the turtles nest on beaches from Greece to Libya. Unfortunately loggerhead turtles are at risk of becoming endangered because of human activity. As more and more coastal resorts are built, nesting sites are destroyed and the turtles' breeding is disrupted. Marine pollution and interference from fishing equipment also kill many loggerhead turtles. It is important that we consider the impact of our actions on other species with which we share this planet.

You will learn about:
- How and why populations change
- The reasons why species become extinct

You will build your skills in:
- Independent research
- Evaluating your work
- Evaluating issues using scientific understanding
- Discussing the global environmental impacts of some uses of science

Chapter 4
Populations and extinction

You will learn:
- To explain ways in which organisms are adapted to their ecosystems
- To describe the effects of an environmental change on the population of a species (including extinction)
- To interpret results and form conclusions using scientific knowledge and understanding
- To present results appropriately
- To evaluate experimental methods, explaining any improvements suggested

Starting point

You should know that...	You should be able to...
A habitat needs to supply an organism with the resources it needs to survive	Know where to look for information when doing research
Organisms can survive in their ecosystems because they are adapted to where they live	Present ordered information in a table
Food chains show the feeding relationships between organisms	Use models, such as food chains
Invasive species can affect populations of species	

Resources and adaptation

To survive and reproduce in an **ecosystem**, organisms need resources. The table shows resources needed by plants and animals.

Resources needed by animals	Resources need by plants
Water	Water
Shelter	Shelter
Resources for reproduction (e.g. finding a mate)	Resources for reproduction (e.g. insects for pollination)
Oxygen (for aerobic respiration)	Oxygen (for aerobic respiration)
	Light (for photosynthesis)
Food	Carbon dioxide (for photosynthesis)
Source of mineral salts (food)	Source of mineral salts
	Warmth

Populations and extinction 67

An **adaptation** is a feature of a species that helps it to survive in its **environment** in an ecosystem.

Animal adaptations include coat colour and thickness, size of the animal and the structure of the feet and claws. Adaptations of plants include leaf shape and size, distribution of stomata and the size of the plant.

An organism's adaptations are caused by the genes in its cells. Different organisms of the same species inherit slightly different combinations of genes, so any adaptations inherited can show differences. For example, one elephant may have a slightly longer trunk than another. We say that they show inherited variation.

> **Key terms**
>
> **adaptation**: characteristic of an organism that helps it to survive in a certain ecosystem.
>
> **environment**: the other organisms and physical factors around a certain organism.

1 a) Give *four* resources that an animal needs to survive and reproduce.

b) Explain why a plant needs water to survive.

2 Explain the term 'adaptation'.

Adaptations to life in a desert

Deserts are extreme environments. They are very dry and may be very hot during the day and cold at night. Due to these conditions, few plants live in the desert. The desert fox in figure 4.1 is well adapted to life in this harsh habitat. The table shows some of its adaptations.

Physical adaptations of desert foxes
Sandy coloured fur for camouflage
Large ears for hearing predators, and to help them lose heat
Fur on the underside of their paws to help protect their feet from the hot sand

4.1 *Desert foxes are adapted to survive in the Sahara desert.*

Cactus plants are well known for growing in American deserts. Cacti have many adaptations that help them to survive where there is very little water. For example, they have:

- spines instead of leaves to reduce water loss through transpiration
- a thick waxy covering to reduce water loss through evaporation
- a special tissue in the stem to store water
- wide-spreading roots that are able to absorb water very quickly

Population change

3 How is a desert fox adapted to live in the desert? List its physical adaptations.

4 When it rains in a desert, the rain is often quite heavy but does not last very long. Explain how a cactus' roots are adapted for this.

Adaptations to life in polar regions

The regions near the Earth's North Pole (Arctic) and South Pole (Antarctic) are very cold, and covered with much snow and ice. Many organisms survive in this extreme environment, including snowy owls (figure 4.3). The table shows some of the ways in which snowy owls are adapted to Arctic life.

4.2 Cactus spines help reduce water loss, and also deter animals from eating the plant.

Physical adaptations of snowy owls
White feathers for camouflage
Thick feathers for insulation
Large talons (claws) on their feet to catch prey

5 Explain how having thick feathers allows snowy owls to survive in the Arctic.

4.3 A snowy owl has adaptations that help it hunt in the Arctic.

Factors affecting the size of populations

Many different factors affect the size of a **population** of organisms.

Some factors are physical (non-living) such as temperature, sunlight, water availability and pollution. For example, a population of gazelles could decrease if there was a period of very cold weather.

If there is a permanent change in a physical factor, it may mean that an organism dies out in that area altogether. For example, imagine that an American desert starts to get rain constantly. The roots of cacti plants are adapted to take in water very quickly, but if they take in too much they start to rot and the plants die. Adaptations for one ecosystem may not help organisms to survive if the conditions in the ecosystem change.

> **Key term**
>
> **population**: the total number of individual organisms of one species living in a certain area.

6 A certain area in the Arctic warms up permanently and the snow now falls as rain. Explain why this may cause snowy owls to stop living in this area.

7 Imagine that the Sahara desert gets very cold and remains cold. Explain why this may cause desert foxes to stop living in this area.

Activity 4.1: Investigating population changes

In this activity, you will use secondary sources to research population changes and consider why these should be used instead of your own first-hand experience and observations.

A1 Find out the name of *one* plant or animal from your country whose population has increased, and *one* whose population has decreased. You will need to find examples with population data for different years.

A2 Present your data as a table.

A3 Draw a line graph to show how the numbers of these organisms have changed over time.

A4 Label your line graph to explain why the population has increased or decreased.

A5 Why is it better to use secondary sources to gather this kind of information, rather than relying on your own experience and observations?

Predator–prey interactions

The size of a population of organisms in an area is also affected by living factors – other organisms. These living factors may spread diseases or compete for resources or they may eat the other organisms in the same area.

For example, look at this food chain:

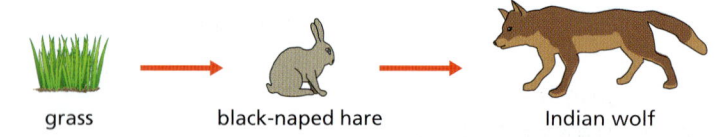

grass → black-naped hare → Indian wolf

The amount of grass increases if there is plenty of rain and sunlight in the habitat. This means that there is plenty of food for black-naped hares and therefore the population grows. Now there is more food for the Indian wolves. So the Indian wolf population increases too. However, more Indian wolves eat more black-naped hares. Therefore, the black-naped hare population decreases. With fewer black-naped hares there is less food for the wolves and so their population decreases too.

Key terms

predator: animal that hunts and eats other animals (called prey).

prey: animal that is hunted and eaten by other animals (called predators).

Figure 4.4 shows the relationship between the population sizes of the **predator** (wolves) and the **prey** (black-naped hares). The graphs of the population sizes are like two waves that follow one another closely.

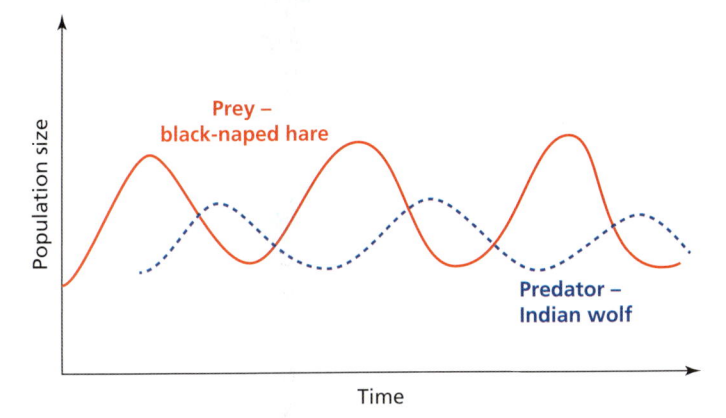

4.4 *A graph to show the changing population sizes of a predator and its prey.*

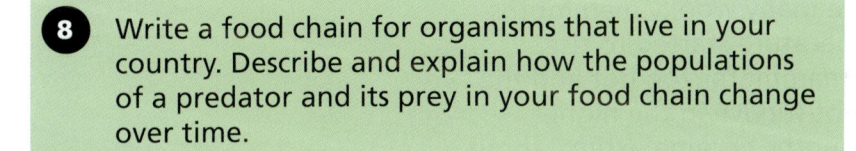

> **8** Write a food chain for organisms that live in your country. Describe and explain how the populations of a predator and its prey in your food chain change over time.

Extinction

Any change in the physical or living factors in an ecosystem will change the populations of organisms. If a change is permanent, then some species may die out altogether and become extinct.

Here are some examples of factors that can cause **extinction**:

- New diseases – a fungus (an organism that reproduces through spores) called *chytrid* has reduced the populations of many frogs and salamanders over recent years. It has even caused the extinction of some species (figure 4.5).

- Competition from an **invasive species** – the numbers of red squirrels in the United Kingdom decreased severely after grey squirrels from North America arrived. Grey squirrels compete with red squirrels for important resources.

- Eaten by an invasive species – in the 1940s brown tree snakes were accidently introduced to the island of Guam in the western Pacific Ocean. Since then scientists think that the snakes have caused the extinction of at least ten native bird species. Plant species are also particularly at risk from farmed animals that are newly brought into an area (such as sheep and goats).

4.5 *The fire salamander is a Dutch species that is on the edge of extinction because of infections by chytrid fungus.*

Key terms

extinction: when a species dies out completely.

invasive species: a non-native species that damages an ecosystem.

4.6 *People brought sheep to Hawaii and these sheep started to eat silversword plants. These plants were then in danger of becoming extinct.*

Populations and extinction   71

- Hunting and poaching – humans hunt animals for their own benefit or for enjoyment. Some humans poach animals because the animal has something 'valuable' – for example, ivory tusks or a beautiful coat. The West African black rhinoceros has been hunted to extinction by poachers who sold its horn for money.

- Catastrophic events – around 250 million years ago there was an extinction of millions of species. One theory about why this happened is that a meteor hit the Earth, which led to a sudden change in the Earth's temperature.

- Habitat destruction – scientists think that the mosaic-tailed rat, only found on one small low-lying island off the coast of Australia, is one of the first mammals to become extinct because of recent global warming. Rising sea levels mean that this rat's habitat has been destroyed.

- Change of physical factors in an environment - about 10 000 years ago, there were many woolly mammoths in the Arctic. Then the temperature started to rise. Their hairy coats made the mammoths too hot and the plants that they ate could not survive in the higher temperatures. Woolly mammoths became extinct about 4000 years ago.

4.7 The horn of the West African black rhinoceros has been sold for money.

Scientists are becoming increasingly worried that global warming will cause changes in the environments of many ecosystems around the world. Some populations of organisms may be able to evolve but evolution by natural selection is often a slow process. (see Topic 3.5). So, many scientists think that many organisms will not evolve fast enough and many species will become extinct.

Scientists go on expeditions to look for species that may be extinct. If they do not find the organisms, this is evidence to support the idea that the species is extinct. If they find small numbers of the species, then the species is said to be **endangered**. Scientists try to find ways of stopping endangered organisms becoming extinct.

> **Key term**
>
> **endangered**: a species is endangered if there are not many individuals left alive.

9 Give *three* factors that may cause extinctions.

10 a) Why were silversword plants in danger of becoming extinct in Hawaii?

b) Suggest what people did to stop the plants becoming extinct.

11 Explain *two* reasons why woolly mammoths became extinct.

Population change

Activity 4.2: Investigating extinction

Why are species becoming extinct?

A1 Scientists think that each of the following species may be extinct. The evidence to support these ideas is in brackets. Discover the reasons why each organism may be extinct. Use different books and the internet for your research.

- Christmas Island shrew (*Crocidura trichura*) (last seen in 1985)
- De Winton's golden mole (*Cryptochloris wintoni*) (last seen in 1937)
- Dinagat Island cloud rat (*Crateromys australis*) (last seen in 2012)
- kouprey (*Bos sauveli*) (last seen in 1988)
- Malabar civet (*Viverra civettina*) (last seen in 1987)
- Kaholuamanu melicope (*Melicope macropus*) (last seen 1995)
- Adams mistletoe (*Trilepidea adamsii*) (last seen in 1954)
- St Helena olive tree (*Nesiota elliptica*) (last seen in 2003)
- Least vermilion flycatcher (*Pyrocephalus dubius*) (last seen in 1987)
- Chinese paddlefish (*Psephurus gladius*) (last seen in 2003)
- Abingdon Island giant tortoise (*Chelonoidis abingdoni*) (last seen 2012)
- *Telefomin cuscus* (*Phalanger matanim*) (last seen in 1997)
- Yangtze river dolphin (*Lipotes vexillifer*) (last seen in 2002)

A2 Present your information as a table.

Science in context: Global pollution

Pollution is when organisms are being harmed by a substance in their habitat. The substance causing the harm is a **pollutant**.

Pollutants include oil from tankers, poisonous substances from factories and substances that make our lives easier (plastics, for example). These pollutants can spread through the atmosphere and oceans, and cause problems all over the world, not just in a few ecosystems.

4.8 *Plastics are a serious threat to some species.*

About 400 million tonnes of plastic are produced each year, and about 40% of that is used to make things that are only used once (such as drinks bottles). Animals get trapped in plastic litter or eat it, which can kill. For example, turtles try to eat plastic bags because they think they are jellyfish.

Australian scientists did a study on the number of small bits of plastic found in the intestines of dead turtles. They found a relationship (correlation) between the amount of plastic and its effect on the animals: the more plastic that a turtle eats the more likely it is to be killed by the plastic.

Populations and extinction

12 Read the information in the Global pollution box. The plastics that end up in the oceans often comes from the disposal of plastics in landfill sites. To reduce the amount of plastic waste ending up in the ocean scientists are looking at alternative ways to dispose of plastics such as incineration or recycling. Discuss the potential global environmental impacts of these methods.

Key terms

pollutant: a substance in an ecosystem that can cause harm to organisms.

pollution: when a substance in an ecosystem causes harm to organisms.

Activity 4.3 Plastic pollution poster

In this activity you are going to work as part of a group to design a poster or a presentation to encourage people to be more careful about what they do with their plastic waste.

A1 Each person should do some brief research to find *one* problem caused by plastic pollution.

A2 In your group:
- discuss what you all found out and what you are going to include
- discuss how you will present your information
- decide on the jobs that different people will do (e.g. drawing, researching information, finding photos, writing words)

A3 Present your work to your class.

A4 Now discuss your work in your group and evaluate your work. Write down:
- a good point about your poster or presentation
- something that could be improved
- a good point about how you worked together as a team
- something that could be improved about your teamwork

Key facts:

✔ Population sizes are altered by changes in physical and living factors in an environment.

✔ Predator and prey populations change constantly when one population depends on the other.

✔ There are many reasons why a species becomes extinct including permanent changes in physical factors, diseases, competition for resources and catastrophic events.

✔ The adaptations of an organism may mean that it is unable to survive in an area if the conditions change.

Making links

In Stage 8 you may have learned about climate change. Explain *two* ways in which climate change caused by human activity may cause some species to become extinct.

Check your skills progress:

- I can carry out independent research and contribute to teamwork.
- I can evaluate teamwork.
- I can find and present ordered information in a suitable graph.

Population change

End of chapter review

Quick questions

1. Which of the following adaptations is a desert animal **least likely to** have?
   - a large ears
   - b claws suitable for digging
   - c thick fur
   - d large feet

2. What is a population?
   - a the number of individuals of one species living in an area
   - b the total number of all the organisms living in an ecosystem
   - c the number of animals living in an area
   - d the number of humans living in the world

3. What provides nutrition for a predator?
   - a plants
   - b soil
   - c prey
   - d energy from light (from the Sun)

4. A species becomes endangered. What does this mean?
   - a This species is adapted to the ecosystem in which it lives.
   - b This species has become dangerous to people.
   - c The number of these organisms is very small.
   - d There are no organisms of this species left.

5. Charles Darwin's theory of evolution says that it occurs by:
   - a endangerment
   - b natural selection
   - c extinction
   - d selective breeding

6. Dodo birds are extinct. What does this mean?

7. In 2006, scientists went to look for Yangtze river dolphins in the Yangtze River in China. They did not find any.
   - (a) What scientific question were the scientists trying to answer?
   - (b) What was their evidence?
   - (c) What idea does this evidence support?

8. What causes inherited variation of the characteristics in members of the same species?

Connect your understanding

9. The lli pika is an animal that looks a bit like a small rabbit. It is a herbivore and lives high in the Tianshan mountains in China. The numbers of the animal are decreasing. Scientists think that it might become extinct.

   (a) Describe *one* adaptation you think the animal has. Explain your reasoning.

   (b) Suggest *one* reason why the lli pika might become extinct.

10. (a) The drawings show an Arctic fox, a desert fox and a red fox.

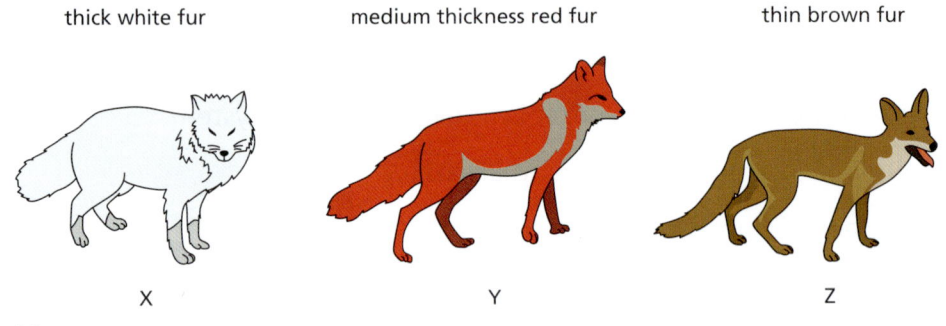

    thick white fur   medium thickness red fur   thin brown fur

    X   Y   Z

    4.9

    (i) Which is the Arctic fox?

    (ii) Explain *two* ways in which the desert fox is adapted to its habitat.

    (b) Arctic hares feed on saxifrage plants. Ermine are prey of snowy owls. Ermine are predators of Arctic hares. Show these organisms in a food chain.

    (c) Explain what may happen to the population of ermine if the population of snowy owls increases.

    (d) A certain area of the Arctic starts to warm up and Arctic hares are no longer found in this area. Explain *one* reason why this happens.

    4.10 *Ermine*

11. Describe *one* way in which an invasive species may cause the extinction of another species in an ecosystem.

Challenge questions

12. 'Biodiversity hotspots' are areas where a great many different species live. Suggest an explanation for why scientists want to protect biodiversity hotspots more than some other areas.

13. Arctic hares have brown fur in the summer and thick white fur in the winter. They have small ears. Imagine that the Arctic ecosystem starts to warm, so there is little snow. Explain how natural selection could cause a population of these hares to evolve into a new species.

    4.11 *An Arctic hare in winter.*

End of stage review

1. (a) A student measured the lengths of some leaves on one type of plant. The student measured the leaves in centimetres (cm) using a ruler.

   10.8   11.0   10.5   12.6   11.7

   12.7   10.2   12.9   12.5   12.0

   12.2   11.9   10.1   11.2   12.6

   11.0   11.7   11.9   12.8   12.1

   11.7   10.8   11.4   11.3   12.0

   (i) Name the type of variation shown by this data.

   (ii) Copy and complete this tally chart for the data.

Grouped lengths of leaves (cm)	Tally	Total
10.1 – 10.5		
10.6 – 11.0		
11.1 – 11.5		
11.6 – 12.0		
12.1 – 12.5		
12.6 – 13.0		

   (iii) Suggest what type of chart or graph you would use to present the data from your tally chart.

   (b) (i) Plants use leaves for photosynthesis. Copy and complete this word equation for photosynthesis.

   carbon dioxide + water → glucose + _____

   (ii) Which *one* of the following words best describes what type of substance glucose is?

   amino acid   carbohydrate   fat   protein

   (iii) Photosynthesis requires chlorophyll. Give the name of the element gained from mineral salts that plants need to make chlorophyll.

End of stage review   77

(c) A student puts celery stems in dyed water. Each stem has a different number of leaves. After 2 hours the student measures the distance the dye has moved. The table shows the results.

Number of leaves on stem	Distance reached by dye (cm)
0	10.1
1	11.2
2	11.9
3	12.7

(i) Make a conclusion from this experiment.

(ii) Outline *one* way in which this conclusion could be further investigated.

(iii) Give the name of the cells that form the water-carrying tubes in a stem.

2. (a) The table shows how the volume of urine produced by someone changes with the volume of water that they drink in a day.

Daily volume of water drunk (cm^3)	Daily volume of urine produced (cm^3)
2400	1700
4800	3100

(i) Predict how much urine would be produced if the person drinks 3600 cm^3 of water each day.

(ii) Give the name of the piece of apparatus that would be used to measure these volumes.

(iii) Give the name of the main waste product in urine.

(iv) Describe how this waste product is put into urine in the body.

(v) Name the tube that carries urine out of the body.

(b) Gerbils are small mammals that are adapted to live in sandy deserts. They have pale brown fur and only produce small amounts of concentrated urine. Give the reason why producing concentrated urine helps them to survive in their ecosystem.

(c) An area of desert starts to get much more rain. Over time, many more plants start to grow and dark soil forms.

(i) Explain what (if anything) would happen to the population of gerbils.

(ii) Due to inherited variation, some of the gerbils have slightly darker fur than others. Explain how natural selection causes the population to change so that more of the gerbils have darker fur.

(iii) Give the name of the molecule, found in the nucleus of cells, that causes inherited variation.

(iv) What is the word used to describe a species that has ceased to exist?

3. (a) The diagram shows a fetus developing in a mother's uterus.

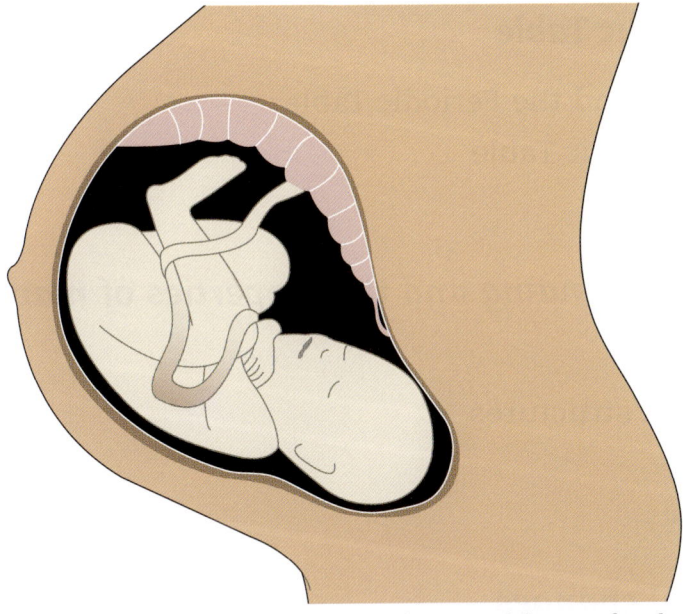

(i) Name *one* harmful substance that could transfer from the mother's blood to the baby's blood.

(ii) Explain *one* problem that this substance can cause.

(b) A fetus develops from a fertilised egg cell. Explain why the fertilised egg cell contains a mixture of genetic material from a male and a female.

(c) The drawing shows all chromosomes in a fertilised egg cell from a mammal.

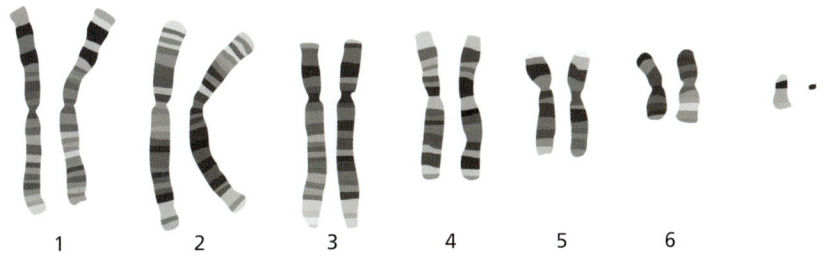

(i) State how you can tell that this fertilised egg cell is not from a human.

(ii) Explain what sex the fetus will be when it grows and develops.

End of stage review 79

Chemistry

Chapter 5: The Periodic Table

5.1:	Atomic structure and the Periodic Table	82
5.2:	Trends in the Periodic Table	87
End of chapter review		90

Chapter 6: Structure, bonding and the properties of matter

6.1:	Chemical bonds	93
6.2:	Simple and giant structures	98
6.3:	Density	103
End of chapter review		107

Chapter 7: Chemical changes

7.1	Changes in chemical reactions	109
7.2	Word and symbol equations	114
7.3	Methods for making salts	118
7.4	Displacement reactions	124
7.5	Rates of reaction	128
End of chapter review		135
End of stage review		138

Chapter 5
The Periodic Table

What's it all about?

Rubidium is an unusual metal compared to ones you will be more familiar with like gold and iron. It is very soft, melts just above body temperature and is very reactive. It can't be stored in the air because it catches fire when it reacts with oxygen.

An element's position on the Periodic Table is linked to its physical and chemical properties. The fact that rubidium is at the bottom of Group 1 explains its strange properties.

You will learn about:
- The structure of the atom
- How the position of an element in the Periodic Table is related to the structure of its atoms
- Trends in groups and periods in the Periodic Table
- How investigations by scientists changed ideas about the atom

You will build your skills in:
- Understanding that models and analogies can change according to scientific evidence
- Describing the uses, strengths and limitations of models and analogies
- Presenting results and using the patterns to predict values between the results collected
- Discussing the development of scientific knowledge
- Describing the use of scientific understanding by individuals and groups working together

Chapter 5 . Topic 1

Atomic structure and the Periodic Table

You will learn:
- To understand how the position of an element in the Periodic Table can be used to predict its atomic structure and chemical and physical properties.
- To describe some uses, strengths and limitations of models
- To understand that models and analogies can change according to scientific evidence
- To represent scientific ideas using symbols and formulae

Starting point

You should know that...	You should be able to...
Elements are made of atoms	Describe the strengths and limitations of a model
Elements are shown in the Periodic Table in an order, in which each element is represented by a symbol with one or two letters	Use symbols and formulae to represent scientific ideas
Rutherford's model was that an atom has a small, central, positively charged nucleus, but most of it is empty space.	
Ideas can be tested by carrying out investigations and collecting evidence	

Using models

A model is a simplified version of reality. Models are used in science to explain things that we cannot see – like the structure of atoms. Atoms make up all substances in the universe so understanding how they behave helps us to explain many different things. However, atoms are very small. If you lined up one million carbon atoms side by side they would be about the same width as a human hair.

This means that atoms are too small to study directly. So, we use a model instead.

Models of the atom

The first model of an atom was a small, hard sphere. However, as scientists collected more evidence they realised that this model could not explain all their observations – it had many weaknesses.

> **Key term**
>
> **Periodic Table**: how the elements are arranged, in order of their atomic number.

82 The Periodic Table

5.1

In 1909 Ernest Rutherford and his team did experiments to test the accepted model of the atom. He got unexpected results that showed the model must be incorrect. So, he developed a new model of the atom to fit the evidence from his experiments. He suggested that the atom had a small, positively charged **nucleus** with the **electrons** arranged further away.

Over time, scientists continued work to improve Rutherford's model. In 1913 Niels Bohr used calculations that supported experimental results from other scientists to explain why electrons were found in a series of **shells** at different distances from the nucleus.

Experiments in the 1920s and 1930s showed that the nucleus was made up of many individual parts – positively charged **protons** and those with no charge called **neutrons**. This simple model of the atom is the one we most commonly use today.

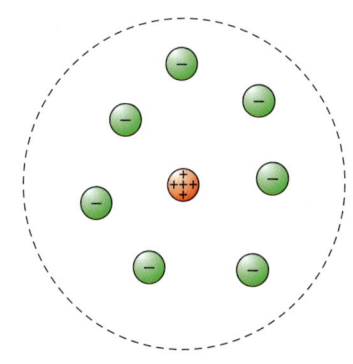

5.1 *Rutherford's model of the atom.*

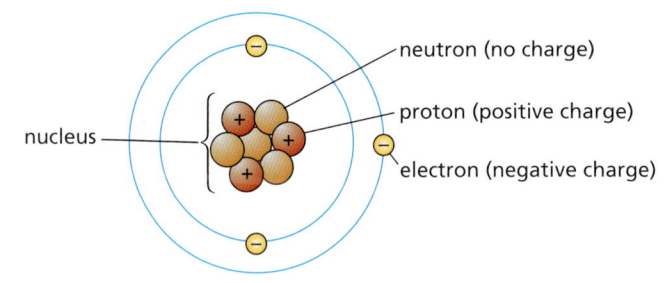

5.2 *A model of the atom we use today. It contains a small, central nucleus surrounded by shells of electrons.*

> **1** Suggest why the neutron was the last particle to be discovered.

Atomic number and mass number

The atoms of an element always have the same numbers of protons and electrons. This means that they have no overall charge – the opposite charges cancel each other out.

- An **atomic number** is the number of protons (and also electrons) an atom of an element has.
- A **mass number** is the total number of protons and neutrons an atom of an element has. This is the total number of particles in the nucleus.

The mass number of an atom is always larger than its atomic number (except for hydrogen which has a mass number and an atomic number of 1). You can find the atomic number and mass number of an element by looking at a **Periodic Table**.

Key terms

electrons: very small negatively charged particles in an atom.

neutrons: particles with no charge in the nucleus of an atom.

nucleus: the central part of an atom – contains protons and neutrons.

protons: positively charged particles in the nucleus of an atom.

shells: the paths or orbits that electrons move along in an atom.

Atomic structure and the Periodic Table

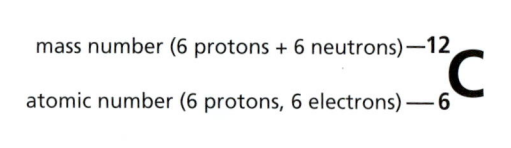

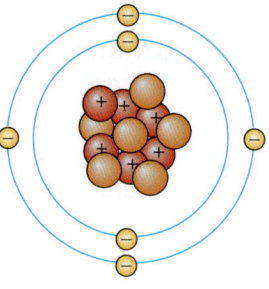

mass number (6 protons + 6 neutrons) — 12
atomic number (6 protons, 6 electrons) — 6 C

5.3 A carbon atom contains six protons and six neutrons in its nucleus, and six electrons in its shells.

> **2** Look at the information about four different atoms.
>
> oxygen   sodium   beryllium   helium
> $^{16}_{8}$O $^{23}_{11}$Na $^{9}_{4}$Be $^{4}_{2}$He
>
> a) Which atom has an atomic number of 4?
> b) How many protons does an atom of oxygen have?
> c) How many electrons does an atom of helium have?
> d) How many neutrons does an atom of sodium have?

Electron arrangement

Electrons are arranged in shells around the nucleus – the first shell can hold up to two electrons; the second and third shells can hold up to eight.

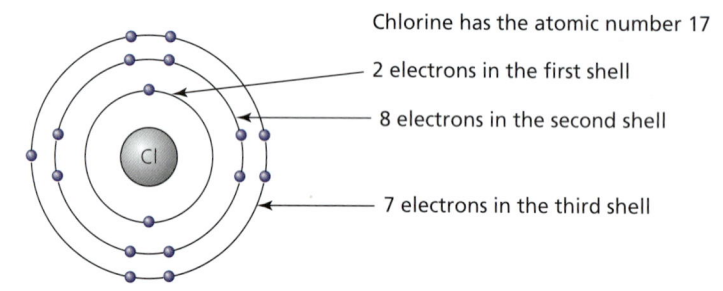

Chlorine has the atomic number 17
- 2 electrons in the first shell
- 8 electrons in the second shell
- 7 electrons in the third shell

5.4 An atom of chlorine contains 17 electrons arranged in three shells.

Activity 5.1: Build an atom

Collect some counters, beans or small sweets of three different colours. These will represent protons, neutrons and electrons.

Your teacher will tell you which element your atom is part of, and also its atomic number and mass number.

A1 Build a model of an atom of your element on a piece of paper. First create the nucleus. Then draw the shells and add the correct number of electrons. Start with the shell closest to the nucleus. Fill each shell with electrons before moving to the next.

A2 Swap your atom with a partner and check their work.

A3 Describe how the atoms of different elements are similar and how they are different.

A4 Discuss the strengths and weaknesses of your model: how is it similar to a real atom? How is it different?

The Periodic Table

5.5 The atomic number of each element is shown in the Periodic Table.

In the Periodic Table the elements are arranged by their atomic numbers going across the **periods** (rows) from left to right. The elements are also arranged in columns, called **groups** (apart from those in the middle part of the table).

As you go across a period the number of protons, and also electrons, in each atom increases by one.

There are two links between an element's position in the Periodic Table and the structure of the atoms in the element.

- The period number tells you how many electron shells the element has. For example, atoms of neon have two electron shells because neon is in Period 2 (second row).
- The group number is the same as the number of electrons in the outer shell. For example, all the elements in Group 1 have one electron in their outer shell.

For example, a fluorine atom has:

- two electron shells – so it is in Period 2
- seven electrons in its outer shell – so it is in Group 7

Key terms

group: column in the Periodic Table.

period: row in the Periodic Table.

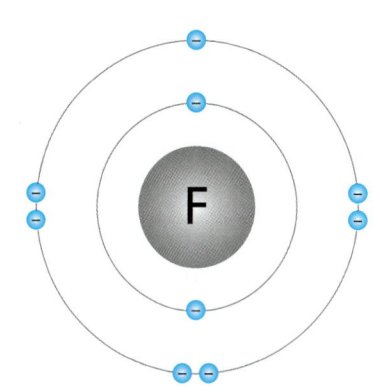

5.6 The structure of an element's atoms relates to its position in the Periodic Table.

Atomic structure and the Periodic Table

3 How many groups are there in the Periodic Table?

4 In which group is each of these elements found?
   a) oxygen
   b) chlorine
   c) magnesium

5 In which period is each of these elements found?
   a) argon
   b) calcium
   c) carbon

6 Draw a diagram to show the electron shells in a silicon atom. Explain how the structure relates to silicon's position in the Periodic Table.

Making links

Topic 6.1 covers how atoms join together by forming bonds. Atoms bond using the electrons in their outer shell – they can either give electrons to another atom or share them. How many electrons can a sodium atom give to a chlorine atom?

Science in context: Discovering new elements

Scientists are still discovering new elements to add to the Periodic Table, although these are now made in the laboratory and are not naturally occurring elements. The last elements were discovered in 2015. They have the atomic numbers 113, 115, 117 and 118.

5.7 The scientist Yuri Oganessian (on the left in this photograph) was part of the team that discovered element 118. It was named oganesson (Og) after him.

Key facts:

✔ The model of the atom we currently use has a nucleus with electrons moving round it in shells.

✔ Elements are arranged in order of atomic number in the Periodic Table.

✔ The Periodic Table can be used to predict an element's structure.

Check your skills progress:

- I can explain that models in science are based on current scientific evidence and understanding, and can change.
- I can discuss the strengths and weaknesses of a model.
- I can use symbols and formulae to represent elements.

The Periodic Table

Chapter 5 . Topic 2

Trends in the Periodic Table

You will learn:
- To understand that trends in chemical and physical properties are seen within the different groups of the Periodic Table and be able to describe these trends using the Group 1 elements as examples
- To describe trends and patterns shown in a set of results, identifying, and explaining, any anomalous results present
- To understand that models and analogies can change according to scientific evidence
- To use observations, measurements, secondary sources of information and keys, to organise and classify organisms, objects, materials, or phenomena

Starting point

You should know that...	You should be able to...
The Periodic Table presents the known elements in an order	Present and interpret observations and measurements appropriately
All substances have chemical and physical properties	

Chemical and physical properties

All elements have **chemical properties**.

One chemical property is reactivity. This is how likely a substance will undergo a chemical reaction.

Another chemical property is flammability. Hydrogen is a flammable element – it will catch fire very easily. Other elements, like gold or nitrogen are not flammable.

The chemical properties of an element depend on the number of electrons in their outer shell. Elements with the same number will have similar chemical properties.

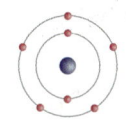

hydrogen   nitrogen

5.9 *Hydrogen atoms have one electron in their outer shell, nitrogen atoms have five. This explains the differences in their chemical properties.*

Elements also have **physical properties** such as melting and boiling point, hardness and colour.

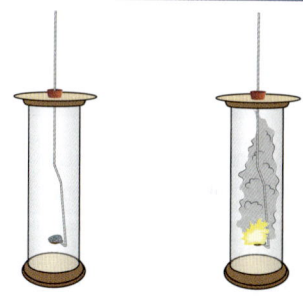

5.8 *Iron and sodium are added to a jar of oxygen. Iron doesn't react but sodium does. This shows that sodium is a more reactive element than iron.*

Key terms

chemical property: a property that is seen when a substance takes part in a chemical change.

physical property: the property that can be observed or measured without changing the basic nature of the substance.

Groups in the Periodic Table

The elements in each group share similar chemical properties. This is because they all have the same number of electrons in their outer shell. The elements in Group 1 are called the alkali metals.

All these elements are reactive metals. They all react with water to produce hydrogen and an alkaline solution. The word equation for the reaction of sodium with water is:

sodium + water → sodium hydroxide + hydrogen

The metals in Group 1 are all soft enough to be cut with a knife and have very low melting points for metals.

Li	lithium
Na	sodium
K	potassium
Rb	rubidium
Cs	caesium
Fr	francium

5.10 *The Group 1 elements.*

1 Write the word equation for the reaction of potassium with water.

Trends and patterns

The properties and reactions of the elements show patterns and trends related to the groups.

Knowing the trends in properties helps scientists to explain and predict the behaviour, properties and reactions of other elements in the group.

Trends and patterns in Group 1

As you go down Group 1 the alkali metals become more reactive. This is a trend in a chemical property.

The reactions between all of the Group 1 metals and water produce hydrogen gas and release heat. This is an example of a pattern of chemical reactivity.

- Lithium reacts slowly with water, so bubbles of hydrogen are produced slowly.
- Sodium reacts more quickly.
- When potassium reacts with water hydrogen is produced quickly. Heat is also released quickly and ignites the hydrogen gas.
- The reaction between caesium and water is explosive and so is never done in a classroom.

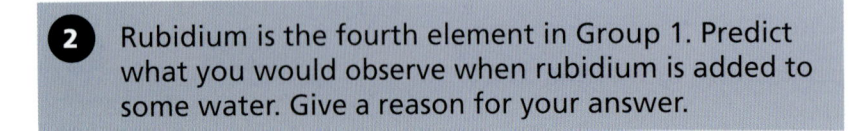

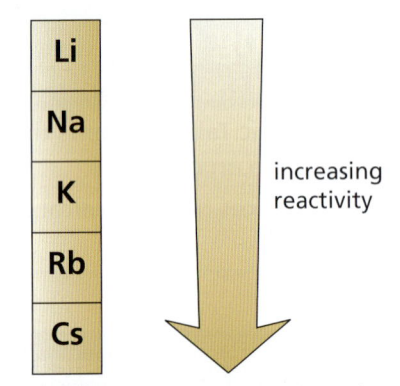

5.11 *As you go down Group 1 the elements get more reactive.*

2 Rubidium is the fourth element in Group 1. Predict what you would observe when rubidium is added to some water. Give a reason for your answer.

5.12 *The reaction between lithium and water (top) and potassium and water (bottom).*

88 The Periodic Table

5.2

Activity 5.2 Physical property trends in Group 1

There are also trends in physical properties in groups.

The table shows the melting points of some of the elements in Group 1.

Element	Melting point (°C)
Lithium	181
Sodium	98
Potassium	64
Rubidium	
Caesium	28

A1 Draw a bar chart to show the data. Remember to leave a gap for rubidium.

A2 Describe the trend in the melting point of Group 1 elements.

A3 Predict the melting point of rubidium. Give a reason for your answer.

Science in context: Developing the Periodic Table

The Periodic Table as we know it is based on the one developed by the Russian scientist Dmitri Mendeleev in 1869. He built on work done by other scientists and placed elements with similar properties in the same groups. He realised that not all the elements had been discovered so left gaps for them in his table. As new elements were discovered his predictions were proved correct.

5.13 *A statue of Dmitri Mendeleev next to his version of the Periodic Table on the side of a building in Russia.*

1. Complete some research to find out more about the Periodic Table and how it has changed over time.

2. Describe the ways in which the Periodic Table has been developed over time and suggest reasons for this. You should consider ideas about scientists working in collaboration, changes in technology and progression in scientific understanding in your answer.

Key facts:

✓ Elements in the same group share similar properties but there are trends, such as reactivity and boiling point, within the groups.

Check your skills progress:

- I can present and interpret results, and predict results between data points.

Making links

Topic 7.4 covers displacement reactions. This type of reaction happens when a reactive metal reacts with a salt of a less reactive metal. Would a displacement reaction happen if sodium was added to potassium chloride?

Trends in the Periodic Table

End of chapter review

Quick questions

1. Where in the atom is each of these particles found?

    (a) protons

    (b) neutrons

    (c) electrons

2. What did Niels Bohr's model show?

3. What words complete these sentences?

    (a) Elements in the Periodic Table are in order of their atomic _____

    (b) Elements in the same _____ in the Periodic Table share similar chemical properties.

4. How does the reactivity of Group 1 metals change as you go down the group?

5. Potassium has the atomic number 19. What does this tell you about the atom's nucleus?

Connect your understanding

6. An aluminium atom has the atomic number 13 and a mass number of 27.

    (a) State how many electrons, protons and neutrons the atom has.

    (b) Draw a diagram of the atom, showing the electrons in their shells.

    (c) State the period and group of aluminium in the Periodic Table.

    Explain how you can use its electron structure to work this out.

7. Use what you know about how electrons are arranged in atoms to explain why elements in the same group share similar chemical properties.

8. The model of the atom has changed over time. Explain why.

9. The table shows the boiling points of some of the Group 8 elements.

Name	Boiling point (°C)
Helium	−272
Neon	−249
Argon	−189
Krypton	
Xenon	−112
Radon	−71

(a) Describe the trend in the data.

(b) Estimate the boiling point of krypton.

Challenge question

10. A scientist adds small pieces of lithium, potassium and sodium to dilute hydrochloric acid. Predict what she will see when she adds each metal. Explain why there is a difference in her observations.

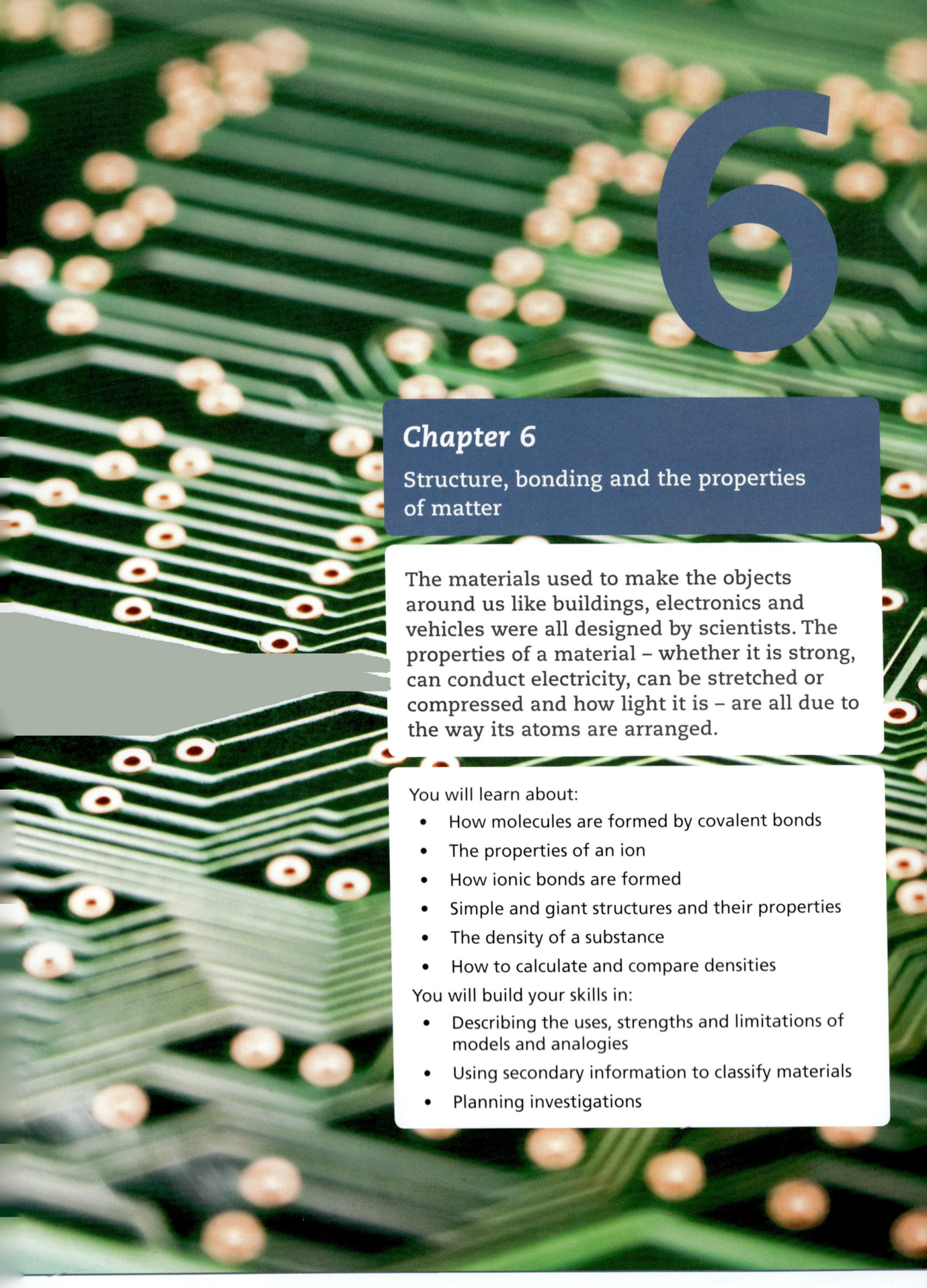

Chapter 6
Structure, bonding and the properties of matter

The materials used to make the objects around us like buildings, electronics and vehicles were all designed by scientists. The properties of a material – whether it is strong, can conduct electricity, can be stretched or compressed and how light it is – are all due to the way its atoms are arranged.

You will learn about:
- How molecules are formed by covalent bonds
- The properties of an ion
- How ionic bonds are formed
- Simple and giant structures and their properties
- The density of a substance
- How to calculate and compare densities

You will build your skills in:
- Describing the uses, strengths and limitations of models and analogies
- Using secondary information to classify materials
- Planning investigations

Chapter 6 . Topic 1
Chemical bonds

You will learn:
- To understand that molecules are formed by covalent bonds
- To describe how a covalent bond is formed
- To describe how negatively charged and positively charged ions are formed from atoms
- To describe an ionic bond
- To describe the strengths and limitations of the dot-and-cross diagram as a model of a molecule
- To represent scientific ideas using recognised symbols or formulae

Starting point

You should know that...	You should be able to...
Compounds contain atoms of more than one element strongly held together	Understand what is meant by a model
Electrons have a negative charge	

Molecules

All substances are made up of particles.

The particles in some substances are atoms.

The particles in other substances are groups of two or more atoms called **molecules**. The atoms in molecules are joined together.

The atoms in a molecule could be the same, or they could be different.

Key term

molecule: a group of two or more atoms joined together.

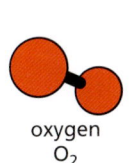

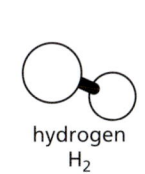

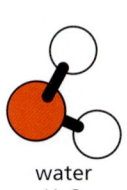

oxygen O_2 hydrogen H_2 water H_2O

6.1 *Oxygen, hydrogen and water all contain molecules.*

1. Explain why oxygen has the formula O_2 and water has the formula H_2O.

2. 'Only compounds are made up of molecules'. Explain why this statement is wrong.

3. Suggest why oxygen is known as a 'diatomic molecule'.

Chemical bonds   93

Covalent bonding

The atoms in a molecule are joined together by a **covalent bond**.

A covalent bond is formed when two non-metal atoms share a pair of electrons in their outer shell.

By sharing electrons, both atoms gain a full outer shell.

For example, hydrogen atoms have one electron shell, which contains one electron. They need one more electron to have a full shell.

So, two hydrogen atoms share their electron. This gives them both two electrons. The shared pair of electrons is a covalent bond.

You can draw a covalent bond using a **dot-and-cross diagram**.

> **Key terms**
>
> **covalent bond**: a bond made when a pair of electrons is shared by two atoms.
>
> **dot-and-cross diagram**: a diagram used to show a covalent bond between atoms in a molecule. Electrons are represented by dots or crosses.

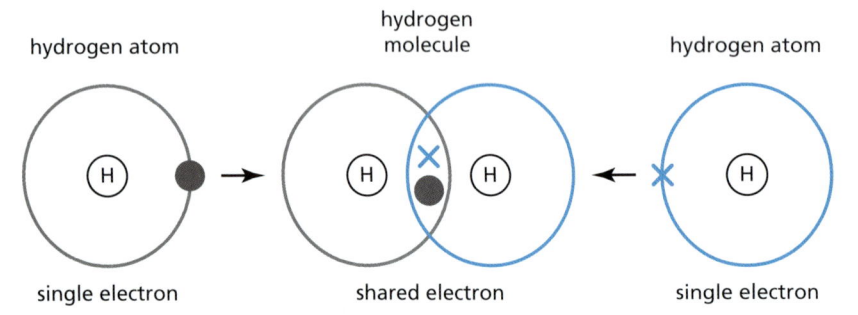

6.2 *This dot-and-cross diagram shows the covalent bond in a hydrogen molecule.*

Activity 6.1: Drawing dot-and-cross diagrams

You are going to draw a dot-and-cross diagram for chlorine (Cl_2).

A1 Draw *one* of the atoms. Only draw its outer shell. Use dots to represent the electrons in its outer shell. You can find out how many electrons to draw by finding what group it is in the Periodic Table.

A2 Draw the other atom. Again, only draw its outer shell. Use crosses to represent its electrons.

A3 Draw the molecule. Show the outer shell of each atom overlapping. Put one electron from each atom in the overlap (one dot and one cross). Make sure each atom now has a full outer shell of electrons.

A4 Repeat the three steps given above to produce a dot-and-cross diagram of hydrogen chloride (HCl).

A5 Now draw a dot-and-cross diagram for a water molecule (H_2O). This has three atoms, so use dots for one element and crosses for the other.

A6 Describe the strengths and limitations of using a dot-and-cross model to represent a molecule.

Structure, bonding and the properties of matter

6.1

The covalent bond exists because of electrostatic attraction between the positively charged nucleus of both atoms and the shared negatively charged electrons. This means that it is very strong.

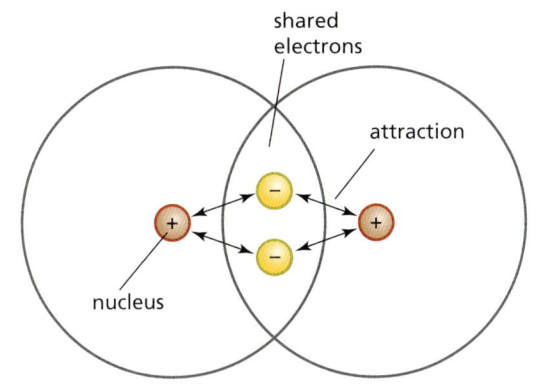

6.3 *A covalent bond exists because there is electrostatic attraction between positive and negative charge.*

Ions

Atoms have an equal number of negatively charged electrons and positively charged protons. These charges cancel each other out so an atom has no overall charge.

When atoms take part in a chemical reaction they can lose or gain electrons from their outer shell to become charged particles called **ions**.

Metal atoms lose electrons to become positively charged ions.

Non-metals gain electrons to become negatively charged ions.

Ionic bonding

When metals react with non-metals in a chemical reaction, electrons are transferred from the metal atoms to the non-metal atoms. Transferring electrons means that both atoms have a full outer shell.

Both atoms become charged ions. There is a strong electrostatic attraction between positive and negative ions. This is called an **ionic bond**.

For example, sodium reacts with chlorine to form the compound sodium chloride.

Sodium atoms have one electron on their outer shell. Chlorine have seven. During the reaction an electron is transferred from each sodium atom to a chlorine atom.

> **Key terms**
>
> **ion**: an atom which has gained at least one electron to be negatively charged or lost at least one electron to be positively charged.
>
> **ionic bond**: an attraction between a positively charged ion and a negatively charged ion.

Chemical bonds   95

Both atoms now have a full outer shell of electrons and are charged ions.

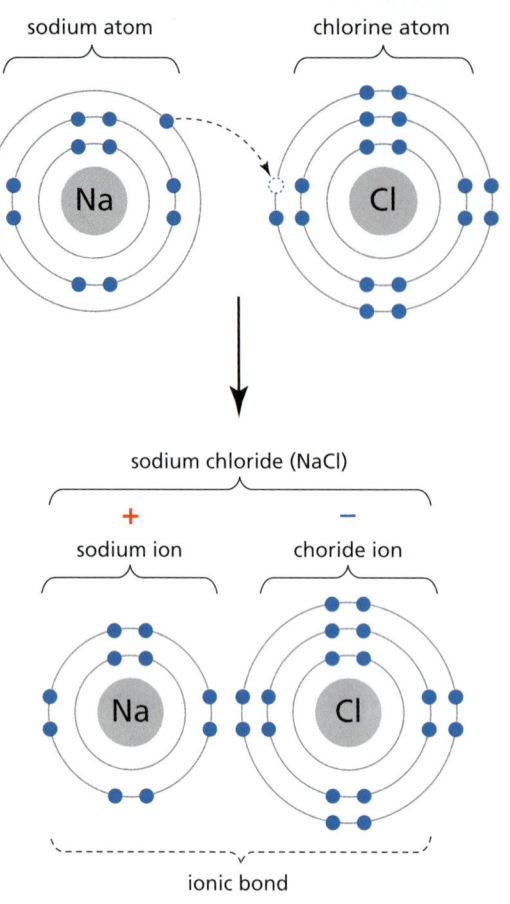

6.4 Sodium chloride contains positive sodium atoms and negative chloride ions held together by ionic bonds.

> **4** Sodium atoms have the atomic number 11.
>
> a) Explain why sodium atoms have no overall charge.
>
> b) When sodium reacts with chlorine ions are formed. Explain why.
>
> **5** Draw a diagram to show what happens when a magnesium atom reacts with an oxygen atom to form magnesium oxide (MgO). What are the charges on each ion?

96 Structure, bonding and the properties of matter

Key facts:

✔ A molecule is formed when two or more atoms join together chemically, through a covalent bond.

✔ A covalent bond is made when a pair of electrons is shared by two non-metal atoms

✔ An ion is an atom that has gained at least one electron to be negatively charged or lost at least one electron to be positively charged.

✔ An ionic bond is an attraction between a positively charged ion and a negatively charged ion.

Check your skills progress:

- I can describe dot-and-cross models and discuss their strengths and weaknesses.

Making links

Chapter 7 covers many different chemical reactions. When substances react the bonds between the atoms are broken in the reactants and then new bonds are formed between the atoms in the reactants. Why do you think reactions need some energy to get started?

Chapter 6 . Topic 2

Simple and giant structures

You will learn:
- To understand how the physical properties of an element or compound may be determined by it's structure (simple or giant)
- To use models to show the structure of giant and simple structures
- To classify substances based on their structure using secondary information
- To use scientific understanding to make predictions

Starting point

You should know that...	You should be able to...
Compounds contain atoms of more than one element strongly held together	Sort and classify materials using secondary information
Physical properties are those that can be observed and measured, such as mass, conductivity and melting and boiling point	

Giant structures

Some elements and compounds are made up of atoms or charged particles called ions. Very strong bonds exist between each atom or ion.

They have a **giant structure**.

Sodium chloride is an example of a compound with a giant structure. It is made up of positive sodium ions and negative chloride ions. Ionic bonds exist between the ions.

Diamond is an element – it only contains carbon atoms. There are four covalent bonds between each element. Diamond also has a giant structure, called a giant covalent structure.

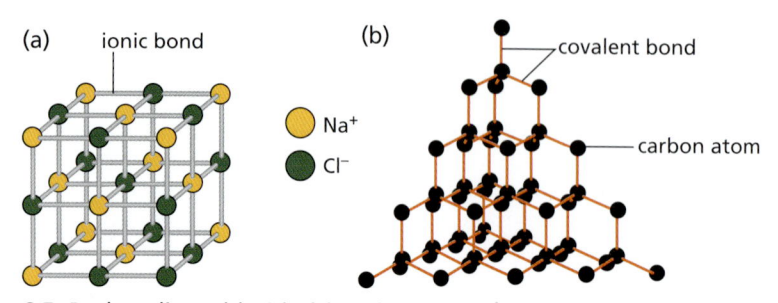

Key term

giant structure: an element or compound that is made up of atoms or ions joined together by strong bonds.

6.5 Both sodium chloride (a) and diamond (b) have giant structures.

98　Structure, bonding and the properties of matter

Metals also have a giant structure. They are made up of positive metal ions surrounded by electrons. The electrostatic attraction between the positive ions and electrons are strong metallic bonds. The electrons are able to move. This is why metals can conduct electricity.

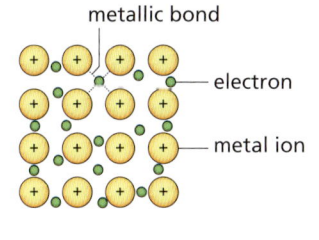

6.6 *Metals have giant structures.*

Properties of giant structures

The bonds that hold together the atoms or ions in giant structures are very strong.

To melt a giant structure these bonds have to be overcome, so the atoms or ions can move around. It takes a lot of energy to do this, which means that giant structures have high melting points (and therefore high boiling points). They are usually solids at room temperature.

1 Giant structures are usually very hard. Use their structure to explain why.

2 When giant structures that contain ions are melted they can conduct electricity. Explain why.

Simple structures

Some elements and compounds are made up of molecules. They have a **simple structure**.

Very strong covalent bonds hold the atoms in the molecules together.

Weaker attractive forces exist between the molecules.

Water is an example of a compound with a simple structure. It contains water molecules (H_2O). When water is a solid (ice) the molecules are held together by weak attractive forces.

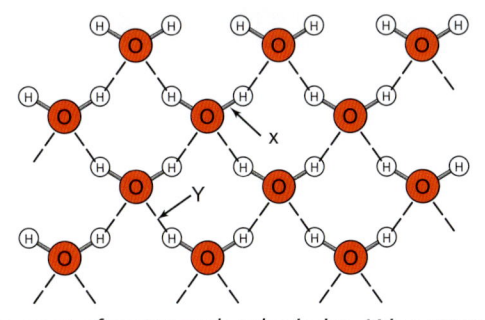

Key term

simple structure: an element or compound that is made up of molecules.

6.7 *The arrangement of water molecules in ice. X is a strong covalent bond, that exists between the atoms. Y is a weak attractive force that exists between molecules.*

Simple and giant structures

Properties of simple structures

Substances with simple structures have low melting and boiling points. Many exist as liquids or gases at room temperature.

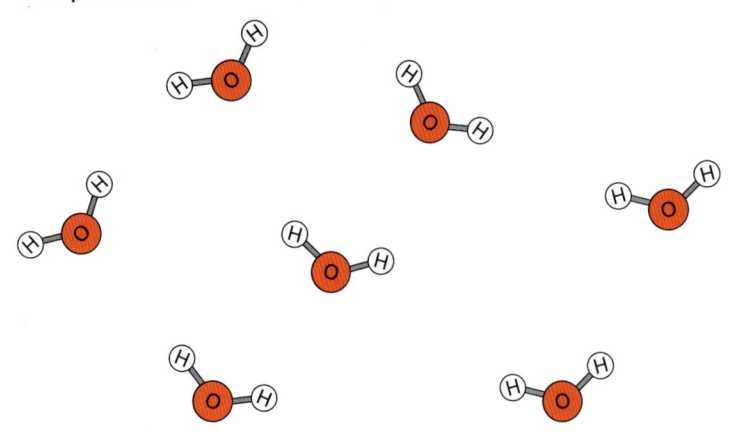

6.8 *The arrangement of water molecules in steam.*

When a simple structure melts it is the weak attractive forces between the molecules that are overcome. The covalent bonds are not affected. This is why liquid water and steam contain water molecules, not hydrogen and oxygen atoms.

> **3** Substances with simple structures cannot conduct electricity. Explain why.

Activity 6.2: Testing properties

A scientist did some tests on four mystery substances. Her results are shown in the table.

Substance	Melting point (°C)	Boiling point (°C)	Can it conduct electricity when solid?	Can it conduct electricity when melted?
A	2852	3600	No	Yes
B	1064	2700	Yes	Yes
C	1710	2230	No	No
D	−7	59	No	No

Keys can be used to identify something by answering a series of questions based on observations. The scientist designs the key below, which can be used to identify each of the structures of substances A–D from her results.

100 Structure, bonding and the properties of matter

```
Does the substance conduct electricity when solid?
├── Yes → Giant metal structure
└── No → Does the substance conduct electricity when melted?
    ├── Yes → Giant structure made of ions
    └── No → Does the substance have a high melting point?
        ├── Yes → Giant structure made of atoms
        └── No → Simple structure
```

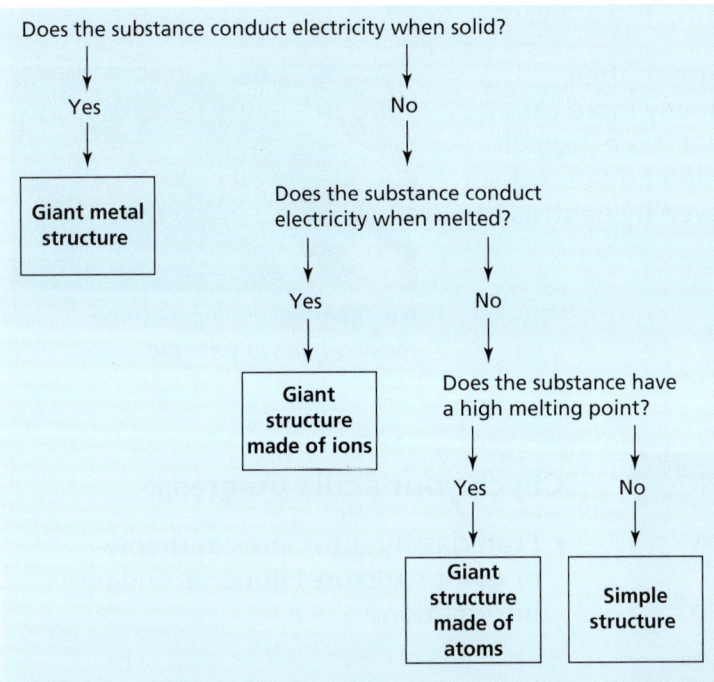

A1 Use the key to identify the structure of compound B. Explain your answer.

A2 Use the key to identify the structure of compound D. Explain your answer.

A3 The scientist concluded that the bonds between ions in giant structures are stronger than the bonds between atoms in giant structures. Does the data support this conclusion?

A4 Explain why this evidence can't prove this relationship.

A5 The properties of three substances are summarised in the table below.

Substance	State at room temperature	Does the substance conduct electricity?
E	Solid	Yes
F	Solid	No
G	Gas	No

The three substances are carbon dioxide, diamond and sodium chloride but it is not known which substance is E, which is F and which is G.

Design your own key that could be used, along with the observations in the table, to work out the identity of each substance.

Simple and giant structures

Science in context: Uses of diamond

Diamonds are used in jewellery because of their sparkling appearance but they have many more uses. One useful property of diamond is that it is extremely hard. Small diamonds are put into drills and saws which are used for engraving, mining and even by dentists to drill holes in teeth.

6.9 *Diamond drilling machine making holes in concrete.*

Key facts:

✔ Some elements or compounds exist as giant structures, which are held together by strong bonds. They have high melting and boiling points.

✔ Some elements and compounds exist as simple structures, which are molecules held together by weak bonds. They have low melting and boiling points.

Check your skills progress:

- I can classify substances as simple or giant structures using secondary information.

Making links

Many giant ionic structures are soluble in water. When this happens the ions in the structure break apart. You may have learned about water and mineral ions in Chapter 1.2. Why is the ability of giant structures to dissolve important for plants?

Structure, bonding and the properties of matter

Chapter 6 . Topic 3
Density

You will learn:
- To describe the mass of a substance in a defined volume as density
- To use the mass and volume of solids, liquids and gases to calculate and compare their densities
- To collect and record observations and measurements appropriately
- To choose the appropriate equipment for an investigation and use it correctly
- To interpret results and form conclusions using scientific knowledge and understanding
- To decide how to obtain sufficiently reliable data from observations and measurements

Starting point

You should know that...	You should be able to...
The weight of an object is due to the force of gravity	Outline plans to carry out investigations considering the variables to control, change or observe
The particle theory of matter can be used to explain the properties of solids, liquids and gases, including changes of state	

What is density?

Density is how much **mass** something has in a certain **volume**. A large piece of polystyrene is very light because it does not have much mass – we say it is not dense. However, a small piece of steel is quite heavy because it has lots of mass – we say it is dense.

6.10 These substances all have the same volume, but they weigh different amounts because they have different densities.

Key terms

density: the mass of an object divided by its volume.

mass: the amount of matter in an object – it is measured in grams or kilograms.

volume: the amount of space an object takes up, measured in cm^3.

Density 103

How do we calculate density?

To calculate a density, we need to know the mass and the volume of an object. We then divide the mass by its volume:

$$\text{density} = \frac{\text{mass}}{\text{volume}}$$

The units for density are usually grams per cubic centimetre (g/cm^3) or kilograms per cubic metre (kg/m^3).

If you have a cube that has a mass of 24 g and a volume of 8 cm^3, to work out its density you do the following calculation:

$$\text{density} = \frac{\text{mass}}{\text{volume}} = \frac{24}{8} = 3 \text{ g/cm}^3$$

So the density is 3 g/cm^3.

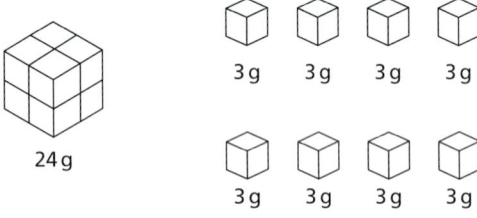

6.11 *The mass of 24 g has been evenly divided between the 8 cubic centimetres to give a density of 3 g/cm^3.*

> **1** A glass prism has a mass of 75 g and volume of 30 cm^3. What is its density?
>
> **2** A ring has a mass of 5 g and occupies a volume of 0.34 cm^3. Pure gold has a density of 19.3 g/cm^3. Is the ring made of pure gold?

How do you measure mass and volume?

Measuring the mass and volume of a liquid

To measure the volume of a liquid, we put it in a measuring cylinder and see how many millilitres of liquid we have – 1 millilitre has the same volume as 1 cm^3. 1 litre has the same volume as 1000 cm^3 or 0.001 m^3 (1 litre is NOT the same as 1 m^3).

To find the mass of a liquid we first have to measure the mass of the empty container that the liquid will have to go into. Then we measure the mass of the container and the liquid together. Then we subtract the mass of the container from their combined mass.

Structure, bonding and the properties of matter

Measuring the mass and volume of a regular solid

To find the mass of a solid, we simply put it on a balance.

To find the volume of a regular solid (a cube or a cuboid) we measure its length, width and height and multiply them together.

Measuring the mass and volume of an irregular solid

We can measure the mass of an irregular solid by simply weighing it again, but we can't do a calculation to work out the volume.

To measure the volume, first you pour some water into a measuring cylinder and read off the volume. Then you immerse the object in the water and read the volume again. The volume of the object is the volume after you put it in minus the volume before you put it in.

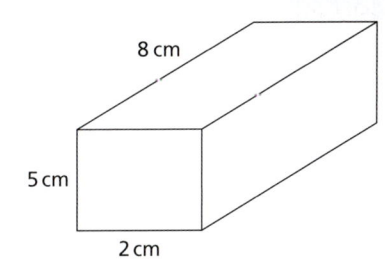

6.12 *The volume of this solid is calculated using 8 cm × 5 cm × 2 cm = 80 cm^3.*

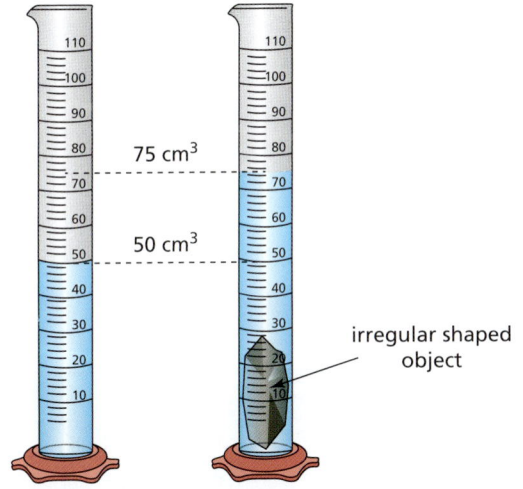

6.13 *The volume of an irregular solid is measured by water displacement. The volume of this solid is 25 cm^3.*

Activity 6.3: Measuring the density of everyday objects

Find some objects where you live. You first need to rank them in order, from the most dense to the least dense. Plan how you will do this.

A1 How will you measure the mass of each object?
A2 How will you measure the volume of regular shaped objects?
A3 How will you measure the volume of irregular shaped objects?
A4 If you have liquids, how will you measure their mass and volume?

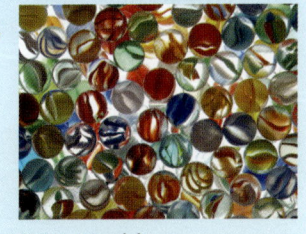

6.14 *Marbles.*

Density and particle theory

You can also think of density as a measure of how closely particles are packed together. All substances are made up of particles.

Density   105

Most substances are densest when they are solid. This is because their particles are packed tightly together so more can fit into a certain volume.

When the substance is melted and forms a liquid its density decreases by a small amount because the particles are able to move and take up slightly more volume.

When substances are a gas they have a much lower density. The particles in a gas are able to move around and fill the container they are in, so they are spread far apart.

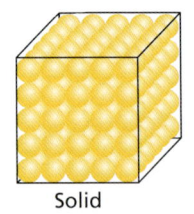

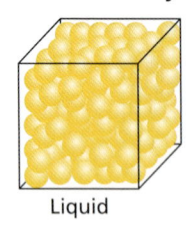

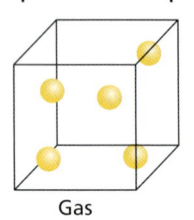

Solid   Liquid   Gas

6.15 *Solids have a higher density than gases because their particles are more tightly packed.*

3 100 cm³ of a liquid has a mass of 120 g. What is its density?

4 A gas has a volume of 2 m³ and a mass of 1.5 kg. What is its density?

Science in context: Low-density materials

Scientists around the globe have developed very low density materials with many useful properties.

One example, developed in Germany, is aerographite. It is made up of a network of extremely thin strands of carbon tubes and has a density of only 0.0002 g/cm³.

Aerographite can be squashed down so it is 1000 times smaller and it will spring back to its original size undamaged. Despite its fragile appearance it can support objects 40 000 times its own mass.

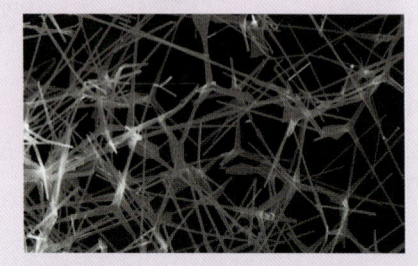

6.16 *Structure of aerographite.*

Key facts:

✔ Density is calculated by mass ÷ volume.

✔ Solids are more dense than liquids and gases because their particles are the closest together.

Check your skills progress:

- I can plan a range of investigations to obtain appropriate evidence.

Structure, bonding and the properties of matter

End of chapter review

Quick questions

1. What is a covalent bond?
2. What happens if an atom gains an electron?
3. What happens if an atom loses an electron?
4. What is an ionic bond?
5. Describe a giant structure.
6. What is density?
7. Calculate the density of the following materials.
    (a) steel, which has a mass of 156 g and a volume of 20 cm^3
    (b) liquid bromine, which has a mass of 21 g and a volume of 7 cm^3
    (c) lithium, which has a mass of 106 g and a volume of 200 cm^3
    (d) xenon, which has a mass of 29.3 kg and a volume of 5 m^3

Connect your understanding

8. Draw a dot-and-cross diagram to show the bonding in a hydrogen fluoride molecule (HF).
9. Describe what happens when a lithium atom reacts with a bromine atom.
10. Why do giant covalent structures have a higher melting point than simple structures?
11. Explain, using particle theory, why solids and liquids are more dense than gases.

Challenge question

12. The elements in Group 8 of the Periodic Table are very unreactive, so do not form compounds with other elements.

    Explain why, using ideas about bonding.

Chapter 7
Chemical changes

What's it all about?

Dyes, medicines, plastics and food preservatives are just a few of the many products that chemists can make using a chemical reaction. To make a particular product chemists have to choose suitable reactants, apparatus and techniques.

You will learn about:
- The conservation of mass and energy in chemical reactions
- Using word and symbol equations to describe reactions
- Preparing common salts by the reactions of metals with acids and metals with carbonates
- How to purify salts using filtration, evaporation and crystallisation
- Identifying examples of displacement reactions and predicting products
- Describing the effects of concentration, surface area and temperature on the rate of reaction

You will build your skills in:
- Representing scientific ideas using recognised symbols or formulae
- Using scientific knowledge to make predictions
- Identifying hazards and ways to minimise risk
- Interpreting results to form conclusions
- Evaluating experimental methods, explaining any improvements suggested
- Describing the use of science in society, industry and research
- Describing the use of scientific understanding by individuals and groups working together
- Discussing the global environmental impacts of some uses of science

Chapter 7 . Topic 1

Changes in chemical reactions

You will learn:
- To understand that mass and energy are conserved in a chemical reaction
- To describe how people develop and use scientific understanding
- To identify hazards and identify ways to minimise risks
- To use scientific knowledge to make predictions
- To collect accurate and precise measurements
- To carry out practical work in a safe manner to minimise risks

Starting point

You should know that...	You should be able to...
During a chemical reaction, reactants react to form products	Describe how scientific knowledge is developed over time
A word equation separates the substances that react and the products that are formed with an arrow	Identify and control risks
Some reactions are exothermic and some are endothermic and this can be identified by temperature change	Make conclusions by interpreting results

Testing theories

Scientists used to think that when a substance burns it loses a substance called phlogiston, which is seen as a flame. Ideas like this are called a **theory**.

Scientists collect evidence to see if their theory is correct.

Charcoal is nearly 100% carbon. When charcoal is burned, its mass decreases. Scientists explained that this happens because the phlogiston leaves the carbon and escapes into the air. This evidence was used to support the phlogiston theory.

However, there are other observations it cannot explain. When magnesium is heated it gives out a bright flame but its mass *increases*. This evidence is not supported by the phlogiston theory.

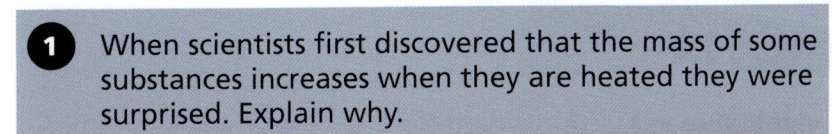

7.1 *Do burning substances lose phlogiston?*

Key term

theory: idea or set of ideas that explains an observation.

1 When scientists first discovered that the mass of some substances increases when they are heated they were surprised. Explain why.

2 Explain why this helped to improve understanding of what happens when substances burn.

Changes in chemical reactions 109

Conservation of mass

We now know that the phlogiston theory is not correct. We know this because of particle theory, which is a newer theory that can explain all the observations. Particle theory explains that everything is made up of atoms. We can use this to explain why the mass of carbon decreases when it is burned and why the mass of other substances, like magnesium, increases.

When carbon is heated in air it reacts with oxygen to form a new compound, carbon dioxide. Energy is transferred as heat and light. This reaction is called **combustion**.

It can be shown as a word equation, and as a particle diagram.

carbon + oxygen ⟶ carbon dioxide

7.2 *When carbon is burned its mass decreases.*

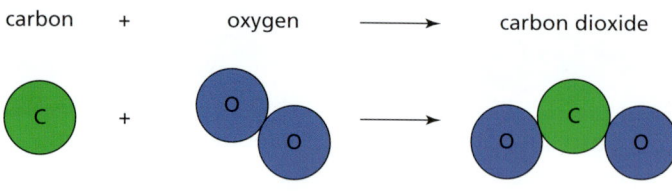

7.4 *The word and particle diagram for the combustion of carbon.*

The mass of the carbon decreases because its atoms are joining with oxygen atoms to form carbon dioxide, which is a gas. The carbon dioxide gas escapes during the reaction and mixes with the air.

The mass of the carbon decreases. But, you can see from the particle diagram that the number of atoms at the start of the reaction is the same as the number of atoms at the end. No atoms have been lost or gained during the reaction. If you could weigh all the reactants and all the products you would find that they have the same mass. This is the law of conservation of mass.

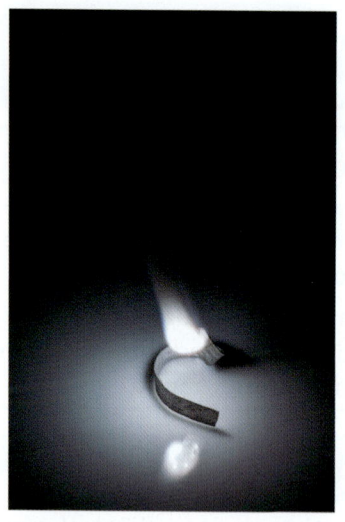

7.3 *When magnesium is burned its mass increases.*

> **3** Explain how a new theory (particle theory) helped change ideas about what happens when substances burn.
>
> **4** Plan a way of collecting evidence to prove that carbon dioxide is made when carbon burns.
>
> **5** When you burn a candle, substances in the wax react with oxygen in the air to produce the products carbon dioxide and water vapour. Explain why a candle gets smaller as it burns.

Key term

combustion: chemical reaction between a substance and oxygen, which transfers energy as heat and light.

When metals are heated in air the metal reacts with oxygen in the air to form an oxide.

Chemical changes

7.1

For example, copper is a shiny orange coloured metal. When it is heated in oxygen it forms a dull, black coating. This is a new compound called copper oxide.

The word equation for this reaction is:

copper + oxygen ⟶ copper oxide

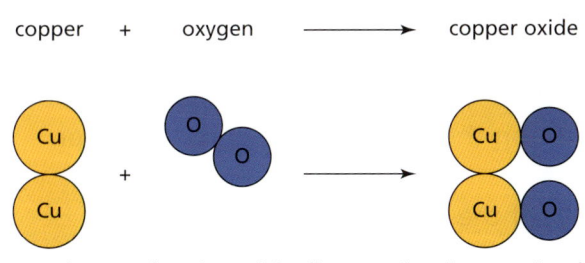

7.6 The word and particle diagram for the reaction between copper and oxygen.

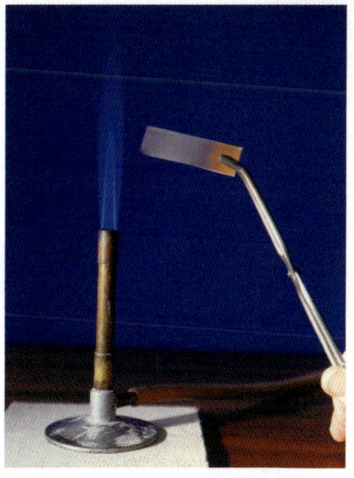

7.5 When copper is heated in air, black copper oxide is formed on the surface.

You can measure the mass of the copper before heating, then again afterwards.

You will find that the mass of the copper has increased.

This is because oxygen atoms from the air have reacted with the copper to form copper oxide.

The mass of the copper and the oxygen equals the mass of copper oxide. This is because of the law of conservation of mass.

copper + oxygen → copper oxide
  10 g   0.5 g   10.5 g

Science in context: Carbon capture

When fuels burn, carbon dioxide is produced and mixes with the air.

Carbon dioxide is a greenhouse gas and is causing climate change. Scientists are working on developing ways to capture carbon dioxide from the air. One idea is to react the carbon dioxide with sodium hydroxide to form sodium carbonate. The mass of the carbon dioxide in the air will decrease, although the atoms have not disappeared, they are part of a new compound.

1. Discuss the potential global environmental impacts of this carbon capture technology.

7.7 Climate change is linked to an increase in flooding.

Changes in chemical reactions 111

Activity 7.1: Heating magnesium

Elin and Yuki wanted to find out what would happen to the mass of magnesium when it was heated in air.

This is the method they followed:

A Measure the mass of a crucible and lid.

B Place a strip of magnesium into the crucible and measure the mass again.

C Put on your eye protection and place the crucible on the tripod over a Bunsen burner. Heat the crucible.

D Every 30 seconds use tongs to lift the lid slightly off the crucible and place it back down. Do not look at the magnesium directly.

E When the magnesium stops glowing (about 5–10 minutes), turn off the Bunsen burner and let the equipment cool down.

F Measure the mass of the crucible and contents again.

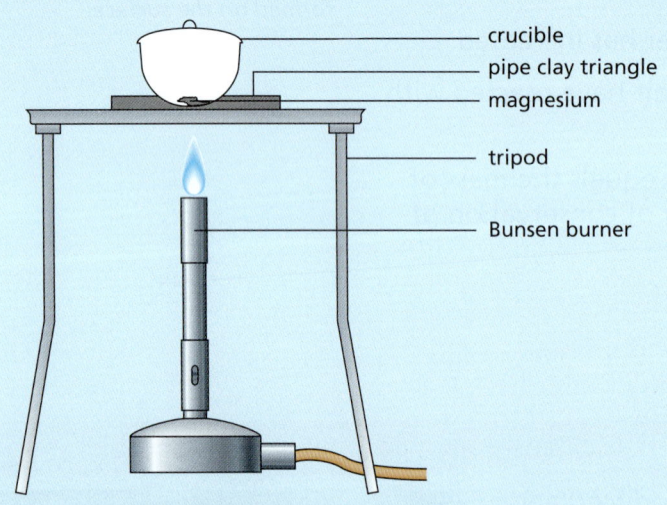

7.8 *Diagram of the equipment needed for this experiment.*

These are their results.

Mass of crucible = 23.4 g

Mass of crucible + magnesium before heating = 24.6 g

Mass of crucible + magnesium after heating = 25.4 g

A1 Write the word equation for the reaction.

A2 Suggest why a lid was used, and why the lid was opened when the magnesium was being heated.

A3 Calculate the change in mass of the magnesium. Give a scientific explanation for this.

A4 Describe how the risks were controlled.

7.1

Conservation of energy

Energy is stored in the chemical bonds in reactants. During a chemical reaction this energy is transferred to the chemical bonds in the products. Some energy may also be transferred to the surroundings as heat.

Energy can flow from store to store but there is always the same amount of energy at the start of a reaction and at the end; energy cannot be created or destroyed. This is the law of conservation of energy.

Key facts:

✔ The mass of products in a chemical reaction equals the mass of reactants.

✔ Energy is not created or destroyed, in a chemical reaction it is transferred from one store to another.

Check your skills progress:

- I can discuss how scientific knowledge is developed through collective understanding and scrutiny over time.
- I can make risk assessments for practical work to identify and control risks.
- I can make conclusions by interpreting results.

Chapter 7 . Topic 2

Word and symbol equations

You will learn:
- To describe chemical reactions using word or symbol equations (not including balancing)
- To represent scientific ideas using recognised symbols or formulae

Starting point

You should know that...	You should be able to...
During a chemical reaction, reactants react to form products	Use symbols and formulae to represent scientific ideas
A word equation separates the substances that react and the products that are formed with an arrow	

Writing word equations

When copper carbonate is heated it breaks down to form copper oxide and carbon dioxide. This can be shown in a word equation:

copper carbonate → copper oxide + carbon dioxide
     reactant   products

> **Key terms**
>
> **product**: substance made during a chemical reaction.
>
> **reactant**: substance that changes in a chemical reaction to form products.
>
> **word equation**: model showing what happens in a chemical reaction, with reactants on the left of an arrow and products on the right.

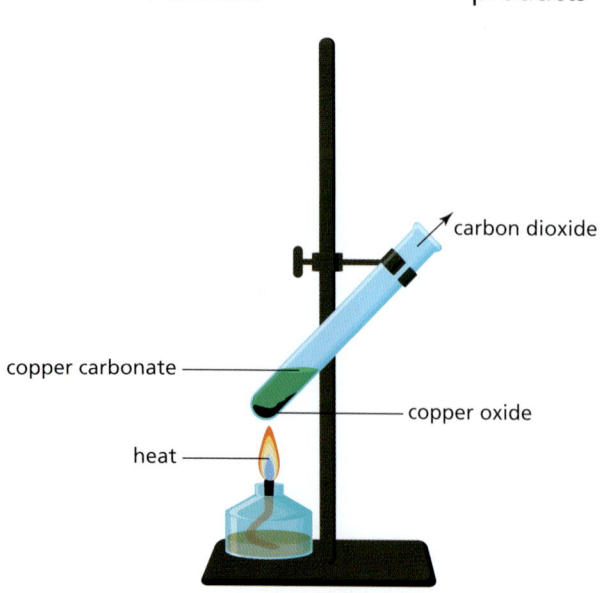

7.9 When copper carbonate is heated it breaks down to form the products copper oxide and carbon dioxide.

A **word equation** shows us the **reactants** and **products** in a reaction. The reactants and products can be elements or compounds. Word equations always have the reactants on the left. The arrow points to the products that are made.

Copper carbonate is the reactant; copper oxide and carbon dioxide are the products.

> **1** Kris adds sodium to a jar of chlorine. There is a bright light and a white powder called sodium chloride is formed.
>
> a) Name the:
>
>   i) reactants
>
>   ii) product
>
> b) Write a word equation for the reaction

Key terms

formula: shows the chemical symbols of elements in a compound, and how many of each type of atom there are.

symbol equation: way of showing a chemical reaction using formulae – a balanced symbol equation has equal numbers of each type of atom on both sides of the equation.

Symbol equations

You can also show reactions using **symbol equations**. These show the **formulae** of the reactants and products. The symbol equation for the breakdown of copper carbonate is:

copper carbonate → copper oxide + carbon dioxide

$CaCO_3 \rightarrow CaO + CO_2$

Whenever a chemical reaction takes place, the atoms in the reactants *rearrange* to form the products. No atoms are *lost* or *created*. This means that the numbers and types of atoms in the reactants are the same as the numbers and types of atoms in the products.

Science in context: Symbol equations

Symbol equations are written using the same symbols in every language. No matter which country you are from you would always use the same symbols to represent the changes that occur during a chemical reaction.

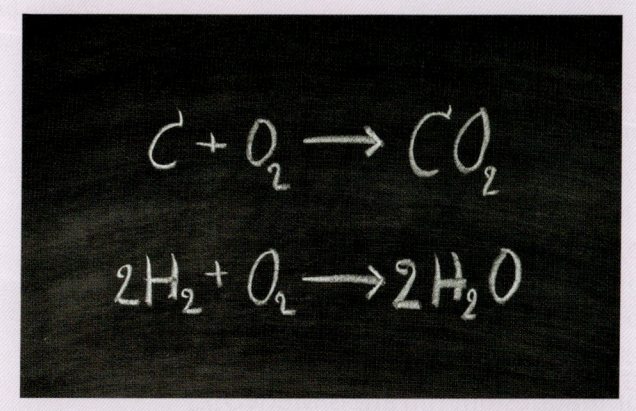

$$C + O_2 \rightarrow CO_2$$

$$2H_2 + O_2 \rightarrow 2H_2O$$

7.10 *These symbol equations are the same in every language.*

1. Explain why it is important for scientists all over the world to use the same symbols regardless of the language they speak.

Writing formulae

Ionic compounds are formed of metal and non-metal ions. You can work out their formulae by using the charge on the ions.

Different elements form ions with different charges, as shown in table 7.1. If the charge is larger than one, a small number next to the charge shows how many charges the ion has. For example, Na^+ has a single positive charge and O^{2-} has a double negative charge. A compound has no overall charge – this is because the positive and negative charges on the ions cancel each other out. You can use these charges to work out the formulae of compounds.

Positive ions	Negative ions
Sodium, Na^+	Chloride, Cl^-
Potassium, K^+	Bromide, Br^-
Magnesium, Mg^{2+}	Oxide, O^{2-}
Calcium, Ca^{2+}	Sulfate, SO_4^{2-}
Zinc, Zn^{2+}	Carbonate, CO_3^{2-}
Copper(II), Cu^{2+}	Nitrate, NO_3^-
Iron(III), Fe^{3+}	Hydroxide, OH^-
Hydrogen, H^+	

Table 7.1 *The charges on some ions.*

Name of compound	Formula
Hydrochloric acid	HCl
Sulfuric acid	H_2SO_4
Nitric acid	HNO_3
Water	H_2O
Carbon dioxide	CO_2

Table 7.2 *The formulae of some common compounds.*

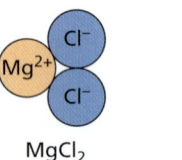

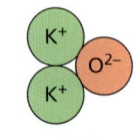

7.11 *Compounds have no overall charge because the numbers of positive and negative charges are equal.*

You can see from table 7.1 that a magnesium ion has a double positive charge, Mg^{2+}, and that a chloride ion has a single negative charge, Cl^-. For the charges to cancel out, the compound magnesium chloride must contain one magnesium ion and two chloride ions.

The formulae of some compounds contain brackets. For example, the formula for magnesium nitrate is $Mg(NO_3)_2$. The brackets around the nitrate ion show that there are two nitrate ions for each magnesium ion. The small number '2' applies to all the element symbols inside the brackets. So $Mg(NO_3)_2$ has 6 oxygen atoms (2 × 3). If you did not write

Chemical changes

the brackets, the formula would look like MgNO$_{32}$ but there are not 32 oxygen atoms!

2 How many atoms of oxygen are represented in each of these formulae?

a) MgO   b) KOH   c) H$_2$O   d) CO$_2$

e) C$_3$H$_6$O$_2$ f) Mg(OH)$_2$ g) CuSO$_4$ h) Ca(NO$_3$)$_2$

3 Write the formula for each of these compounds. You will need to use table 7.1.

a) sodium chloride   b) calcium oxide
c) magnesium bromide   d) potassium nitrate
e) zinc carbonate

4 Explain why the formula of potassium oxide is K$_2$O.

Making links

Chemical reactions also take place in living organisms. In Topic 4.4 you may have learned about photosynthesis, a process involving a series of reactions where carbon dioxide and water are converted into glucose and oxygen. Can you write the word equation to summarise this process?

Key facts:

✔ A word equation shows us the reactants and products in a reaction.

✔ A symbol equations show the formulae of the reactants and products.

Check your skills progress:

- I can use symbols and formulae to represent scientific ideas.

Word and symbol equations   117

Chapter 7 . Topic 3

Methods for making salts

You will learn:
- To describe the methods used to prepare and purify salts from the reactions between acids and metals, acids and metal carbonates
- To represent scientific ideas using symbols and formulae
- To choose the appropriate equipment for an investigation and use it correctly
- To carry out practical work in a safe manner to minimise risks
- To identify and control risks
- To present results appropriately

Starting point

You should know that...	You should be able to...
When an acid and base react they form a salt, in a neutralisation reaction	Make conclusions by interpreting results
Some metals react with acids	Identify and control risks

Making salts

A **salt** is formed when metals and metal carbonates react with acids. The type of salt made in the reaction depends on the acid used.

The first part of the salt's name is always the name of a metal element. The metal comes from the metal or base used.

The second part of the salt's name is from the acid used.

Acid used	Type of salt made
Hydrochloric	Chloride
Sulfuric	Sulfate
Nitric	Nitrate

Reaction of acid with metals

Zinc reacts with sulfuric acid to form the salt zinc sulfate. Hydrogen is also made. The word equation is:

zinc + sulfuric acid → zinc sulfate + hydrogen

This can also be written as a symbol equation:

$Zn + H_2SO_4 \rightarrow ZnSO_4 + H_2$

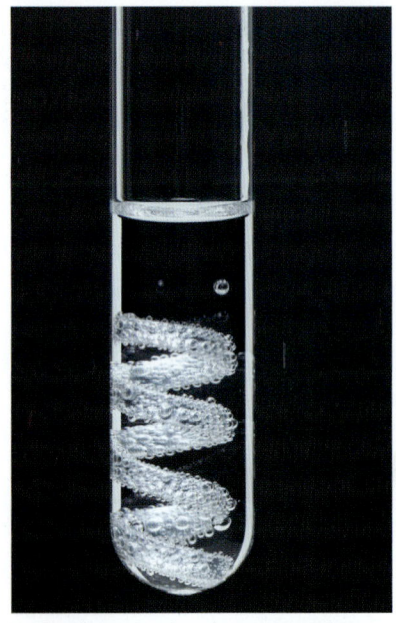

7.12 The reaction between zinc and an acid produces bubbles of hydrogen gas.

Key term

salt: a type of compound that consists of metal atoms joined to non-metal atoms, e.g. sodium chloride.

118 Chemical changes

Reactions between acids and carbonates

Metal carbonates such as calcium carbonate are compounds that are **bases** – they neutralise acids. Some metal carbonates, such as sodium carbonate, are soluble. Bases which are soluble are known as alkalis and dissolve into water to form **alkaline solutions**. Metal carbonates react with acids to produce a salt, water and carbon dioxide.

For example, the word equation for the reaction between calcium carbonate and hydrochloric acid is:

calcium carbonate + hydrochloric acid → calcium chloride + water + carbon dioxide

The carbon dioxide is released as bubbles.

> **Key terms**
>
> **alkali**: a base that is soluble.
>
> **alkaline solution**: a solution formed when a base dissolves in water.
>
> **base**: a compound that can react with an acid and neutralise it.

7.13 *Marble is a rock that contains calcium carbonate. It reacts with hydrochloric acid to produce bubbles of carbon dioxide.*

---

1 Copy and complete the word equations for the reactions.

  a) _____ + sulfuric acid → magnesium _____ + _____

  b) zinc + _____ acid → zinc nitrate + _____

2 Write word equations for the reactions between:

  a) zinc carbonate and sulfuric acid
  b) iron carbonate and hydrochloric acid.

3 Indigestion is caused by too much stomach acid. It can be stopped by taking indigestion tablets that contain magnesium carbonate.

  a) Write a word equation to show the reaction that happens between indigestion tablets and stomach acid (hydrochloric acid).
  b) Explain why they help stop indigestion.

Methods for making salts

4 Marble (calcium carbonate) statues can be damaged over time because of acid rain. Suggest why this happens.

7.14 *This marble statue has been damaged by acid rain.*

Activity 7.2: What is the powder?

Iman and Arianna were given four different powders. They had to design a way of finding out if the powders were metals, carbonates or neither.

Here is their plan:

A Add one spatula of powder to a test tube.

B Add 5 cm³ of hydrochloric acid to the test tube.

C Fit a bung loosely on top of the test tube.

D If the powder bubbles, remove the bung and hold a lighted splint close to the top of the tube.

E Repeat steps **A** and **B**. Fit a bung with a delivery tube into the test tube – put the other end of the delivery tube into a test tube of limewater.

Here are their results:

Powder	Observations when the acid was added	Observations when a lighted splint was used	Observations when the gas was bubbled through limewater
1	Lots of bubbles produced quickly	Heard a pop noise	No change
2	No bubbles	No change	No change
3	A few bubbles produced slowly	Heard a pop noise	No change
4	Lots of bubbles produced quickly	Flame went out	Limewater went cloudy

A1 Use your scientific knowledge and understanding to explain what the results show about the four powders.

A2 Explain how Iman and Arianna should control risks when following their plan.

Chemical changes

7.3

Making a soluble salt

You can make a salt by reacting a metal or solid carbonate with acid.

First, pour some dilute acid into a beaker. Then add a spatula of the metal or solid metal carbonate and stir with a glass rod. If a metal is used it will be in the form of small pieces or a powder. Eye protection will be required.

The reaction will produce a soluble salt. You will see fizzing because bubbles of gas are made. The gas will mix with the air and leave the beaker. The salt dissolves to form a solution.

You need to keep on adding the solid, one spatula at a time, until no more reacts. There will be some solid left over in the solution because you have used an excess of the solid reactant. This means that all the acid has reacted.

7.15 How to react an acid with a metal or an insoluble metal carbonate.

Purifying the salt

You will now have a mixture of a salt solution and solid. To purify the salt, the other substances need to be removed.

Using filtration

You remove the solid by **filtering** the mixture. The excess, or unreacted, solid stays in the filter paper. The salt solution goes through the filter paper and collects in the container below.

7.16 How to perform filtration.

Using evaporation

The final step is to remove the water from the salt solution by **evaporation**. Because this process forms the salt crystals it is called **crystallisation**.

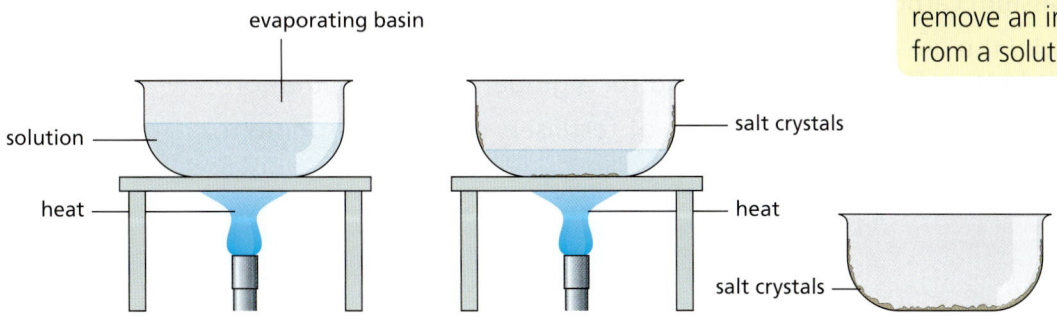

Key term

filtration: separating technique used to remove an insoluble solid from a solution.

7.17 How to use evaporation to crystallise salt crystals from a solution.

Methods for making salts

To do it you pour the salt solution into an evaporating basin and heat it very gently using a Bunsen burner. As water evaporates, the salt solution becomes more concentrated. You will see small salt crystals forming round the edge of the basin.

You then turn off the Bunsen burner and leave the evaporating basin to cool before moving it to a warm place to let the rest of the water evaporate. This allows crystallisation to happen slowly, resulting in larger crystals.

7.18 Copper sulfate forms blue crystals.

> **5** When reacting a solid with an acid to make a salt, explain why:
> a) filtration is used
> b) evaporation is used
> c) stirring the mixture helps the reaction to happen more quickly
> d) adding the metal in excess results in just salt crystals with no acid

Key terms

crystallisation: the formation of crystals from their solution.

evaporation: separating technique used to remove water from a solution.

Science in context: Feeding the world

The human population is increasing – making sure everyone has enough food is getting more and more difficult.

Farmers add fertilisers to the soil to help their crops grow bigger or stronger. They can double the amount of crop (such as grains or seeds) produced from an area of land, providing more food. Artificial fertilisers are salts that contain ions that plants need to grow – such as nitrate, magnesium, iron and potassium. They can be made by using chemical reactions. For example, potassium nitrate fertiliser can be made by reacting potassium carbonate with nitric acid.

7.19 Adding fertilisers to soil increases the amount of food that can be grown.

1. Explain why the use of fertilisers is so important in the effort to provide food for a global human population?
2. Discuss the potential negative impacts of fertilisers on the environment.

Chemical changes

7.3

Key facts:

- ✔ A salt is formed when metals and metal carbonates react with acids.
- ✔ The type of salt made in the reaction depends on the acid used.
- ✔ Salts can be purified using filtration, evaporation and crystallisation.

Check your skills progress:

- I can make conclusions by interpreting results.
- I can make risk assessments.

Making links

In Stage 8 you may have learned about the reactivity series – that some metals are more reactive than others. A chemist wants to make the salt copper sulfate. Why would they use copper carbonate as a reactant rather than copper?

Methods for making salts

Chapter 7 . Topic 4

Displacement reactions

You will learn:
- To identify displacement reactions, and predict their products (involving zinc, magnesium, calcium, iron, copper, gold and silver salts only)
- To represent scientific ideas using symbols and formulae
- To describe the uses, strengths and limitations of models and analogies
- To use scientific knowledge to make predictions
- To carry out practical work in a safe manner to minimise risks
- To describe trends and patterns shown in a set of results, identifying, and explaining, any anomalous results present
- To collect and record observations and measurements appropriately

Starting point

You should know that...	You should be able to...
The reactivity series of metals lists them in order of their reactivity	Plan investigations to test ideas, including deciding which measurements and observations are necessary

Understanding displacement reactions

A more reactive element will displace (take the place of) a less reactive element in a chemical reaction. This is called a **displacement reaction**. Both metals and non-metals can take part in displacement reactions.

You can use displacement reactions to compare how reactive metals are.

Figure 7.20 shows an iron nail being added to blue copper sulfate solution. You can see that, after some time, the solution has become green, and that the iron nail has a coating of brown copper.

In this reaction, iron has displaced copper from copper sulfate solution to make iron sulfate. The copper is now on its own as an element and the iron is part of a compound. This reaction can be shown using a word equation:

iron + copper sulfate → iron sulfate + copper

This displacement reaction happens because iron is more reactive than copper.

Key term

displacement reaction: chemical reaction in which a more reactive metal displaces (takes the place of) a less reactive metal from a compound, to form a new compound.

7.20 *When iron is added to copper sulfate solution, iron slowly displaces copper from the copper sulfate.*

124 Chemical changes

1 How can you see that a chemical reaction has taken place between iron and copper sulfate in figure 7.20?

2 When magnesium is added to a test tube containing copper sulfate solution a chemical reaction happens, but this time the solution changes colour much quicker. Which is more reactive, iron or magnesium?

3 Explain whether or not adding copper powder to iron sulfate will produce a reaction

The reactivity series

The **reactivity series** lists metals in order of their relative **reactivity**. Figure 7.21 shows the reactivity series for seven metals. Calcium is the most reactive and gold is the least reactive. Gold is **inert** and takes part in very few chemical reactions. Some gold **salts** are known, such as gold chloride, but you are very unlikely to use these in the school laboratory.

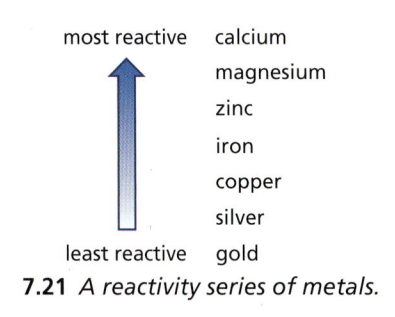

most reactive — calcium
magnesium
zinc
iron
copper
silver
least reactive — gold

7.21 A reactivity series of metals.

Making predictions about displacement reactions

You can use the reactivity series to predict whether displacement reactions will happen and, if so, what the products will be. For example, you can use the reactivity series to predict whether the following displacement reaction will take place:

copper + magnesium sulfate → magnesium + copper sulfate

Magnesium is higher than copper in the reactivity series, which means it is more reactive. So the reaction above between copper and magnesium sulfate would not happen. Copper cannot displace magnesium from magnesium sulfate because copper is less reactive than magnesium.

4 Predict whether a displacement reaction would happen between each of the pairs of reactants below:

calcium and copper sulfate

magnesium and calcium chloride

silver and iron nitrate

calcium and zinc chloride

> **Key terms**
>
> **inert**: unable to take part in a chemical reaction.
>
> **reactivity**: how likely it is that a substance will undergo a chemical reaction.
>
> **reactivity series**: series of metals written in order from the most reactive to the least reactive.

Activity 7.3: Comparing the reactivity of metals

You can use displacement reactions to compare how reactive metals are and produce a reactivity series of metals.

A group of students carried out a series of experiments using four metals and solutions of their salts. They added each metal to the other solutions, one at a time, and observed what happened.

Jamila predicted that magnesium and iron sulfate would react, producing iron and magnesium sulfate.

A1 Is she correct? Give a reason.

A2 Hassan predicted that copper and zinc sulfate would react, producing zinc and copper sulfate.

Is he correct? Give a reason.

The table shows their results.

	Magnesium sulfate	Zinc sulfate	Iron sulfate	Copper sulfate
Magnesium		✓	✓	✓
Zinc	✗		✓	✓
Iron	✗	✗		✓
Copper	✗	✗	✗	

✓ = reaction happened
✗ = no reaction happened

A3 Explain why the students did not add the metals to the salt solutions of the same metal. For example, they did not add magnesium to magnesium sulfate.

A4 Use the students' results to produce a reactivity series of the four metals. Put the most reactive at the top and the least reactive at the bottom.

A5 Justify your reactivity series – why have you put the metals in that order?

A6 How could the students have improved this experiment? Explain your proposed changes.

A7 Write word equations for the reactions between:

  a magnesium and zinc sulfate

  b zinc and iron sulfate

  c iron and copper sulfate

A8 A student was trying to identify a metal. She found that it reacted with copper sulfate, but not with magnesium sulfate or zinc sulfate. What metal could it be?

7.4

Science in context: Global dimension

Extension Iron, the most widely used metal worldwide, is found in the ground as an ore that contains iron oxide. Iron is extracted from its ore using a displacement reaction. The process is done in a large furnace, called the blast furnace. A carbon-based substance is added to the furnace, along with the iron oxide. Carbon is more reactive than iron. Molten iron is produced in the reaction.

1. Describe how displacement is used to make iron in this reaction.

7.22 Molten iron from a blast furnace.

Key facts:

✔ A more reactive metal will displace a less reactive metal from its compounds.

✔ Displacement reactions can be used to compare the reactivity of different metals.

Check your skills progress:

- I can make conclusions from results.
- I can make predictions and evaluate these against evidence.
- I can evaluate experiments by others and suggest improvements.

Making links

You may have learned about sodium and potassium in Stage 8 Topic 6.5 and you will learn more about them in your future Chemistry studies. Give reasons that explain why sodium and potassium cannot be used in displacement reactions like these.

Displacement reactions

Chapter 7 . Topic 5

Rates of reaction

You will learn:
- To describe and explain how the rate of reaction is affected by changes in concentration, surface area and temperature
- To plan investigations used to test hypotheses
- To describe the uses, strengths and limitations of models and analogies
- To identify hazards and ways to minimise risks
- To carry out practical work in a safe manner to minimise risks
- To use scientific knowledge to make predictions
- To describe trends and patterns shown in a set of results, identifying, and explaining, any anomalous results present
- To collect and record observations and measurements appropriately
- To interpret results and form conclusions using scientific knowledge and understanding
- To decide how to obtain sufficiently reliable data from observations and measurements

Starting point

You should know that...	You should be able to...
Different metals react at different speeds with oxygen, water and dilute acids	Describe trends and patterns in results
	Explain results using scientific knowledge and understanding

How can you compare rates of reaction?

You have seen that different chemical reactions happen at different speeds. A **rate of reaction** is the speed at which the reaction happens. This can be compared in different ways – for example, you can measure how quickly a reactant is used up or how quickly a product is made.

If a chemical reaction produces a gas, you can measure how quickly that gas escapes from an open container. You put the container and its contents on a balance (figure 7.23). As the gas escapes the mass of the flask and its contents reduce. The faster the mass of the reaction mixture decreases, the faster the rate of the reaction.

> **Key term**
>
> **rate of reaction**: how fast a chemical reaction happens.

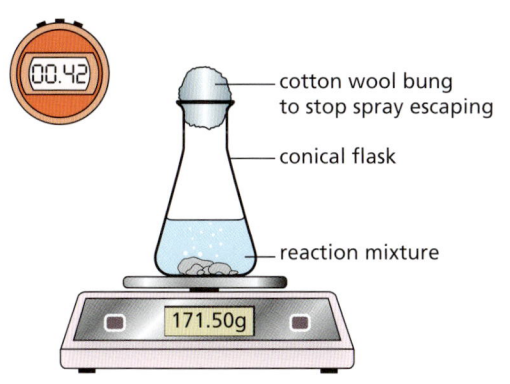

7.23 *Measuring the decrease in mass over time. The cotton wool allows gas to escape, but not liquids.*

Carbon dioxide is given off when calcium carbonate reacts with dilute hydrochloric acid. The table shows the results of an experiment to measure the rate of this reaction. The mass of the flask and its contents was measured every 30 seconds until the reaction stopped.

An alternative method is to measure how much gas is produced over time, using a measuring cylinder or a gas syringe (figures 7.24 and 7.25). The volume of gas collected in the gas syringe can be measured over a time interval, such as every 10 seconds. The faster the gas is collected, the faster the rate of the reaction.

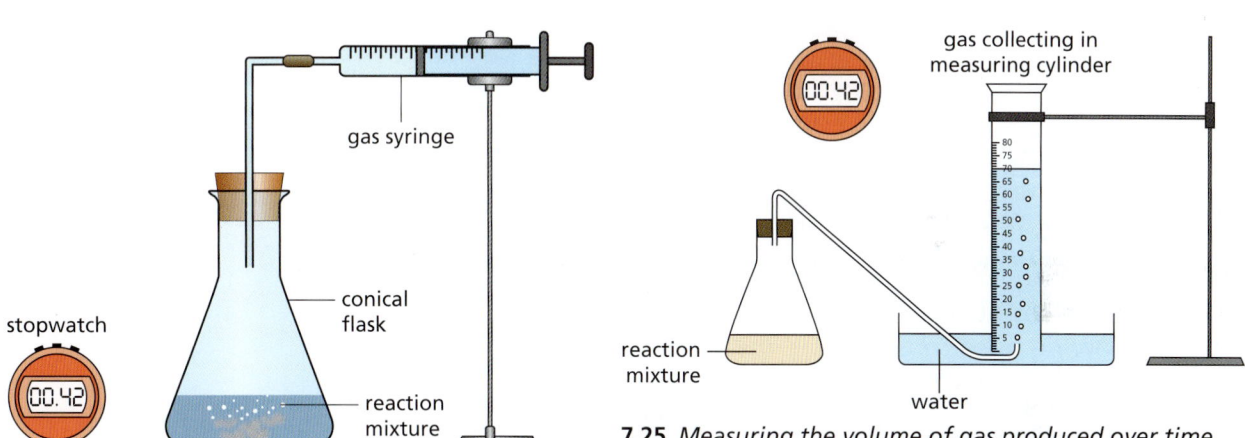

7.24 *Measuring the volume of gas produced over time using a gas syringe.*

7.25 *Measuring the volume of gas produced over time using a measuring cylinder. As the gas collects in the measuring cylinder it pushes water out.*

> **1** Describe what 'rate of reaction' means.

Rates of reaction

2 Look at the table below.

a) Explain why the reaction mixture lost mass.

b) State the time taken for the reaction to stop.

Time (s)	Total mass (g)
0	123.50
30	122.29
90	121.91
120	121.78
150	121.71
180	121.68
210	121.78
240	121.63
270	121.61
300	121.61

3 Hydrogen is produced when zinc reacts with a dilute acid. State *two* different ways you could measure the rate of this reaction.

4 A student reacted magnesium with some hydrochloric acid and collected the gas produced. She measured the volume of gas every 10 seconds. The table shows her results.

Use the results to answer the following questions.

a) During which 10 seconds was the largest volume of gas produced?

b) What volume of gas was produced between 0 and 30 seconds?

Time (s)	Volume of gas (cm^3)
0	0
10	5
20	9
30	13
40	16
50	18
60	19
70	20
80	20
90	20

c) When did the reaction end? Explain your answer.

d) At what stage was the reaction happening fastest? Explain your answer.

Chemical changes

7.5

Changing the rate of a reaction

For a chemical reaction to happen, the reactant particles have to collide with each other. To speed up a chemical reaction, particles have to collide with each other more often or they have to collide with more energy. You can do this by changing the reaction conditions. There are three key factors that affect the rate of reaction. These are:

- temperature
- concentration
- surface area

If any of these factors are changed then the rate of the reaction will change.

5 What factors can affect the rate of a chemical reaction?

Activity 7.4: Which reaction is the fastest?

A group of students investigated the reaction between calcium carbonate and hydrochloric acid. They were trying to find out how the concentration of the acid affected the rate of reaction.

The students added 10 g of powdered calcium carbonate to 50 cm^3 of hydrochloric acid in a conical flask. Each experiment had a different concentration of acid. They put the conical flask on a balance and measured the change in mass over time.

The table shows their results.

Time (s)	Mass of reactants (g)		
	Experiment 1	Experiment 2	Experiment 3
0	60.0	60.0	60.0
20	59.8	59.2	59.5
40	59.5	58.4	58.9
60	59.0	57.7	58.3
80	58.8	57.0	57.9
100	58.5	56.3	57.3

A1 State the independent variable in this investigation.
A2 State *one* control variable in this investigation.
A3 Write a word equation for this reaction. Use the equation to explain why the mass decreases.
A4 Calculate the decrease in mass after 100 s for each experiment.

Rates of reaction 131

A5 Which experiment had the greatest rate of reaction? Explain how you know.

A6 Explain what the students would observe if the fastest reaction was allowed to continue for 5 minutes.

How do the factors affect the rate of reaction?

The temperature at which a chemical reaction happens is very important. If you increase the temperature of the reactants, their particles gain energy and move around faster. They collide with each other more often, and more of these collisions have enough energy to cause a reaction. The more often particles collide with enough energy, the greater the rate of reaction.

So increasing the temperature of a reaction increases the rate of the reaction.

6 State and explain how increasing the temperature affects the rate of a chemical reaction.

The **concentration** of a substance is the number of its particles in a given volume. If you increase the concentration of one reactant you are increasing the number of particles of that reactant in the same volume.

If there are more particles of that reactant present then there is an increased chance that these particles will collide with the other reactant particles. The more often the particles collide, the faster the reaction.

So increasing the concentration of a reactant increases the rate of the reaction.

low temperature

high temperature

● reacting particle of substance **A**
● reacting particle of substance **B**

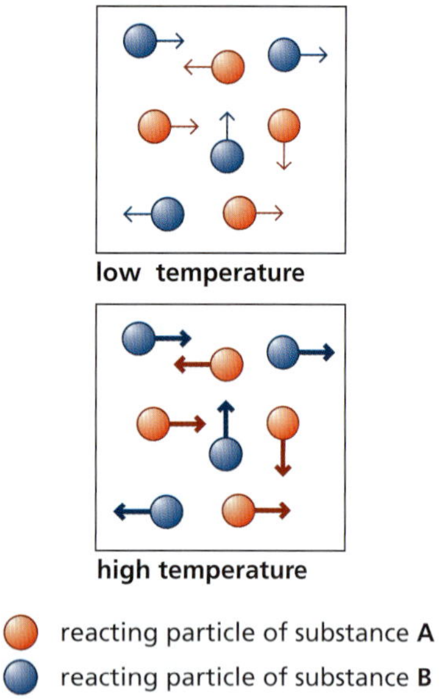

7.26 *The particle model showing increasing the temperature of a reaction mixture.*

Key term

concentration: a measurement of how many particles of a certain type there are in a volume of liquid or gas.

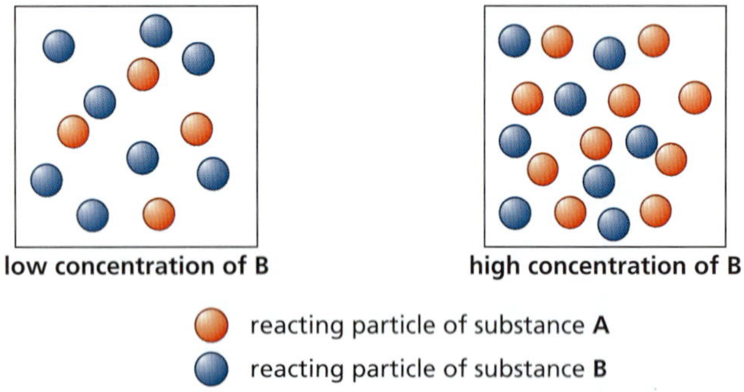

low concentration of B   high concentration of B

● reacting particle of substance **A**
● reacting particle of substance **B**

7.27 *The particle model showing increasing the concentration of a reactant.*

7 State and explain how increasing the concentration of the reactants affects the rate of a chemical reaction.

132   Chemical changes

7.5

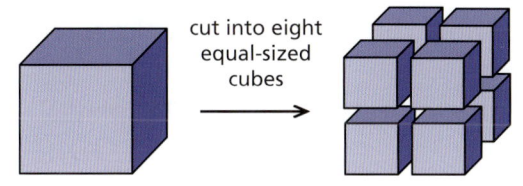

7.28 Increasing the surface area of a solid reactant.

The particle size of a solid reactant also affects the rate of a chemical reaction. The bigger the piece of solid, the slower it will react. If you break a solid into smaller pieces, or if you grind it into a powder, the **surface area** of the solid is increased. This means there is more chance that particles of the solid can collide with the other reactant particles, so collisions happen more often and the reaction is faster.

> **Key term**
>
> **surface area**: the area of a surface, measured in squared units such as square centimetres (cm^2).

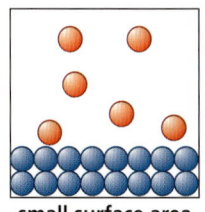

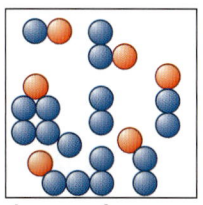

- particle of substance **A**
- particle of substance **B**

7.29 In the first particle model diagram, only the particles at the surface of substance B can react with particles of substance A. In the second diagram more particles of B can react with particles of A.

So increasing the surface area of a solid reactant increases the rate of reaction. If you think about cooking, it is very similar. When you boil potatoes, if you cut them into smaller pieces they cook more quickly. Putting the potatoes into boiling water whole would mean they cooked much more slowly.

8 State and explain how decreasing the size of pieces of a solid reactant affects the rate of a chemical reaction.

Activity 7.5: Investigating the effect of surface area

You have been provided with three samples of the same indigestion tablet and some dilute hydrochloric acid. One tablet is full size, one is broken into small pieces and the other is ground up into powder. You are to plan an investigation to determine which of these samples has the greatest rate of reaction with the acid.

A1 State the independent variable in this investigation.

A2 State the variables you will need to keep the same.

A3 State the apparatus you will need for this experiment and make a risk assessment to identify and control risk.

Rates of reaction

A4 Write a step-by-step method for this reaction. State how you are going to make sure that your results are reliable.

A5 Which experiment do you predict would have the greatest rate of reaction? Explain your answer.

Science in context: Refrigeration

Food gradually goes off during storage. Chemical reactions produce substances with unpleasant tastes and smells, and allow mould to grow. These reactions happen more quickly at warm temperatures. Storing food at low temperatures in fridges and freezers reduces the rate of these reactions, keeping the food safe to eat for longer. Refrigeration reduces food waste when transporting food from farms to shops, and allows people to live in areas once thought to be too hot or too far from other towns and cities.

7.30 *Vaccines and some medicines must be kept cold or frozen.*

Key facts:

✔ The rate of a reaction increases as temperature increases; when the concentration of reactant particles increases; and when the surface area of the reactants increases.

✔ Chemical reactions only occur when the reactant particles collide with each other and with enough energy.

✔ An increase in temperature increases the rate of a reaction because reactant particles collide more often and with more energy.

✔ An increase in the concentration of a soluble reactant, or in the surface area of a solid reactant, increases the rate of a reaction because reactant particles collide more often.

Check your skills progress:

- I can make risk assessments for practical work to identify and control risks.
- I can make predictions based on my scientific knowledge and understanding.
- I can make conclusions by interpreting results.

Chemical changes

End of chapter review

Quick questions

1. A piece of magnesium with mass 2.4 g was heated in air to form magnesium oxide with a mass of 4.0 g. Calculate the mass of oxygen that reacted with the magnesium.

2. Lithium is added to water. Lithium hydroxide and hydrogen are formed. Write the word equation for this reaction.

3. What salt is formed when calcium reacts with sulfuric acid?

    a sulfur calcate
    b sulfuric calcium
    c calcium sulfuric
    d calcium sulfate

4. What *two* reactants can be used to make the salt magnesium chloride?

    a magnesium
    b sulfuric acid
    c hydrochloric acid
    d oxygen

5. What gas is formed when acids react with metals?

    a oxygen
    b nitrogen
    c hydrogen
    d carbon dioxide

6. This is a list of separating techniques:

    distillation   evaporation   filtration

    For each of the stages used in making a salt below, choose the separating technique you would use:

    (a) removing excess metal from a salt solution

    (b) crystallising salt crystals from a salt solution

7. Some metals are more reactive than others.

    Copy and complete the following sentences.
    Metals react _____ quickly as you go down the reactivity series.
    A _____ reactive metal will displace a _____ reactive metal from its compounds.

8. List *three* factors that can change the rate of a chemical reaction.

9. What must reactant particles do for a reaction to happen?

Connect your understanding

10. A teacher measured the mass of a piece of iron wool (fine strands of iron) as 3.6 g.

    She used tongs to hold the iron in a Bunsen burner flame. She noticed it turned darker and dull in colour. She let it cool and then measured the mass again. It was now 3.9 g.

    (a) Describe what happened to the mass of the iron when it was heated.

    (b) Use the particle model to explain why this happened.

11. When paper burns its mass decreases. Explain why.

12. A carbonate was added to an acid to make the salt potassium chloride.

    Write the word equation for this reaction.

13. Mo wants to make the salt called sodium nitrate. He could react sodium metal or sodium carbonate with an acid.

    (a) What acid should he use?

    (b) Should he use sodium metal or sodium carbonate? Give a reason for your answer.

14. A chemist mixes a piece of calcium with some hydrochloric acid.

    (a) Write a word equation for the reaction.

    (b) State the symbol or formula for each substance involved in the reaction.

15. Describe the steps you would take to make crystals of zinc sulfate from zinc granules and sulfuric acid.

16. Use the reactivity series to predict whether a reaction will occur when the following chemicals are mixed. If you predict a reaction, write the name of the products. If you predict the substances will not react with each other, write 'No reaction'.

    (a) zinc and copper sulfate solution

    (b) silver and magnesium chloride solution

    (c) magnesium and silver sulfate solution

    (d) calcium and copper sulfate solution

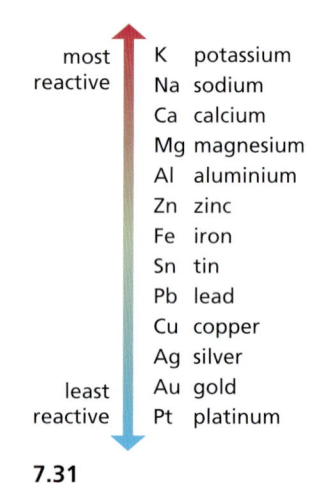

most reactive
K potassium
Na sodium
Ca calcium
Mg magnesium
Al aluminium
Zn zinc
Fe iron
Sn tin
Pb lead
Cu copper
Ag silver
least reactive
Au gold
Pt platinum

7.31

17. A student reacts sodium carbonate with dilute hydrochloric acid and measures the volume of gas produced in a measuring cylinder. The student measured the volume of gas produced every minute.

   (a) Draw a diagram of the apparatus that would be needed for this experiment.

   (b) What gas is produced in the reaction?

   The table shows the results collected by the student.

Time (min)	Volume of gas collected (cm³)
0	0
1	24
2	45
3	60
4	72
5	76
6	76
7	76

   (c) After how many minutes had all the acid been used up?

   (d) A second experiment was carried out for comparison at a higher temperature. Give *two* variables that should be controlled in this experiment.

   (e) Will more or less gas be collected in the second experiment? Explain your answer.

   (f) Explain how increasing the temperature will affect the rate of a chemical reaction.

Challenge questions

18. Use the formulae below to draw a particle diagram to show the reaction between calcium and sulfuric acid.

    sulfuric acid: H_2SO_4

    calcium sulfate: $CaSO_4$

19. In the past, the copper industry used pieces of scrap iron to extract copper from dilute copper sulfate solution: $Fe + CuSO_4 \rightarrow FeSO_4 + Cu$

    (a) Explain why this reaction happens.

    (b) Explain, using the particle model, *two* ways to make this reaction happen faster without increasing the temperature.

End of stage review

1. Scientists use models to show the structure of atoms.

   (a) This diagram shows a model of a lithium atom.

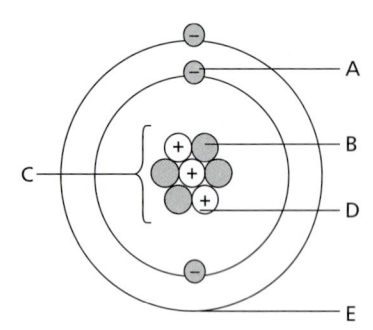

   What does each letter, A, B, C, D and E, label?

   Choose from the following words:

   | neutron | proton | nucleus | electron | shell |

   (b) Sodium's atomic number is 11.

   Use the structure of both atoms to explain why lithium and sodium are in the same group in the Periodic Table.

2. Three metals in order of increasing reactivity are: copper, zinc, magnesium.

   (a) Emily added a piece of zinc to copper sulfate solution.
   Copy and complete this word equation to show the products formed during the reaction.

   zinc + copper sulfate → _____ _____ + _____

   (b) Name this type of reaction.

   (c) Predict whether a reaction will occur when zinc is added to magnesium chloride solution. Give a reason for your answer.

   (d) Emily felt the test tube during the reaction. It felt warm. She concluded that energy must have been taken in during the reaction. Explain why this is not correct.

3. Rajiv and Jamila reacted some magnesium ribbon with dilute hydrochloric acid. They saw that bubbles of gas were produced.

   (a) Write a word equation for this reaction

   (b) They planned to repeat the experiment one more time using a different concentration of acid. Describe how they could compare the rate of the reaction at the two different concentrations.

138 Chemical changes

(c) Explain why increasing the concentration of the acid would increase the rate of the reaction.

(d) Give one other way in which the rate of this reaction could be increased.

4. Copper chloride is a solid at room temperature. Chlorine is a gas.
   Use their structure to explain why.

Physics

Chapter 8: Energy

8.1: Energy conservation	142
8.2: Heating and cooling	148
8.3: Conduction, convection, radiation and evaporation	152
End of chapter review	161

Chapter 9: Forces

9.1: Floating and sinking	165
End of chapter review	173

Chapter 10: Electricity

10.1: Voltage and resistance	176
10.2: Measuring current and voltage in series and parallel circuits	184
End of chapter review	190

Chapter 11: Sound

11.1: Loudness and pitch	193
11.2: Interference	200
End of chapter review	205
End of stage review	207

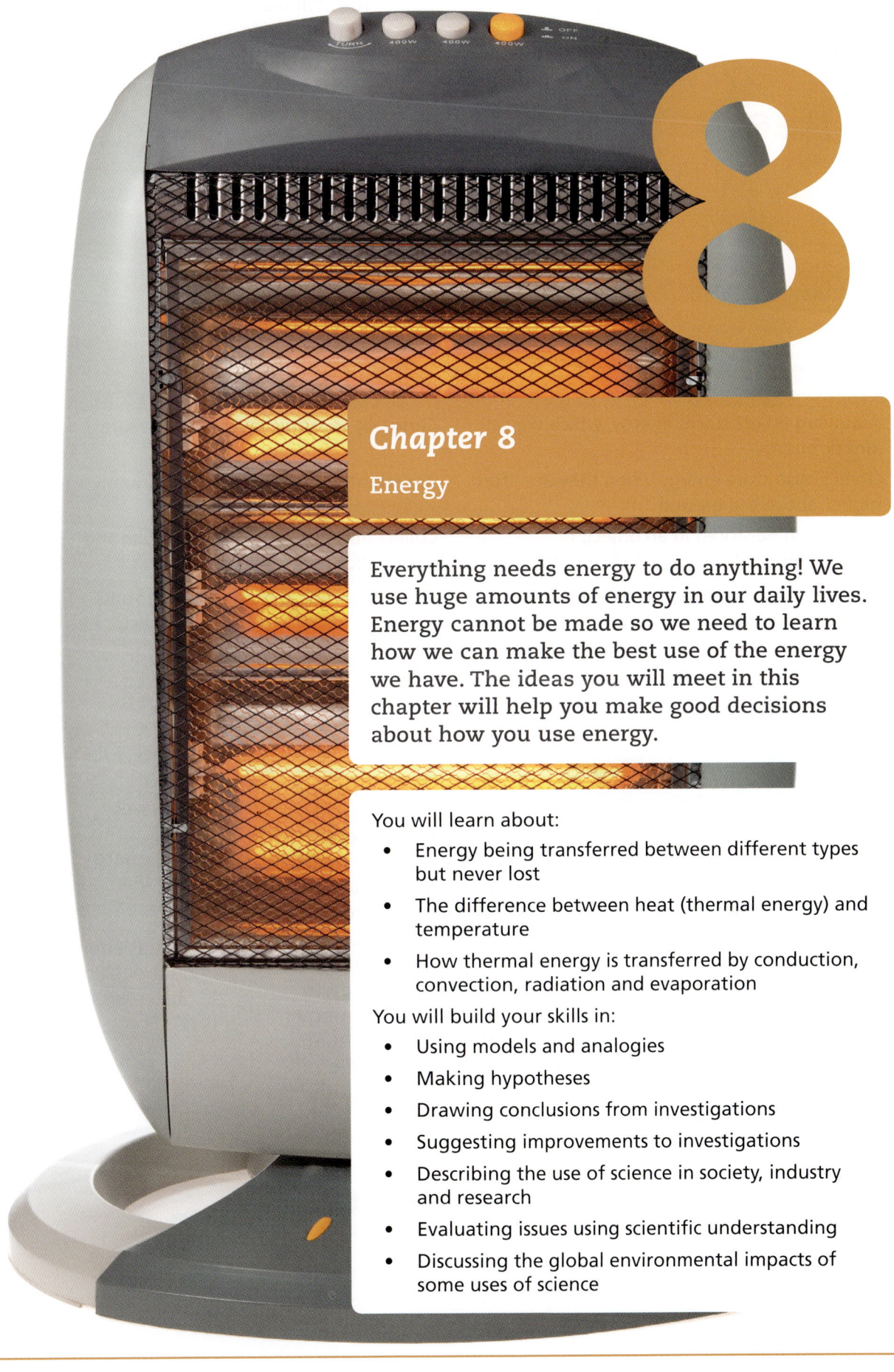

Chapter 8
Energy

Everything needs energy to do anything! We use huge amounts of energy in our daily lives. Energy cannot be made so we need to learn how we can make the best use of the energy we have. The ideas you will meet in this chapter will help you make good decisions about how you use energy.

You will learn about:
- Energy being transferred between different types but never lost
- The difference between heat (thermal energy) and temperature
- How thermal energy is transferred by conduction, convection, radiation and evaporation

You will build your skills in:
- Using models and analogies
- Making hypotheses
- Drawing conclusions from investigations
- Suggesting improvements to investigations
- Describing the use of science in society, industry and research
- Evaluating issues using scientific understanding
- Discussing the global environmental impacts of some uses of science

Chapter 8 . Topic 1

Energy conservation

You will learn:
- To understand that energy cannot be created or destroyed
- To use scientific knowledge to make predictions
- To describe the uses, strengths and limitations of models and analogies
- To decide whether evidence from first-hand experience or secondary sources should be used

Starting point

You should know that...	You should be able to...
A moving object stores energy, which we call kinetic energy	Carry out scientific investigations safely
Objects also store energy when they are lifted higher above the ground	Use scientific equipment appropriately
Energy can be stored in an object, or transferred from one object to another	Collect and record sufficient results and observations
When energy is transferred from one object to another, there is usually also some energy transferred into the surroundings as sound, light or thermal energy	Describe trends and patterns in results
Energy is never created or destroyed	Identify anomalous results

Energy and the pendulum

When a pendulum is moving it has **kinetic energy**. Where does this kinetic energy come from? To answer this we need to think about what has to happen before the pendulum can move. To start a pendulum moving you first have to lift the pendulum bob. To do this you have to do work against gravity. While the bob is at a high position it has stored energy, called **potential energy**. It uses this stored energy to move once you release the bob, converting potential energy to kinetic energy. The higher the bob is, the more potential energy it has. The faster the bob moves, the more kinetic energy it has. At most points in its swing, the bob has both some kinetic and some potential energy.

Key terms

kinetic energy: energy stored by an object because it is moving.

potential energy: the amount of stored energy an object has because of its position.

142 Energy

8.1

Activity 8.1: Observing the motion of a pendulum

Observe a swinging pendulum.

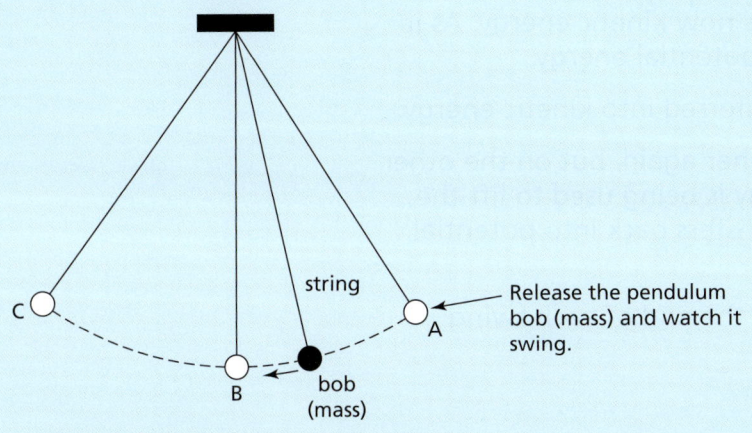

8.1 Observing the motion of a pendulum.

A1 When is the bob highest and when is it lowest?

A2 It is hard to judge the speed of the bob and to tell when it stops moving.

Suggest at which point in its swing the bob will:
a) move fastest
b) stop moving for an instant

A3 How would you change your investigation to confirm if your answers to part A2 were correct?

A4 What kinds of energy does the bob have at points **A**, **B** and **C** in its motion?

A5 What can you say about the kinds of energy the bob has when it is between points **A**, **B** and **C**.

A6 Draw a labelled diagram, similar to figure 8.1 to present your observations.

A pendulum will swing backwards and forwards for a long time. Its motion demonstrates an important principle. Energy is not destroyed or lost. This is the principle of **conservation of energy**.

The pendulum's total energy stays the same all through the swing.

At point **A**, the mass is at its highest point. The mass has potential energy. At that instant, it has stopped moving upwards and is about to start moving downwards. This means it stops for a very short time so it can change direction. As it is not moving, all its energy is potential energy.

> **Key term**
>
> **conservation of energy**: energy cannot be created or destroyed. The total amount of energy is constant.

Energy conservation 143

The mass swings back down and its speed increases. This means it gains kinetic energy. At the same time it loses potential energy as it is not as high as it was.

At point **B**, the mass is at its lowest point. Its speed is at its largest value. All its energy is now kinetic energy. As it cannot go any lower, it has no potential energy.

Potential energy has been transferred into kinetic energy.

Next, the mass begins to go higher again, but on the other side of the swing. Kinetic energy is being used to lift the mass. So, the kinetic energy transfers back into potential energy.

No energy is lost. The height at the end of each swing should be the same.

Energy dissipation

In practice, the bob will not keep swinging back to the same height every time. This is because some energy will be dissipated to the surroundings, for example, through friction with the air. Whenever energy is transferred some is always dissipated. For example, in a motor, some energy will be useful (turning the motor) and some will be wasted through sound and thermal transfer.

> **1** Look at the diagram shown in figure 8.1.
>
>   a) At a point somewhere between point **A** and point **B**, state the *two* types of energy that the mass has.
>
>   b) Describe what the principle of conservation of energy tells you about the total energy.
>
> **2** If a pendulum swings in a vacuum it might swing for ever. In air, the swings become gradually shorter. Suggest where some of the energy may have gone. Remember, the conservation principle means that it cannot have been lost altogether.

8.1

Activity 8.2: Energy changes when bouncing a ball

Read the instructions carefully and, before you carry out this activity, predict what you expect the results to show.

Drop a bouncy ball from a height of 1 m onto the floor.

Measure how high it bounces.

If it bounces more than once, measure the height of each bounce.

Repeat at least three times.

Record your results in a table.

A1 What is your prediction?

A2 What pattern can you see in your results?

A3 Suggest a reason for this pattern.

A4 Draw a labelled diagram showing at which points the ball:
   a) has the most potential energy
   b) has the most kinetic energy
   c) is increasing its potential energy
   d) is increasing its kinetic energy

A5 Why is it important to repeat this experiment at least three times before forming a conclusion?

A6 How precise were your results? How could you make them more precise and more accurate?

A7 From where does the ball get its original potential energy?

Measuring energy changes

Energy and energy transfers are measured in **joules** (J). A joule is quite a small unit, so we often use kilojoules (kJ). 1 kJ = 1000 J. You will often see those units used on food packaging. If the ball you used in Activity 8.2 had a mass of 100 g, it would have had 1 joule of potential energy when you held it 1 m above the ground.

Remember that energy is always conserved. The total energy that is transferred in must equal the total energy transferred out. Another way of saying this is:

   total energy input = total energy output

Key term

joule: the scientific unit for energy. Its abbreviation is J. 1000 J = 1 kilojoule (kJ); 1 000 000 J = 1 megajoule (MJ).

Energy conservation 145

3 A car burns fuel with an energy value of 85 kJ. 68 kJ of this is output from the engine as wasted thermal energy. Calculate how much useful energy is left for moving the car. (Ignore any energy wasted as sound.)

4 What percentage of the chemical fuel energy used by the car described in question 3 will eventually end up as thermal energy?

Science in context: All-electric vehicles

All-electric vehicles (EVs) are powered by electricity.

EVs convert about 60% of the electrical energy they are supplied with to power the car. Petrol vehicles only convert about 20% of the energy stored in the fuel to power the car. Although it looks like EVs are more efficient than petrol vehicles, we must remember that there is likely to be energy wasted when the electricity is generated. For example coal-fired power stations are usually about 35% efficient, meaning that about 65% of the energy stored in the fuel does not become useful electrical energy. So if electricity from a coal-fired power station is used to charge an EV, only about 21% of the original chemical energy of the coal is used usefully to power the EV.

8.2 *An electric car being charged.*

EVs do not emit any pollution. We must remember, though, that the power plant producing the electricity may emit pollutants. If the electricity is generated from some sources, such as solar or wind power, no pollutants will be emitted from them.

Scientists and engineers are trying to find ways of producing large amounts of electricity from efficient and non-polluting sources, but most of the world's electricity is still generated by fossil-fuelled power stations.

5
a) Which parts of the information about EVs would you use if you were trying to persuade a friend that EVs were a good thing?

b) Which parts of the information about EVs would you use if you were trying to persuade a friend that EVs were a bad thing?

c) Do you have enough information to decide whether EVs are a good or bad thing? If not, could you find more relevant information by doing scientific experiments yourself or would you need to look for more secondary sources? Give reasons for your answer.

Key facts:

✔ The units of energy are joules (J), kilojoules (kJ) and megajoules (MJ).

✔ Energy is conserved: it is never created or destroyed but just transferred from one energy type to another.

✔ The amount of energy that has been wasted can be calculated from the difference between the total energy input and the useful outputs of energy.

Check your skills progress:

- I can use my knowledge of energy to predict what will happen when a ball is bounced.
- I can collect sufficient accurate and precise measurements to test my prediction.
- I can evaluate my investigations and suggest improvements.

Chapter 8 . Topic 2
Heating and cooling

You will learn:
- To describe how heat and temperature are different
- To understand how heat dissipation refers to the movement of thermal energy
- To understand that models and analogies can change according to scientific evidence
- To collect and record observations and measurements appropriately
- To identify hazards and identify ways to minimise risks
- To carry out practical work in a safe manner to minimise risks
- To use scientific knowledge to make predictions
- To interpret results and form conclusions using scientific knowledge and understanding

Starting point

You should know that...	You should be able to...
Thermal energy is emitted during many energy transfers	Collect sufficient evidence and record it in a suitable form
Dissipation means to transfer energy in a wasteful way	Make conclusions by interpreting results

The difference between 'heat' and temperature

Temperature is a measure of the average **thermal energy** of the particles in a substance. This is related to how hot or cold something is and it can be measured using a thermometer. Thermal energy is the energy stored in an object because of its temperature and is transferred from a hotter object to a colder object.

The Atlantic Ocean has lots of thermal energy stored in it, but it still feels cold. It has a low temperature because the thermal energy is spread over a very large amount of water.

A hot cup of coffee has less thermal energy in it than the Atlantic Ocean, but the average thermal energy is much higher because there is less water in the cup of coffee. So a cup of coffee has a higher temperature than the Atlantic Ocean.

Key terms

temperature: a measure of how hot or cold something is. It is the average amount of thermal energy in a substance.

thermal energy: energy stored in an object due to its temperature.

148 Energy

Temperature and thermal energy

In figure 8.3 we can see that the particles in part b are at a higher temperature than those in part a because they have more energy.

In figure 8.4, we can see that the particles in both parts of the diagram are at the same temperature but there is more thermal energy in total in part b. This is because there are more particles.

We can see that each particle vibrates; the more the particles vibrate, the greater the temperature; the more particles there are, the more total energy there is.

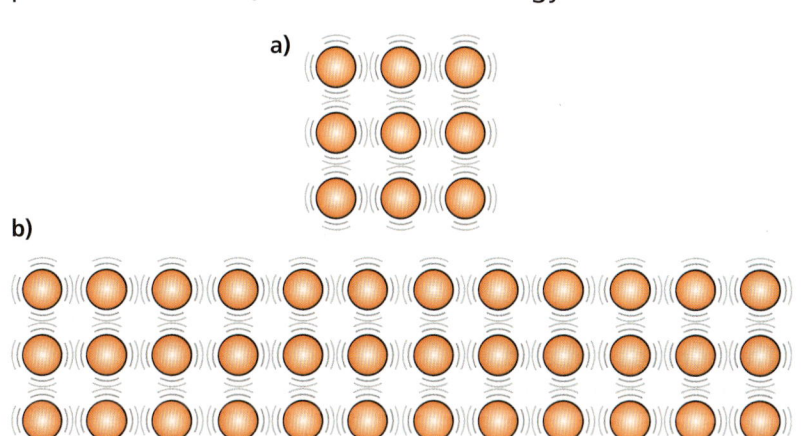

8.4 Temperature and thermal energy – same temperature, more particles.

8.3 Temperature and thermal energy – same number of particles, higher temperature.

Movement of thermal energy

When two objects at different temperatures come into contact, thermal energy flows from the hotter object to the cooler object until their temperatures are the same.

When both objects, or areas, are at the same temperature, there is no more overall flow of thermal energy.

Activity 8.3: Thermal transfer

Place one of your hands in
- cold water (about 10 °C)
- water at room temperature
- warm water (about 45 °C)

Describe what you feel each time and, in each case explain the direction of energy transfer between your hand and the water.

Heating and cooling 149

1. Does thermal energy move from hot objects to cooler objects or from cool objects to hotter objects?

2. Which has the most thermal energy, a litre of water at 30 °C or 200 cm^3 of water at the same temperature? Explain your answer.

3. Jo lives in a country that has very cold winters. Jo says that it is important to make sure that all the windows in her house have very thick curtains to stop the cold coming in. Explain why what Jo has said is not correct.

4. Why does putting your hand into hot water burn your hand but cool water doesn't?

5. Why shouldn't you put hot objects into a fridge?

Dissipation of thermal energy

Whenever energy is transferred, some thermal energy is dissipated into the surroundings. This spreads out and makes the surroundings warmer. We cannot capture all this dissipated thermal energy so it is wasted.

Science in context: Heat and energy

In the late 1700s scientists believed that heat was a substance that couldn't be destroyed but flowed from hot objects to cooler objects. They called this substance 'caloric'. Benjamin Thompson (also known as Count Rumford) challenged this theory. During his work he discovered that friction made objects hotter. This couldn't be explained by the caloric theory. Thompson concluded that heat was a form of energy (now known as thermal energy). Many scientists were interested in Thompson's theory.

In the 1800s, Julius Mayer made some important observations during his work as a ship's doctor. His work made a clear link between heat and energy, supporting Thompson's theory.

At the same time, James Prescott Joule, who had been investigating the link between heat and energy too, published his theories and findings. These also supported the idea that heat was a form of energy. The unit of energy (the joule) is named after him because his work was so important.

Key facts:

✔ I know the difference between thermal energy and temperature.

✔ I know that thermal energy is dissipated when it is transferred.

✔ I know that thermal energy always transfers from hotter objects and areas to cooler ones.

Check your skills progress:

- I can describe how scientific theories about thermal energy have changed over time.
- I can make conclusions and thermal energy transfer by interpreting the results of an investigation.

Chapter 8 . Topic 3

Conduction, convection, radiation and evaporation

You will learn:
- To understand how heat dissipation refers to the movement of thermal energy
- To describe the movement of thermal energy during conduction, convection, and radiation
- To explain how evaporation causes cooling
- To use scientific knowledge and understanding to suggest a testable hypothesis
- To plan investigations used to test hypotheses
- To collect accurate and precise measurements
- To carry out practical work in a safe manner to minimise risks
- To identify and control risks
- To collect and record observations and measurements appropriately
- To interpret results and form conclusions using scientific knowledge and understanding
- To describe the uses, strengths and limitations of models and analogies
- To use scientific knowledge and understanding to make predictions

Starting point

You should know that...	You should be able to...
Matter is made up of particles	Make predictions and review them against the evidence
In solids the particles are close together and held together in a regular pattern; in liquids the particles are close together but they can move; in gases the particles are far apart and can move around	Make predictions referring to previous scientific knowledge and understanding
A vacuum contains no matter	Make careful observations
During evaporation some of the particles in the liquid leave as a gas	Make conclusions from data that is collected

Conduction

Conduction occurs when thermal energy is transferred through a substance. It occurs mainly in solids. In particular, metals are good thermal conductors. This means that thermal energy moves through metals faster than it does through other substances.

Not all solids are good thermal conductors. For example, non-metals are not good thermal conductors. We call these substances **insulators**. Wool, plastic and wood are examples of insulators. Insulators are useful when we need to keep

8.5 *Traditional Mongolian yurt.*

heat trapped in something. Trapped air is also a good insulator.

For example, cold weather clothing is made of insulators. Usually these are made of fabrics, like wool or felt, which trap air. In Mongolia, felt is traditionally used as insulation in yurts as well as for winter clothing. Hair is also added to mud walls to improve insulation.

In nature, polar bears, which live in very cold regions have hollow hair fibres, which makes their coat a good insulator.

At home, the handles of cooking pans are made of an insulating material so that we do not burn our hands when we pick them up.

> **1** Explain why frying pans are made of a metal.
>
> **2** Explain why pan handles are made of plastic or wood and not from metal.
>
> **3** To keep warm, you are told to wear several layers of clothes. This traps air between the layers. Why is this good at keeping you warm?

Key terms

conduction: form of heat transfer in which thermal energy passes through a substance from particle to particle. Conduction occurs mainly in solids.

insulator: a material which is a poor thermal conductor.

Using the particle model to explain conduction

In conduction, thermal energy moves from one particle to its neighbouring particles (see figure 8.6). Conduction occurs mostly in solids because the particles in solids are close together, so it is easy for thermal energy to transfer from one particle to another. This happens because when thermal energy transfers to a particle, it vibrates more than before. This makes the particles next to it vibrate more, which then makes the particles next to them vibrate more.

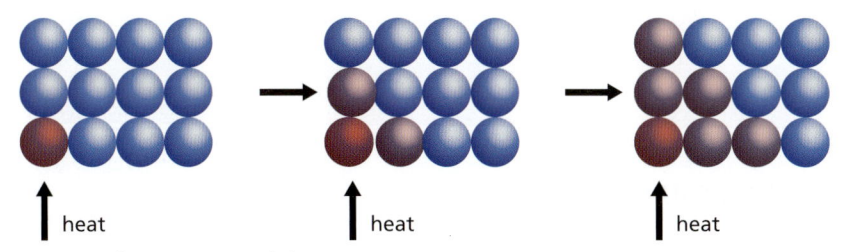

8.6 *Conduction in a solid.*

Liquids and gases are not very good at conducting thermal energy. This is because the particles in liquids move around each other and are further apart, making it harder for thermal energy to transfer from one particle to another. In gases the particles are even more spaced out, which means it is very difficult for thermal energy to transfer from one particle to another.

Conduction, convection, radiation and evaporation

4 Use the particle model to explain why solids are the best conductors; why liquids can conduct thermal energy, but not as well as solids; and gases are the worst conductors of all.

Activity 8.4: Conductors and insulators at home

Find objects in your house that either conduct thermal energy or insulate from thermal energy. Write down what they are made of and why they are needed to either conduct thermal energy or something from insulate it.

A1 What are the insulators made from?
A2 List some examples of why thermal insulators are useful.
A3 What were the conductors you found made from?
A4 List some examples of why we need good conductors.

Convection

Convection is a type of thermal transfer that occurs in **fluids** – gases and liquids. Convection is a process that involves several steps (see figure 8.7).

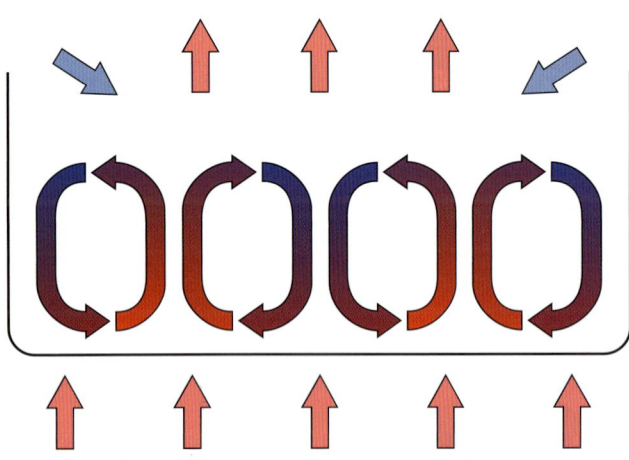

8.7 *How thermal energy moves in convection.*

- When a fluid is heated, its particles move around faster.
- When the particles move faster they spread out, so they become further apart.
- When particles move further apart, the substance becomes less dense.
- Materials that are less dense float on materials with a higher density – the hot fluid floats to the top.
- When the hot fluid is at the top it begins to cool.
- When the fluid cools its particles slow down.

Key terms

convection: form of thermal transfer in which thermal energy causes a substance to expand and rise. This then cools and sinks. Convection only occurs in gases and liquids.

convection current: the movement of particles in a fluid due to convection.

fluid: a substance that can flow from one place to another – a gas or a liquid.

Making links

The idea of density is discussed in Stage 9 Chemistry. The density of a substance determines whether it floats or sinks in another substance.

Balsa wood floats on water. What does this tell you about the density of balsa wood?

154 Energy

- When the particles slow down they get closer together.
- The substance becomes more dense.
- Now that the substance is more dense it begins to sink.

The overall process is described as a **convection current**.

Where do we find convection currents?

Convection currents occur when we heat water. For example, figure 8.8 shows a pan of water being heated. The water is heated at the bottom, becomes less dense and rises. When it reaches the top surface of the water it cools, becomes denser and sinks towards the bottom.

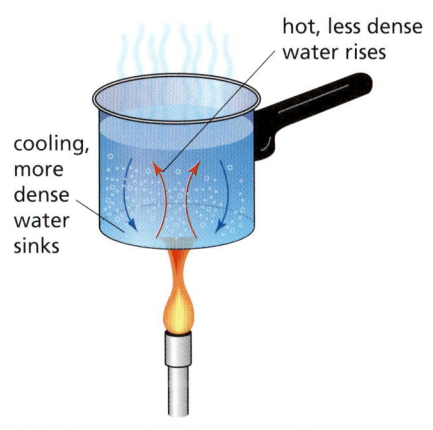

8.8 *Convection in a pan of water.*

It is convection that causes wind and air currents (figure 8.9). Solar energy from the Sun heats up the ground, which then heats up the air above it. The air becomes less dense and rises upwards. When it reaches the upper part of the atmosphere it cools and sinks. The moving air is what we call wind.

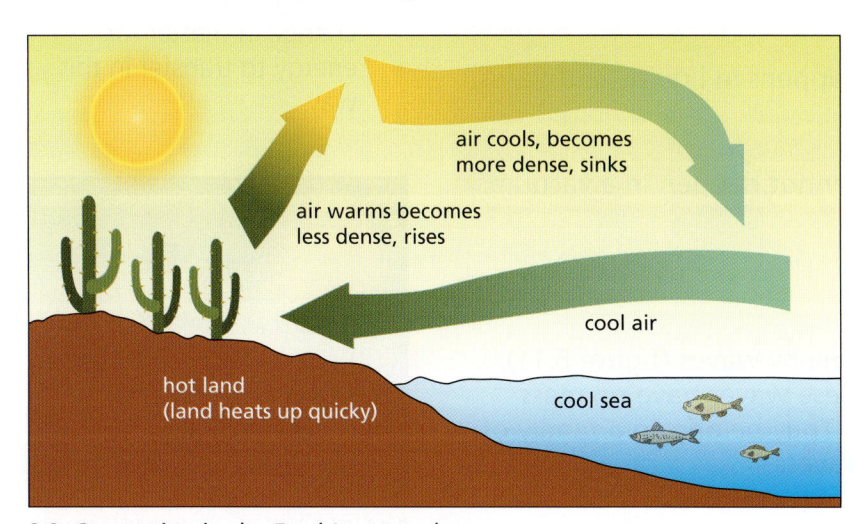

8.9 *Convection in the Earth's atmosphere.*

Making links

In Chapter 12 (Earth in space) you will meet the idea of plate tectonics. In this chapter convection currents in the Earth's mantle are discussed. What does this tell you about the Earth's mantle?

Conduction, convection, radiation and evaporation

Wall radiators heat rooms by convection. Even though they are called 'radiators', they don't heat a room by radiation. Figure 8.10 shows that they warm up the air above them, which becomes less dense, rises and travels across the room. When it cools, it sinks and goes back to where the radiator is.

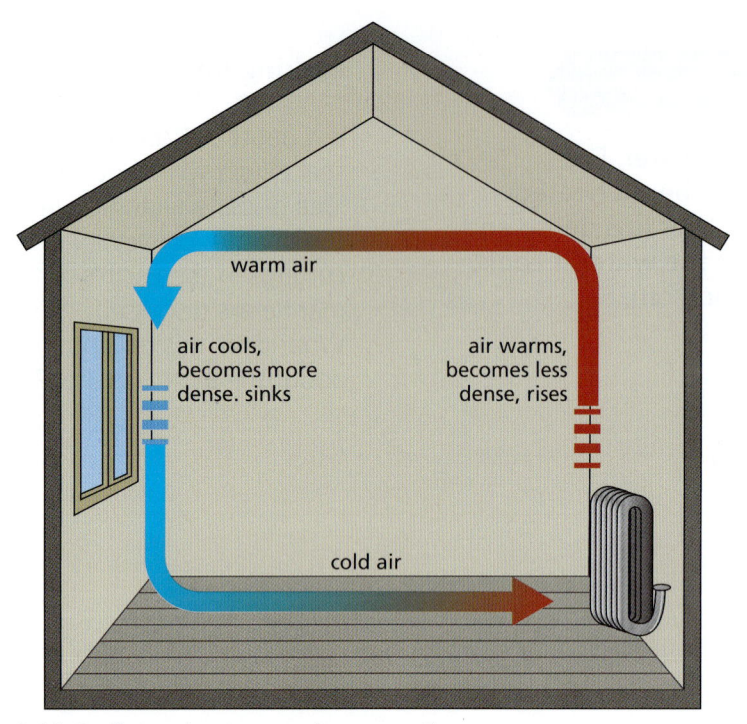

8.10 *Radiators heat rooms by convection.*

> **5** When liquids and gases are heated, the particles in them start to move around faster. What does this do to the distance between the particles?
>
> **6** When a fluid is heated, what happens to the density of the liquid or gas?
>
> **7** Explain why convection happens in liquids and gases, but not in solids.
>
> **8** Explain why convection cannot happen in a vacuum.

Key term

radiation: form of energy transfer in which thermal energy is released as infra-red radiation. There is no change in matter for energy to transfer in this way.

Radiation

Radiation is the transfer of energy by waves (figure 8.11), in particular infra-red waves. These waves have no mass and travel at the speed of light. They belong to a family of waves called electromagnetic waves.

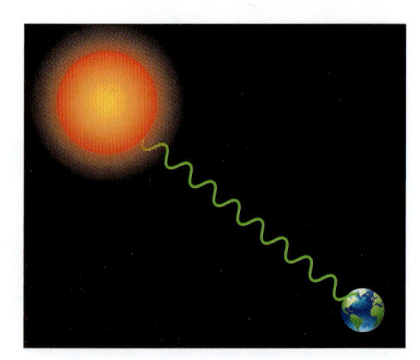

8.11 *The energy emitted by the Sun reaches the Earth by radiation.*

156 Energy

8.3

The best colours for absorbing and emitting thermal energy

Objects **absorb** energy from radiation. They can also let out the energy or **emit** it. Some colours are better at absorbing and emitting energy than others. Shiny white surfaces are the worst at absorbing or emitting energy, and dull black surfaces are the best (figure 8.12).

This means that we make insulators using materials with shiny white surfaces. For example, aluminium foil is good at keeping food hot because it can reflect back radiated energy.

Computer processors create heat. Heat sinks on computers are black because they need to emit as much energy as possible to make sure the electrical circuits inside the processors don't get damaged.

Radiation is the only heat transfer that can happen when there are no particles (a vacuum). This means that the energy from the Sun reaches us by radiation.

> **Key terms**
>
> **absorb**: take in energy.
>
> **emit**: give out energy in the form of radiation.

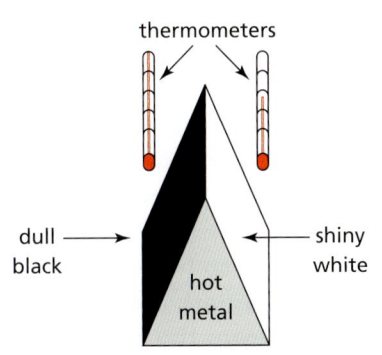

8.12 *Dull black surfaces emit more thermal energy than shiny white ones.*

9 Explain why you can feel the warmth from a fire if you are standing sideways to it.

10 Why does heat from the Sun not reach us by conduction or convection?

Activity 8.5: How well do different coloured surfaces absorb thermal radiation?

You have been given two metal cans. These cans are identical except that the outside of one is painted dull black and the outside of the other is painted shiny white. You also have some water, two thermometers and an infra-red electric heater.

A1 Design an experiment to investigate whether the colour of the can affects how well it absorbs thermal radiation. Explain how you would use the equipment, what you would measure and how you would make sure it was a fair test.

A2 What would you expect the result to show? Explain your answer.

Conduction, convection, radiation and evaporation

11 Look at figure 8.13 and spot all the ways that a vacuum flask keeps hot liquids hot, and cold liquids cold.

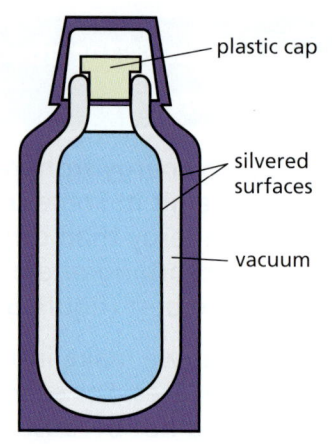

8.13 A vacuum flask.

Science in context: Solar energy

Solar water heaters are used widely in China, Europe, Japan and India. They are a renewable way of providing hot water to houses and factories. Solar water heaters are painted a dark colour to absorb as much radiated thermal energy from the Sun as possible. They then transfer this thermal energy into water which increases the water's temperature.

8.14 A solar water heater.

Evaporation

If you leave a glass of water out in the open, over time you will notice that the water level drops. This is because some of the water has **evaporated** and turned into a gas.

The difference between evaporation and boiling

A liquid is made up of particles (atoms or molecules) that are moving around. Not all the particles have the same amount of energy. This means that they do not all move at the same speed – some are moving faster than others (figure 8.15). When the fastest ones (those with the most energy) reach the surface of a liquid, they can break free from the liquid and fly off into the air – this is evaporation.

It happens slowly and on its own. Evaporation can also happen at any temperature below the boiling point of the liquid. It happens more slowly at cooler temperatures.

> **Key term**
>
> **evaporation**: when a liquid turns into a gas, at a temperature lower than the boiling point. An evaporating liquid takes energy with it and so it cools the surface it was evaporating on.

158 Energy

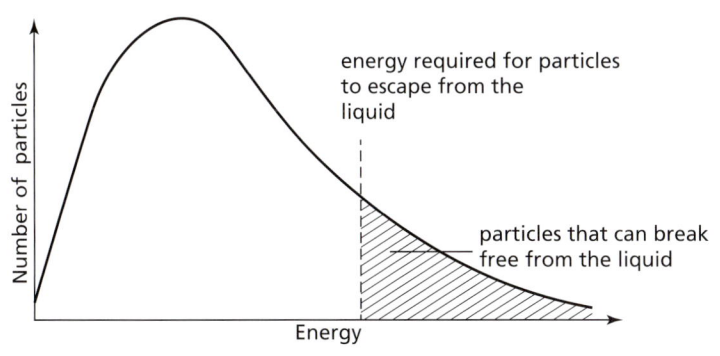

8.15 *A graph showing that the particles in a liquid have a range of energies.*

When a liquid is heated its particles move faster. When the temperature of the liquid reaches its boiling point, the particles have enough energy to leave the surface of the liquid and form a gas. Boiling happens faster than evaporation and it needs an external source of thermal energy. Boiling only occurs when a liquid is at its boiling point.

Cooling by evaporation

If you put a drop of water on your skin, your skin will start to feel cold. This is because the water absorbs thermal energy from your skin. The increase in the energy of the water particles causes some of them to evaporate and form a gas. Because the water has removed thermal energy from your hand, the water cools your skin by evaporation.

Unless it is very cold, water will evaporate from a container if left long enough. During evaporation some of the particles in the liquid that have a high enough energy leave the liquid as a gas. Because the water particles left behind have less energy than those which have left, the water left in the container is cooler than it was.

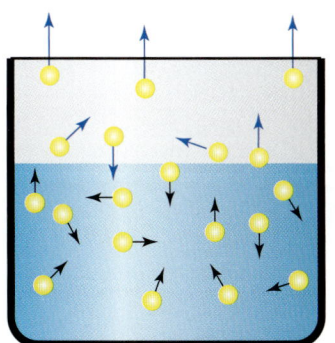

high energy = evaporating

medium energy = can be pulled back into the water

low energy = stay in the liquid

8.16 *A particle diagram for cooling by evaporation.*

> **Making links**
>
> In Stage 8 Chemistry you learned how to determine whether a process or chemical reaction is exothermic or endothermic based on the temperature change. Is evaporation an exothermic or an endothermic process? Give a reason for your answer.

Conduction, convection, radiation and evaporation

12 What is the difference between evaporating and boiling?

13 When you put some water on the back of your hand, your hand starts to feel cold. Explain why this happens.

Science in context: Clay pot coolers

Traditional clay pot coolers keep food cool without electricity. They work because of evaporation.

There are two pots, separated by a layer of sand. Water is poured onto the sand.

As the water evaporates from the sand, it transfers energy away from inner pot, keeping the food cool.

8.17 *A traditional clay pot cooler.*

Key facts:

✔ Thermal energy is transferred by conduction, convection, radiation and evaporation.

✔ Conduction occurs in solids and happens when thermal energy is passed from particle to particle.

✔ Convection occurs in fluids and happens when the particles move around because of having more energy.

✔ Radiation is caused by thermal energy being transferred by waves and can occur in a vacuum.

✔ Silver, shiny objects reflect thermal energy well; black, matt objects absorb and emit thermal energy well.

✔ Evaporation causes cooling.

Check your skills progress:

- I can use the particle model to explain how conduction works.
- I can use the particle model to explain how convection works.
- I can use the particle model to explain how evaporation cools things.

Energy

End of chapter review

Quick questions

1. How many joules of energy are there in a kilojoule?

2. Malia is playing on a swing.

   Select the *two* correct statements.

   a At the highest point Malia has maximum kinetic energy.

   b At the lowest point Malia has maximum potential energy.

   c At the highest point Malia has no kinetic energy.

   d At the lowest point Malia has no potential energy.

   8.18

3. Give the definitions of the following terms:

   (a) temperature
   (b) conduction
   (c) evaporation
   (d) radiation

4. Which thermal energy transfer is most likely to take place in the following situations?

   (a) a beaker of water being heated over a Bunsen burner flame

   (b) thermal energy travelling through the vacuum of space from the Sun to the Earth

   (c) thermal energy travelling through a metal spoon

5. Which colour surface, shiny white or matt black is the best for each of the following:

   (a) emitting thermal radiation

   (b) absorbing thermal radiation

   (c) reflecting thermal radiation

Connect your understanding

6. Fridges have a cooling fluid to absorb thermal energy. This cooling fluid then emits this thermal energy through some pipes at the back of the fridge.

    (a) Why are these pipes painted black?

    (b) How does the thermal energy travel from the cooling fluid to the surface of the pipes?

7. An electric motor in a vacuum cleaner uses 300 J of electrical energy every second. The amount of thermal energy wasted in the motor is 60 J every second.

    How much useful energy is transferred every second?

8. The Atlantic Ocean has more thermal energy in it than a cup of hot coffee. Why does the cup of coffee feel hotter than the Atlantic Ocean?

9. Explain the following:

    (a) why thermal radiation from the Sun reaches the Earth by radiation only

    (b) why convection cannot happen in solids

    (c) why gases conduct thermal energy better when they are compressed into small spaces

Challenge questions

10. The photograph shows a wood-burning stove used to heat a room. The stove is positioned on an outside wall.

8.19

(a) Explain why the outlet pipe from the stove is painted black.

(b) Explain why the outlet pipe goes vertically upwards out through the ceiling and not horizontally back through the wall.

(c) Explain why the stove is placed near to the ground and not further up the wall.

(d) Some thermal energy is wasted by passing through the wall. Does the thermal energy transfer through the wall by conduction, convection or radiation? Explain your answer.

(e) How could you reduce the amount of thermal energy that is wasted by passing through the wall. Explain your answer.

Chapter 9
Forces

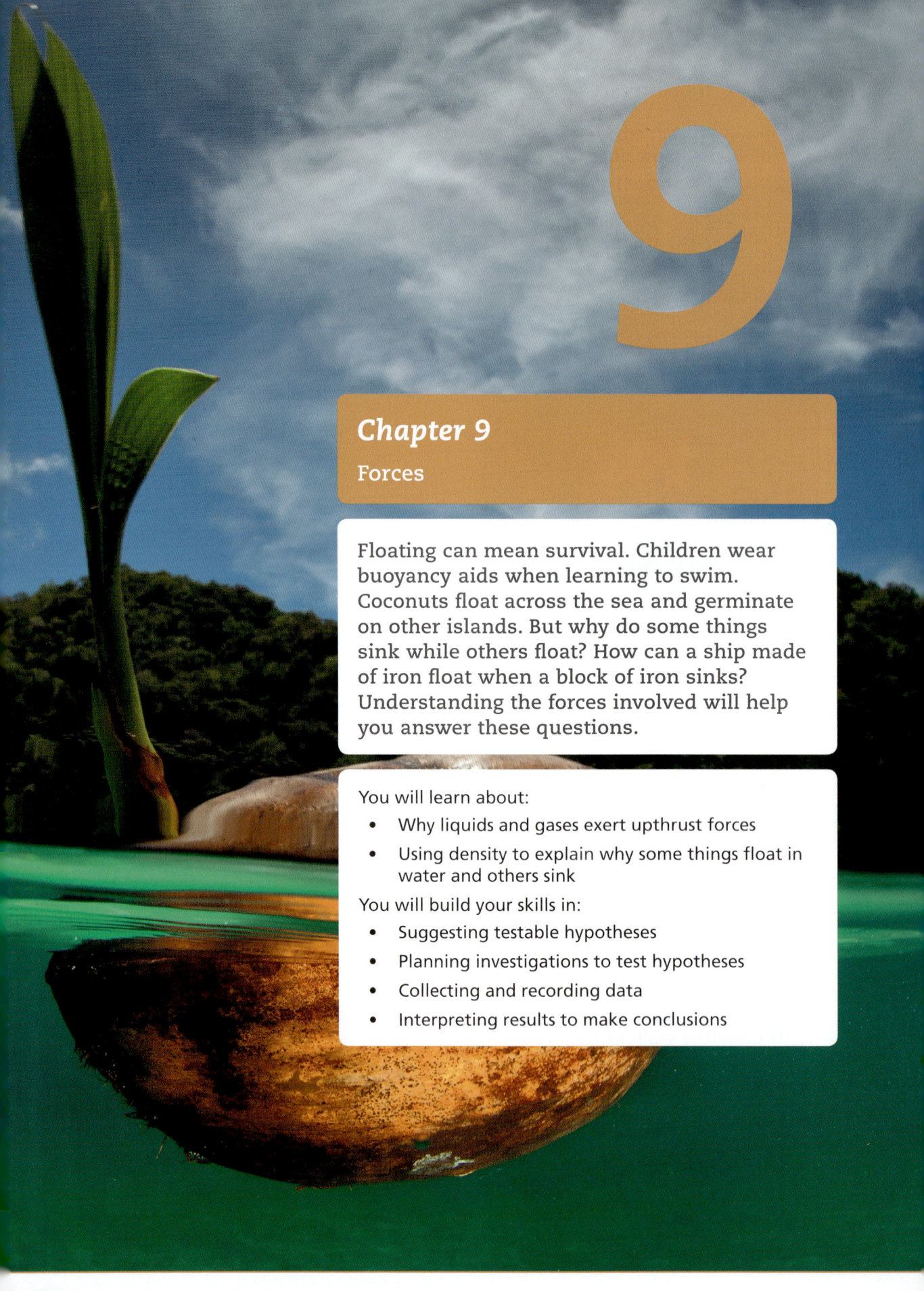

Floating can mean survival. Children wear buoyancy aids when learning to swim. Coconuts float across the sea and germinate on other islands. But why do some things sink while others float? How can a ship made of iron float when a block of iron sinks? Understanding the forces involved will help you answer these questions.

You will learn about:
- Why liquids and gases exert upthrust forces
- Using density to explain why some things float in water and others sink

You will build your skills in:
- Suggesting testable hypotheses
- Planning investigations to test hypotheses
- Collecting and recording data
- Interpreting results to make conclusions

Chapter 9
Floating and sinking

You will learn:
- To explain how an object floats or sink using density
- To use scientific knowledge to make predictions
- To use observations, to organise and classify objects
- To collect and record observations and measurements appropriately
- To interpret results and form conclusions using scientific knowledge and understanding
- To use scientific knowledge and understanding to suggest a testable hypothesis
- To plan investigations used to test hypotheses

Starting point

You should know that...	You should be able to...
The weight of an object is due to the force of gravity	Suggest a testable hypothesis based on scientific understanding
When an object is immersed in water, water particles collide with it causing pressure	Plan a range of investigations of different types to obtain appropriate evidence when testing hypotheses
Water pressure increases with depth	Make predictions and use scientific knowledge to explain these
Balanced forces on an object result in steady motion in the same direction, or staying at rest	Evaluate the strength of the evidence collected and how it supports, or refutes, the prediction
The mass and shape of an object can affect if it floats or sinks	Describe trends and patterns in results, identifying any anomalous results and suggest why results are anomalous
	Collect, record and summarise sufficient observations and measurements, in an appropriate form

Floating and upthrust

You may have noticed that when you are in water such as a swimming pool, you feel lighter. This is because water pushes up with a force called **upthrust**. This helps you to float in water.

Some solid substances sink in water, others float. Floating objects may float high or low in the water.

> **Key term**
>
> **upthrust**: the upwards force on an object from the liquid or gas in which it is floating.

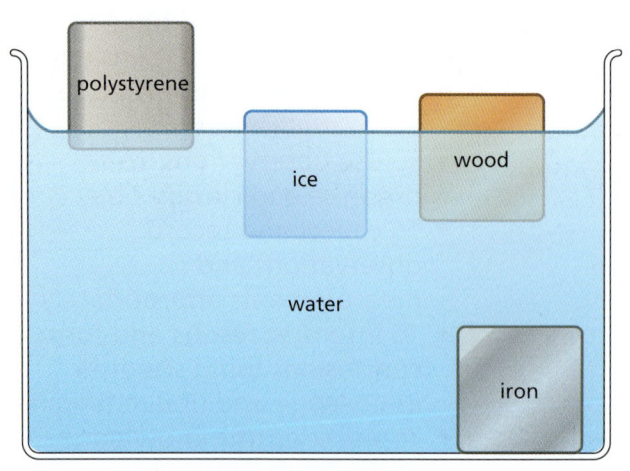

9.1 Floating and sinking in water.

9.2 Most of an iceberg floats below the water surface.

Activity 9.1: Investigating floating and sinking

You can investigate floating and sinking by immersing objects made of different materials in water. Look at blocks made of different materials. Predict which will float and which will sink. Place them in turn into a beaker of water and observe what happens.

A1 For objects which float, draw a diagram to record how much of the block floats above the water.

A2 Which block floats highest in the water?

A3 Which floats lowest?

166 Forces

1 Sonja and Arik tested a hypothesis that the heavier an object is, the more likely it is to sink. Here are their results:

Object	Mass	Does it float or sink?
Cork	10 g	Floats
Wooden block	400 g	Floats
Copper block	300 g	Sinks
Copper bowl	300 g	Floats
Iron nail	10 g	Sinks

a) Do their results support the hypothesis? Explain your answer using data from their results.

b) Sonja thinks they should improve their hypothesis. She says they had too many independent variables. Suggest a better hypothesis and describe how it could be tested. Think about what variables would need to be kept the same (the control variables).

Why do things float?

When an object is immersed in water, the water exerts pressure on it. This is because the moving water particles hit the surface of the object. In figure 9.3 the pressures on the vertical sides of the block are equal but opposite, so the horizontal forces are **balanced** and there is no sideways **resultant force**.

However, the pressure of water increases with depth. Since the top and bottom surfaces have the same area the force on the bottom of the block is greater than the force on the top. This means there is an **unbalanced force** upwards. This is what causes the upthrust.

> **Key terms**
>
> **balanced forces**: when the resultant force is zero.
>
> **resultant force**: shows the single total force acting on an object when all the forces acting on it are added up.
>
> **unbalanced forces**: when there is a resultant force.

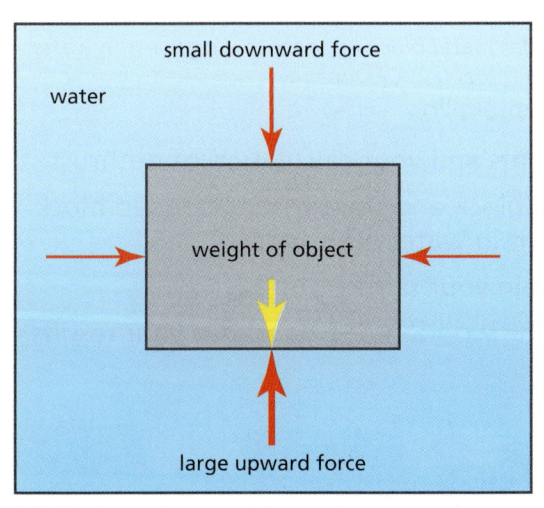

9.3 *Upthrust is caused by the increase of pressure with depth.*

Floating and sinking 167

The upthrust acts in the opposite direction to the force of gravity on the object (its weight). If the upthrust is equal to or larger than the weight the object will float. If the weight is larger than the upthrust, it will sink.

Activity 9.2: Investigating upthrust

Newton meters (also known as force meters) are used to measure the weight (force of gravity) of an object.

The newton meter contains a spring which is attached to a metal hook.

The object being tested is attached to, and hung from, the metal hook. The force of gravity causes the object to move downwards and the spring inside the newton meter stretches.

On the outside of the newton meter case there is a scale. The position of the pointer on the scale is used to give a value for the size of the force.

The greater the weight of the object, the further the spring will stretch and the larger the value read from the scale on the newton meter.

A1 Hang a metal block from a newton meter and measure its weight.

A2 Slowly lower the block into a beaker of water.

A3 What do you notice about the reading? What forces cause this?

A4 Explain how this force affects the reading on the newton meter.

A5 Explain how you can calculate the upthrust force from the water on the iron block.

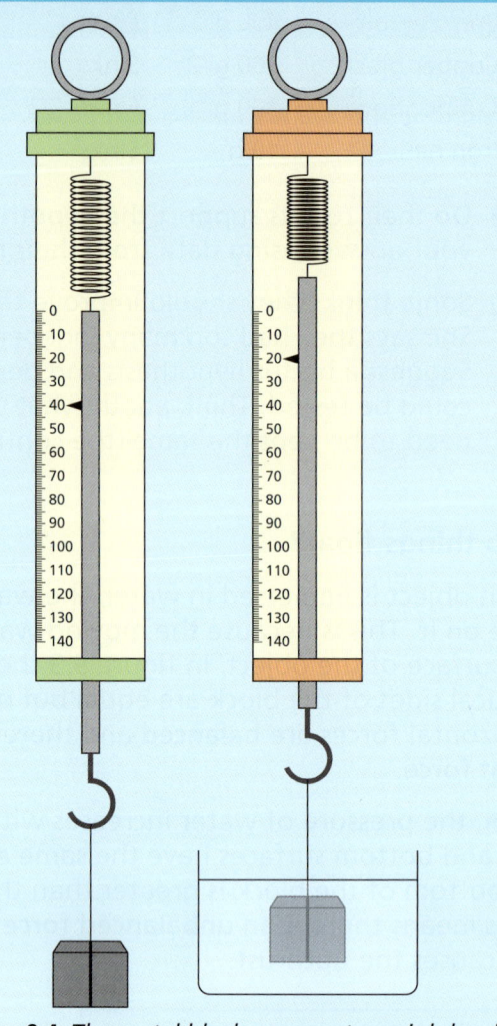

9.4 *The metal block appears to weigh less in water.*

A6 Draw a suitable table to record your measurements and your calculation of upthrust.

A7 Repeat the investigation using a different metal block and then with a wooden block. Record the weight in air and the apparent weight in water each time.

A8 Calculate the upthrust each time and record this in your table.

A9 Explain why the metal blocks do not float, but the wooden one does. Use your results and the idea of balanced or unbalanced forces.

168 Forces

2 Metal objects appear to lose weight when immersed in water.

Jack thinks the upthrust might be affected by the depth of the water, or by the area of the base of the block lowered into the water.

a) Write a hypothesis you could test about one of these ideas or another factor you think might affect the loss of weight.

b) How could you test this hypothesis?

3 Draw a force diagram for a person floating in water. Use the diagram to explain why they float.

4 An inflated ball floats in water. Describe and explain what will happen if the ball is held underwater, then released.

Floating and density

In everyday language we say iron is heavier than wood. We all understand what this means, but a tree is heavier than an iron nail. In this case By 'heaviness', we really mean density – the mass of a fixed volume of the material. Density is a measure of the mass of a material for a specified unit volume.

Density can be calculated using the equation:

$$\text{density} = \text{mass} \div \text{volume} \quad \text{or} \quad \text{density} = \frac{\text{mass}}{\text{volume}}$$

This equation can also be written in symbols:

$$\rho = m \div V \quad \text{or} \quad \rho = \frac{m}{V}$$

You may remember from Stage 7 that the symbol m is for mass. We use the symbol V for volume. ρ is the Greek letter rho which physicists use as the symbol for density.

Density is normally measured in g/cm^3 or in kg/m^3.

Objects which are less dense than water will float in water, and objects which are more dense than water will sink in water. So, it is not the mass of an object which determines if it sinks or floats, but the density. This means that a heavy steel ship can float if the total density of the whole ship (all the metal of the hull plus all the air in the spaces inside the hull) is less than the density of water. The hull is the body of the ship that is watertight and does not allow water to enter.

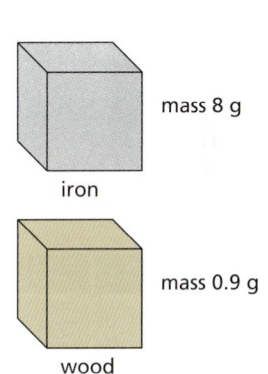

iron — mass 8 g

wood — mass 0.9 g

9.5 These blocks are the same size, but the iron has a greater mass. Iron is more dense than wood.

Floating and sinking   169

If the hull of a ship is damaged and punctured (as happened when the Titanic hit an iceberg on its first voyage in 1912), water enters the hull and the overall density increases, and the ship may sink.

We can work out if a substance will float or sink in water by comparing the densities of the substance and water. If the substance is more dense than water then it will sink; if it is less dense then it will float.

Substances less dense than water can float if their shape is changed. A ball of modelling clay will sink in water, but when made into a bowl shape, it will float.

9.6 *A steel ship can float if it is mainly filled with air, giving it an average density less than water.*

> ### Activity 9.3: Linking density and floating
> Liquids have different densities, and this affects whether they float or sink in water. Cooking oil has a density of 0.9 g/cm³ and syrup has a density of 1.4 g/cm³.
> **A1** Predict what will happen when both are poured into water.
> **A2** Half fill a beaker with water. Add a spoonful of oil and a spoonful of syrup.
> **A3** Draw a diagram to show your results.
> **A4** Comment on whether your predictions were correct.

Table 9.1 shows the densities of some materials.

Material	Density (g/cm³)
Iron	8.0
Wood (pine)	0.4–0.7*
Wood (ebony)	1.1–1.3*
Brass	8.7
Polystyrene	0.01
Lead	11.0
Polythene	0.8
Aluminium	2.7
Gold	19.0
Wax	0.9
Water	1

*The density of wood depends on species and it varies because moisture content varies.

Table 9.1

> **5** Put the materials from table 9.1 in order of density, and determine which will float and which will sink.
>
> **6** Hot water is less dense than cold water. Describe how this affects water in a pan on a hot plate.

170   Forces

7 Explain how hitting a rock may cause a boat to sink.

8 A scuba diver has a tank of compressed air. He releases some air under water and sees the air bubbles rise to the surface. Explain why the bubbles rise.

Floating in air

Chemistry topic 6.3 explains that density is how closely particles are packed together.

9 Use this idea to explain why hot air is less dense than cold air.

10 Ice floats in water. What does this tell you about the spacing of ice particles?

Solids and liquids which are less dense than water float in water. A similar thing happens with gases in air. Gases which are more dense than air will sink and gases which are less dense than air rise.

Table 9.2 shows the density of some gases.

Gas	Density (kg/m^3)
Air	1.30
Hot air (approximately 100°C)	0.95
Helium	0.17
Carbon dioxide	1.98
Nitrogen	1.20

Table 9.2

11 Omar filled balloons with different gases and observed what happened when he let them go. He used air, helium, nitrogen and carbon dioxide and recorded his results in the table below. Unfortunately he forgot to put the names of the gases in his table.

Match each gas to the correct observation.

Balloon	Observation
A	Fell quickly to the floor
B	Fell slowly to the floor
C	Rose quickly to the ceiling
D	Rose slowly to the ceiling

12 a) Draw a force diagram to show the forces on a hot air balloon which is tied to the ground.

   b) Use the data in table 9.2 to explain why hot air balloons rise through air when not tied down.

13 A balloon which is blown up by using the air from your lungs will sink more quickly than one inflated using an air pump. Use the information in table 9.2 to explain why.

Science in context: Weather balloons

Weather balloons are used around the world to take measurements in the atmosphere for weather forecasting. They are also used to monitor pollution and for taking aerial photos.

Weather balloons are filled with helium, which is less dense than air. This means that they can rise up high into the upper atmosphere. Research is also being conducted into using high-altitude balloons filled with helium or hydrogen for travel at heights between aircraft and spacecraft.

9.7 *A weather balloon being released at a research station in Australia.*

Key facts:

✔ Density is calculated by mass ÷ volume.
✔ Objects that are less dense than water float on it.
✔ Objects that are more dense than water sink in it.

Check your skills progress:

- I can predict whether a substance will float or sink in water depending on its density.
- I can suggest a hypothesis and plan an investigation to test my hypothesis.
- I can interpret results and draw conclusions.

Forces

End of chapter review

Quick questions

1. Copy and complete these sentences: A substance will float in water if it is ____ dense than water. It will sink if it is ____ dense than water.

2. Determine which of the objects in table 9.3 will float in water. Water has a density of 1.0 g/cm³.

Object	Density (g/cm³)
Gold coin	19
Ice cube	0.92
Iron nail	8
Polythene bag	0.8

Table 9.3

3. A lump of a material sinks in water. What does this tell you about the density of the material?

4. The diagram shows the forces on a solid toy being held under water.

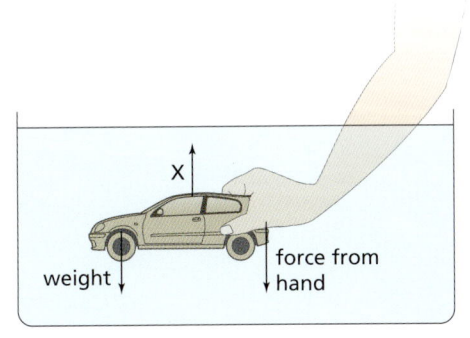

9.8

(a) What is the name of the force marked X?

(b) If force X is greater than the downwards force on the toy due to its weight, what will happen to the toy when it is released?

(c) Which of these materials could the toy be made from: wood, with density 0.9 g/cm³ or aluminium with density 2.7 g/cm³?

5. Mercury is a metal that is liquid at room temperature. It has a density of 13.5 g/cm³. Determine which of the objects from table 9.3 will float in mercury.

Connect your understanding

6. Lead has a density of 11 g/cm³. Draw and label a force diagram for a piece of lead at the moment it is placed in water. Include a resultant force arrow on your diagram and use this to explain why the piece of lead will sink.

Challenge question

7. When gases become hot, their particles move further apart. Use this to explain why hot air balloons rise in air.

Chapter 10
Electricity

Electricity powers much of our lives. The high-voltage wires deliver energy to make current flow. The light-dependent resistors on streetlights change their resistance as the light changes. This changes the current in the streetlamp, causing it to switch on when sunlight fades.

In this topic you will use lower safer voltages and will learn about how voltage, current and resistance are connected and how we use this to control circuits.

You will learn about:
- How current divides in parallel circuits
- How to measure current and voltage in series and parallel circuits
- How to calculate resistance
- How resistance affects current

You will build your skills in:
- Using and evaluating a scientific model
- Constructing circuits using the appropriate apparatus safely
- Collecting and recording sufficient measurements to identify patterns and trends

Chapter 10 . Topic 1

Voltage and resistance

You will learn:
- To understand how to draw circuit diagrams using conventional symbols for the components
- To understand how current and voltage can be measured in series and parallel circuits
- To describe how the addition of cells and lamps affects the measurement of voltage
- To understand how to calculate resistance and describe the effect of resistance on current
- To represent scientific ideas using recognised symbols or formulae
- To describe the uses, strengths and limitations of models and analogies
- To carry out practical work in a safe manner to minimise risks
- To collect accurate and precise measurements
- To record observations and measurements appropriately
- To interpret results and form conclusions using scientific knowledge and understanding

Starting point

You should know that...	You should be able to...
A cell provides energy to make charge flow in a circuit	Draw and interpret circuit diagrams
Current is the flow of charge around a circuit	Identify components from their circuit symbols
Current is measured in amps using an ammeter	Use an ammeter to measure current
	Use a simple model such as the rope loop model to explain current flow

Measuring voltage

Cells supply the energy to make current flow in an electric circuit. Current is the flow of charge around a circuit, carried by electrons.

Voltage is a measure of how much energy the electrons have at different points around the circuit. Electrons leave the cell with a lot of energy which is delivered to components such as lamps. Electrons return to the cell with less energy.

Voltage is measured using a **voltmeter**. Voltage is measured in volts, usually written as V. A voltmeter measures the difference in energy at different points.

Using a model can help us understand how voltage and current are linked.

> **Key terms**
>
> **voltage**: a measure of energy in a circuit.
>
> **voltmeter**: device for measuring voltage.

10.1

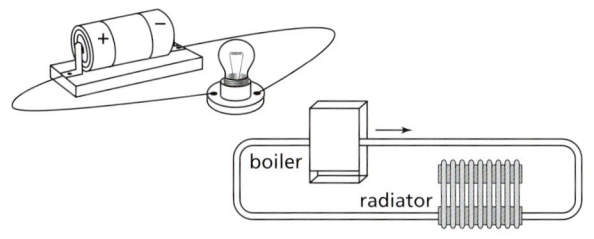

10.1 *Compare the different parts of a simple electrical circuit and a simple central heating system.*

A useful model to help understand the flow of energy in a circuit is a central heating system model. In this model, the boiler supplies energy, which is carried as heat by the water. The water flows through the pipes to the radiator. As the water goes through the radiator it loses heat to the room. The water going back to the boiler is cold – it has less energy.

Feature of central heating system	What it represents in a circuit
Boiler	Cell or battery
Water	Charges
Flow of water	Current
Radiator	A lamp or another component which converts energy such as a buzzer or a motor

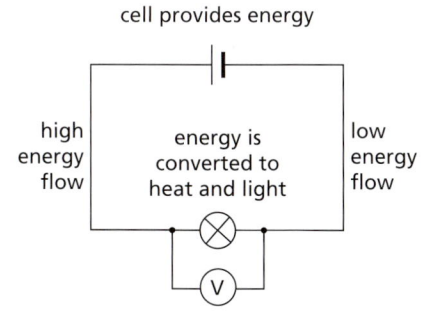

10.2 A voltmeter is used measure the energy drop across the lamp. It is connected across the terminal of the lamp.

10.3 Analogue voltmeters show the voltage using a needle on a scale. Digital voltmeters show the numbers.

Activity 10.1: Using a voltmeter

A1 Use a voltmeter to measure the voltage across one cell, as shown in figure 10.4.

10.4 *A voltmeter.*

Voltage and resistance 177

A2 Make the circuits shown in figures 10.5a and 10.5b to investigate what happens to the voltage if you connect two or three cells together in series.

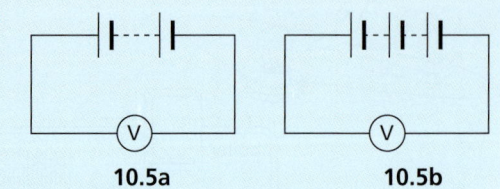

A3 Make the circuits shown in figures 10.6a, 10.6b and 10.6c.

A4 Measure the voltage across the battery and then across each lamp in turn.

A5 What do you notice about the voltage across the battery, and about the voltages across each of the lamps?

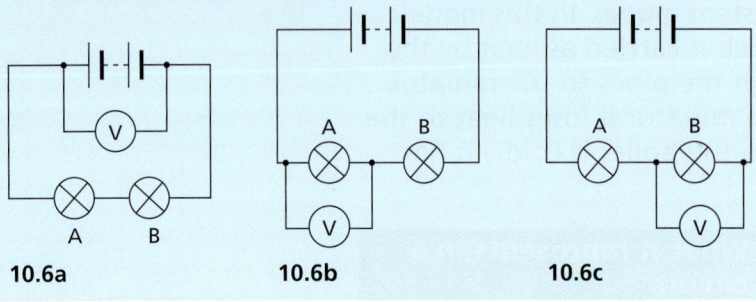

10.5a 10.5b

10.6a 10.6b 10.6c

1 What is the voltage of two 1.5 V cells connected together?

2 Why is it important for all the cells to be connected the same way round?

3 What would you change in the central heating model to represent using a battery of three cells rather than just one cell?

Electrical resistance

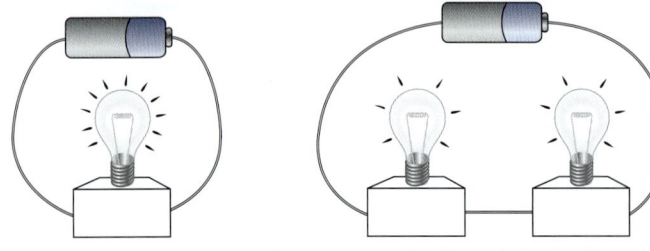

10.7 The second circuit has an extra bulb and the bulbs are less bright than in the circuit with only one bulb.

Figure 10.7 shows a simple circuit with one cell and one bulb. Adding an extra lamp to this circuit makes it harder for charges to flow. This means that current is less.

Resistance is a measure of how hard it is for charge to flow through a component. The bigger the resistance, the more energy or voltage is needed to make a current flow.

Key term

resistance: a measure of how difficult it is for current to flow. Measured in ohms.

178 Electricity

Resistance is measured in ohms, usually written using the Greek letter omega, Ω.

Running through mud needs a lot of energy. The mud resists the runner. Some materials resist current in a similar way. In the central heating model this is like having a big radiator to heat a large room. More heat energy will be transferred as the water flows through the radiator.

Most components in electrical circuits have some resistance. Lamps, buzzers, and motors resist current and change the energy carried by the charges to other useful forms of energy.

A **resistor** is a component added to a circuit to control the flow of current. Most resistors are made of carbon, which conducts electricity but not very well, or very thin metal wire. Resistors can be fixed or variable. The resistance of a variable resistor can be changed.

10.8 *The runner is encountering resistance as he tries to run through the mud.*

10.10 *The symbol for a resistor.*

> **Key term**
>
> **resistor**: a device which resists the flow of current.

10.9 *Fixed resistors as used in electrical circuits. The colours are a code which tells the user the value of the resistance in ohms.*

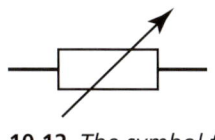

10.12 *The symbol for a variable resistor.*

10.11 *Variable resistor as used in classroom experiments. Turning the dial changes the resistance.*

There are also special types of resistors which change their characteristics with different conditions. The resistance of light-dependent resistors (LDRs) changes as the amount of light falling on them changes, and the resistance of thermistors changes as their temperature changes. These types of resistors can be used in sensors used to detect and monitor changes in light and temperature.

Activity 10.2: Dimming the lights

Adding resistors to a circuit changes the current. This can be used to control the brightness of a lamp.

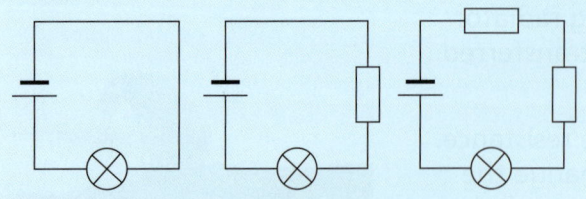

10.13 *Resistors in a circuit.*

A1 Make the first circuit shown in figure 10.13 and notice the brightness of the lamp.

A2 Add one 10 Ω resistor and note the effect this has on the brightness.

A3 Add another 10 Ω resistor and note the effect.

A dimmer switch is a variable resistor. Increasing the resistance makes it hard for current to flow, so less current flows through the lamp.

A4 Set up a circuit like the one you made in A2 above using a variable resistor instead of a fixed resistor to control the brightness of the lamp.

A5 Draw the circuit diagram for your new circuit.

A6 Investigate the effect of a variable resistor on a buzzer and on a motor.

Science in context: Using variable resistors

The resistance of a light-dependent resistor (LDR) changes depending on the light level. This can be used to switch on lights as it gets dark.

A thermistor is a resistor whose resistance changes with temperature. This can be used to measure and control the temperature of a home.

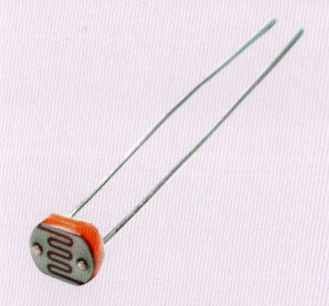

10.14 *Light-dependent resistor (LDR).*

10.15 *A domestic heating thermostat.*

4. What effect would adding a variable resistor have on a) a motor and b) a buzzer?

5. What name is given to materials which have very low resistance?

6. What name is given to materials which have extremely high resistance?

Resistance, voltage and current

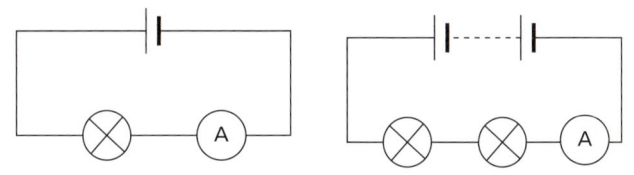

10.16 *Series circuits with the same proportions of cells and bulbs have the same current.*

Adding an extra lamp doubles the resistance in this circuit. To get the same current the voltage has to be doubled as well. This is done by adding an extra cell.

In any circuit:

- Voltage is a measure of the energy supplied to the charges in the circuit.
- Current is a measure of the flow of charges around the circuit.
- Resistance is a measure of the opposition to the flow of charges.

These three quantities are related using a simple formula.

To calculate resistance in a circuit, we divide voltage by current:

$$\text{resistance} = \frac{\text{voltage}}{\text{current}}$$

You can rearrange this equation to calculate voltage:

$$\text{voltage} = \text{current} \times \text{resistance}$$

You can also rearrange the equation to calculate current:

$$\text{current} = \frac{\text{voltage}}{\text{resistance}}$$

A 2 V cell is connected to a 20 Ω resistor. What current flows in the resistor?

$$\text{current} = \frac{\text{voltage}}{\text{resistance}} = \frac{2}{20} = 0.1 \text{ A}$$

Activity 10.3: Calculating resistance

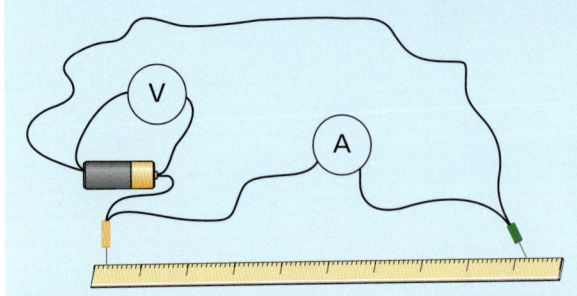

10.17 A diagram showing the equipment needed to measure the resistance of different lengths of wire.

In this activity you will use the circuit shown in figure 10.17 to measure the resistance of different lengths of wire.

A1 The wire can get hot when current flows. Describe how you will make sure your experiment is safe.

A2 Use a voltmeter to measure and record the voltage of the cell.

A3 Connect the circuit with 100 cm of wire. Record the current.

A4 Calculate the resistance of the wire using the formula

$$\text{resistance} = \frac{\text{voltage}}{\text{current}}$$

A5 Repeat steps 2 and 3 for 80 cm, 60 cm, 40 cm and 20 cm of wire.

A6 What effect does decreasing the length of wire have on the resistance?

A7 How could this wire be used as a dimmer switch?

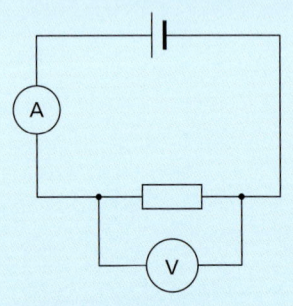

10.18 A circuit.

A8 Make the circuit shown in figure 10.18 using fixed resistors.

A9 Measure the current and voltage.

A10 Calculate the resistance of the resistor.

7 A 1.5 V cell is connected to a lamp with a resistance of 15 Ω. Calculate the current through the lamp.

8 What voltage battery would be needed to make a 0.5 A current flow through a 10 Ω resistor?

Key facts:
✔ Voltage is measured in volts using a voltmeter.
✔ Voltage, current and resistance are linked by the equation voltage = current × resistance
✔ A resistor will decrease the flow of current in a circuit.

Check your skills progress:
- I can measure current and voltage in circuits.
- I can calculate resistance, current and voltage.

Chapter 10. Topic 2

Measuring current and voltage in series and parallel circuits

You will learn:
- To understand how to draw circuit diagrams using conventional symbols for the components
- To describe current in series and parallel circuits
- To understand how current and voltage can be measured in series and parallel circuits
- To describe how the addition of cells and lamps affects the measurement of voltage
- To represent scientific ideas using recognised symbols or formulae
- To describe the uses, strengths and limitations of models and analogies
- To use scientific knowledge to make predictions
- To carry out practical work in a safe manner to minimise risks
- To collect accurate and precise measurements
- To record observations and measurements appropriately
- To interpret results and form conclusions using scientific knowledge and understanding

Starting point

You should know that...	You should be able to...
Increasing the voltage of a battery increases the brightness of a lamp	Observe and explain patterns such as how the number of cells affects the loudness of a buzzer
Components in a circuit can be represented by symbols	Construct simple circuits from a circuit diagram

Series and parallel circuits

In the **series circuit** in figure 10.19 all the charge which flows through the first lamp must also flow through the other. This means that the current is the same all round a series circuit. This can be modelled using the rope loop model.

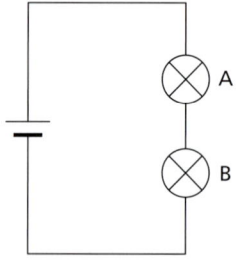

10.19 *All the charge which flows through lamp A also flows through lamp B.*

> **Key term**
>
> **series circuit**: a circuit made up of a single loop.

10.20 *This class are using the rope model to investigate a series circuit.*

A parallel circuit is made up of more than one loop.

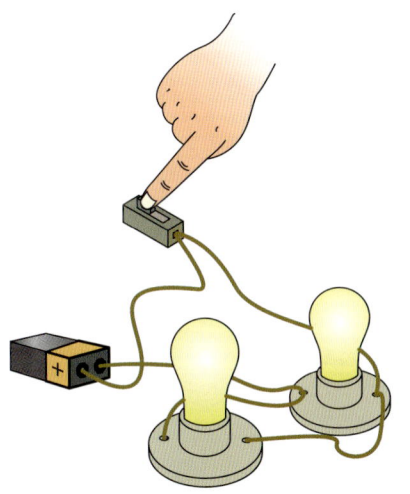

10.21 *In this parallel circuit, the two lamps are connected in more than one loop.*

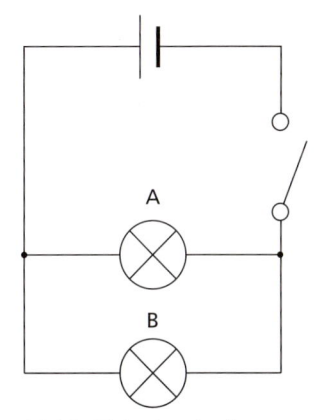

10.22 *This circuit diagram shows the parallel circuit with two lamps shown in figure 10.21.*

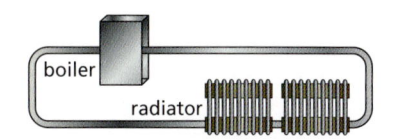

10.23 *The parallel circuit shown in figure 10.21 can be modelled with this simple central heating system with two radiators.*

In this **parallel circuit** some charge will flow through lamp A and some will flow through lamp B.

In the central heating model the water will divide between the two radiators.

> **Key term**
>
> **parallel circuit**: a circuit made up of more than one loop.

Activity 10.4: Connecting lamps in series and parallel circuits

In this activity you will investigate different ways of connecting lamps and switches in circuits. You will evaluate the advantages of each type of circuit.

A1 Connect the circuit shown in figure 10.24.
A2 What happens when you open and close the switch?
A3 What happens if you unscrew one lamp?

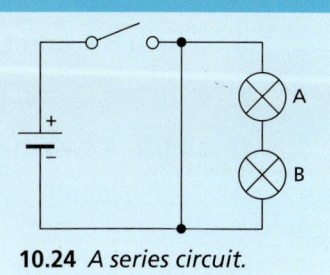

10.24 *A series circuit.*

Measuring current and voltage in series and parallel circuits   **185**

A4 Now make the circuit shown in figure 10.25.

A5 What happens when the switch is opened and closed?

A6 Which circuit makes the lamps brighter?

A7 What happens if you unscrew one lamp?

A8 Where would you put the switch if you wanted to keep lamp A on all the time but wanted to be able to switch lamp B on and off?

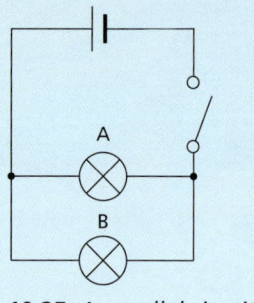

10.25 *A parallel circuit.*

1 In the central heating model, what would represent:

  A voltage

  B current

  C resistance?

2 Household lights are connected in a parallel circuit. Explain why this is better than a series circuit.

3 Draw a diagram for a circuit with two lamps and two switches arranged so that the lamps can be controlled separately.

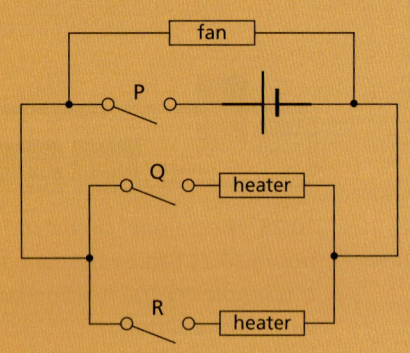

10.26 *A circuit.*

4 Figure 10.26 shows the circuit used in a hairdryer. Describe what will happen when each of these combinations of switches are closed:

  a) switch P

  b) switch Q

  c) switches P and Q

  d) switches Q and R

  e) all three switches

186   Electricity

10.2 Making measurements in series and parallel circuits

Activity 10.5: Measuring current in series and parallel circuits

An ammeter measures current through a component so the current must flow **through** the ammeter.

A1 Make the circuit shown in figure 10.27.

Investigate how the current varies around the circuit.

A2 Change the placement of the ammeter in the circuit to measure the current before, between, and after the lamps.

A3 What do you notice about the current around the circuit?

A4 The charge leaving the battery has lots of energy. What happens to this energy as the charge goes through the lamps?

A5 Make the circuit shown in figure 10.28.

Investigate how the current varies around the circuit.

A6 What do you notice about the current around this circuit?

A7 Which loop gets most current? Why do you think more charge takes this route?

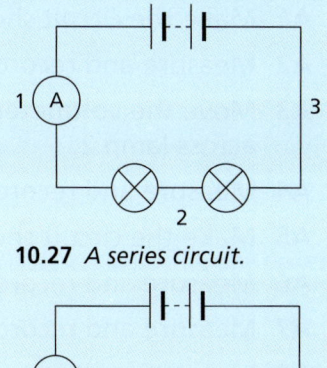

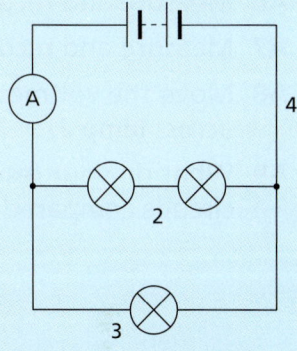

10.27 *A series circuit.*

10.28 *A parallel circuit.*

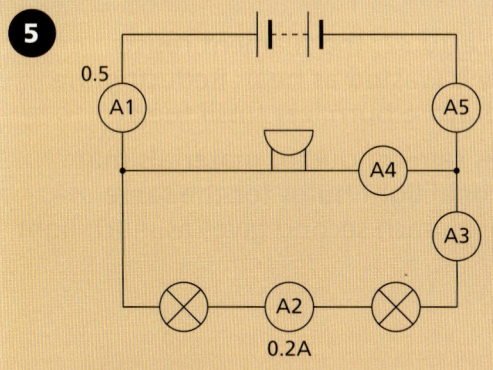

5

10.29 *A circuit.*

What will the current be on:

a) ammeter A3?

b) ammeter A4?

c) ammeter A5?

d) Does the buzzer have more or less resistance than the two lamps?

Measuring current and voltage in series and parallel circuits

Activity 10.6: Measuring voltage in series and parallel circuits

A voltmeter measures the drop in energy of the charges across a component so the voltmeter must be connected **across** the component.

A1 Make the circuit shown in figure 10.30.

A2 Measure and record the voltage across lamp 1.

A3 Move the voltmeter and measure and record the voltage across lamp 2.

A4 Measure and record the voltage across the cell.

A5 Make the circuit shown in figure 10.31.

A6 Measure and record the voltage across the battery.

A7 Measure and record the voltage across lamp 1.

A8 Move the voltmeter and measure and record the voltage across lamp 2.

A9 What do your results show about the voltage in series circuits compared to the voltage in parallel circuits?

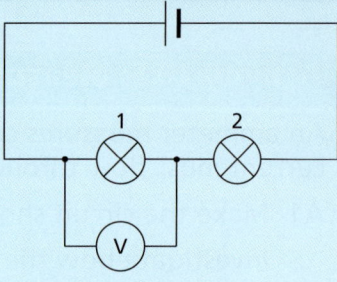

10.30 *A series circuit.*

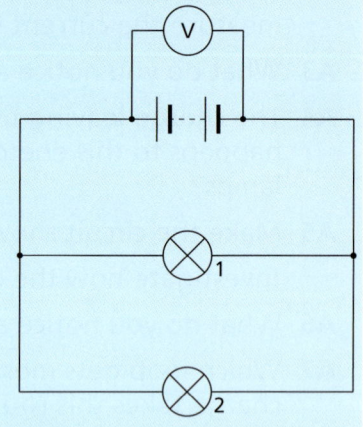

10.31 *A parallel circuit.*

Science in context: Developments in electric lighting

In lamps like the traditional filament light bulb in figure 10.32, the filament resists current flow to produce heat and light. A lot of energy is wasted as heat. Reducing the waste energy means we can use less electricity and therefore burn less fossil fuels.

The light-emitting diode (LED) bulb in figure 10.33 uses semiconductor materials that emit light and produce much less heat than the traditional light bulbs for the same amount of light. An LED bulb that uses 9 joules of energy each second gives as much light as a traditional bulb, which uses 60 joules each second.

10.32 *A traditional filament light bulb.*    10.33 *An LED light bulb.*

188   Electricity

6 Copy and complete this table to summarise what you have learnt about series and parallel circuits.

Type of circuit	Number of loops	Effect of switches	Brightness of lamps	Current	Voltage
Series			Adding lamps makes the lamps dimmer		
Parallel		Switches can control components independently		Current is shared between the loops	

7 A cell in a parallel circuit can light two lamps as brightly as one lamp on its own. Sajid says that this will save him money on buying cells. Explain why he is wrong.

Key facts:
✔ In a series circuit the current is the same at all points.
✔ In a series circuit the voltage is shared between the components.
✔ In a parallel circuit the current is shared between the loops.
✔ In a parallel circuit the voltage is the same across the battery and each loop.

Check your skills progress:
- I can draw and make series and parallel circuits.
- I can consider the advantages and disadvantages of different circuit models.

Measuring current and voltage in series and parallel circuits

End of chapter review

Quick questions

1. What is a series circuit?

2. What is a parallel circuit?

3. Draw lines to match each quantity to its unit:

Current		Ohms
Voltage		Amps
Resistance		Volts

4. Draw a circuit you could use to measure the resistance of a lamp.

5. State whether each of the following apply to a series or a parallel circuit:

   A The current is the same all the way round the circuit.

   B If one lamp goes out the others will all work.

   C Each lamp can be operated by a separate switch.

   D The voltage across each lamp is the same as the voltage across the cell.

6. A 12 V battery is connected to a lamp with a resistance of 100 Ω. How much current will flow?

Connect your understanding

7. A student made the circuit shown in figure 10.34.

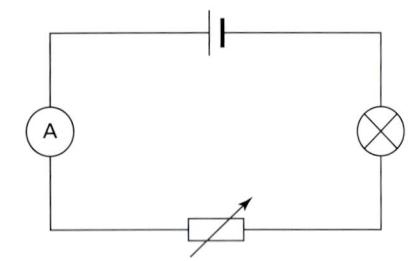

   10.34

   Describe and explain what will happen if the student changes the variable resistor so that the current has less wire to flow through.

8. Using two lamps and three switches, design a parallel circuit which will let you:

   • switch off both lamps using just one switch and

   • control each lamp separately.

Challenge questions

9. Sunita and Maryam did experiments to find the effect of changing the number of cells and the number of lamps on the current in a series circuit. They made some mistakes.

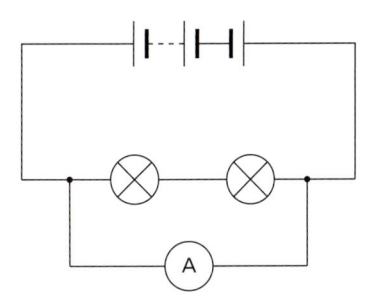

10.35

(a) They made *two* mistakes with their circuit. What are the mistakes?

(b) Draw a circuit diagram to show the correct way to connect this circuit.

Their results are shown in the table below.

Number of cells	Number of lamps	Current (A)
1	1	0.8
2	2	0.8
3	3	0.8
4	4	0.8
5	5	0.8

(c) Maryam said that their results show that changing the number of cells doesn't change the current. Explain why she is wrong.

(d) What should the girls do to test Maryam's idea?

They repeat the experiment and get these results:

Number of cells	Number of lamps	Current (A)
1	1	0.8
1	2	0.4
1	3	0.3
2	1	1.5
2	2	0.8
2	3	2.8
3	1	2.3
3	2	1.1
3	3	0.8

(e) There is *one* anomalous result. Which result is it?

(f) Write *two* conclusions they can make from their results.

Chapter 11
Sound

The same tune sounds different when it is played on different instruments. Some sounds are higher or louder than others. When two loudspeakers simultaneously play the same sound there are some positions between them where the sound is quiet and some positions where the sound is loud. These facts can be explained by learning what decides how high or loud a sound is and what happens when two or more sound waves combine.

You will learn about:
- What determines the pitch of a sound
- What determines the volume of a sound
- What happens when two sound waves combine

You will build your skills in:
- Suggesting a hypothesis that can be tested
- Making and explaining predictions using scientific ideas
- Planning an investigation, including how you will collect evidence to answer your question
- Evaluating how well evidence supports or contradicts a prediction
- Describing the use of science in society, industry and research
- Evaluating issues using scientific understanding

Chapter 11 . Topic 1

Loudness and pitch

You will learn:
- To understand how to draw and label waveforms and describe the links between loudness and amplitude and pitch and frequency
- To describe trends and patterns shown in a set of results, identifying, and explaining, any anomalous results present
- To use scientific knowledge and understanding to suggest a testable hypothesis
- To plan investigations used to test hypotheses
- To use scientific knowledge to make predictions
- To collect and record observations and measurements appropriately
- To interpret results and form conclusions using scientific knowledge and understanding
- To evaluate how the prediction is supported by the evidence collected

Starting point

You should know that...	You should be able to...
Sound is produced by vibrations	Describe how we can represent and explain sound waves using a model or analogy
	Plan an investigation to test a hypothesis
	Use your scientific knowledge to predict the results of an experiment or investigation
Sound travels as a wave	
Sound travels at about 340 m/s through air	
Pitch describes how high or low a sound is	
High- and low-pitched sounds can be soft or loud	
Volume describes how soft or loud a sound is	

Why do sounds have different pitches and loudness?

If you pluck a guitar string, it will make a sound. If you shorten the string it will make a different sound. If you pluck it harder it will make a louder sound. Sounds made by a violin have a higher **pitch** than those made by a double bass. Why is this?

It is because their sound waves are different. How loud a sound is depends on the **amplitude** of vibration of the sound wave. The greater the amplitude of the sound wave,

Key terms

amplitude: the maximum height of the wave, from the centre to the top or bottom.

pitch: how high or low a sound is.

the louder the sound. The amplitude of a sound wave depends on how much energy the sound wave has. For a musical instrument, this depends on how hard you hit, blow or pluck the instrument. Amplitude is measured in metres (m) though sound waves usually have a very small amplitude, much less than a millimetre.

The pitch of a sound depends on the **frequency** of vibration of the sound wave. The greater the frequency, the higher the pitch. Sounds made by a flute have a higher frequency (and a higher pitch) than those made by a cello. The more waves you make every second, the higher the frequency is.

Frequency is measured in **hertz** (Hz). One wave every second gives a frequency of 1 Hz.

Waves with a high frequency will have a short **wavelength** because they will be close together. The shorter the wavelength, the higher the sound. The wavelength of a wave means how long one wave is. One wavelength is the distance between a point on one wave (for example, where the particles are closest together) and the same point on the next wave. The vibrating strings of a double bass are longer than those of a violin. A double bass, therefore, can make sound waves with longer wavelengths and lower frequencies than a violin can.

Wavelength is measured in metres (m).

11.1 *The wavelength of sound.*

> **Making links**
>
> Energy is needed to make waves, like sound waves. Waves transfer energy from one place to another. The amplitude of a sound depends on how much energy the sound wave has.
>
> Give an example of *one* other type of wave that transfers energy from one place to another.

> **Key terms**
>
> **frequency**: the number of waves per second.
>
> **hertz**: the unit of frequency. 1 Hz = one complete wave every second.
>
> **wavelength**: the length of one complete wave.

1 Two of the strings on a guitar can be used to play two different sounds.

Sound 1 is produced by playing a string that vibrates 300 times in 2 seconds.

Sound 2 is produced by playing a string that vibrates 1000 times in 5 seconds.

The amplitudes of the two sounds was measured, and sound 1 had an amplitude which was twice that of sound 2.

a) Which sound was the loudest?

b) Which sound had the highest frequency?

c) which sound had the longest wavelength?

d) Which sound had the lowest pitch?

11.1

Looking at sound waves on an oscilloscope screen

You can use a signal generator or microphone to send electrical impulses to an oscilloscope. Signal generators can make electrical waves with different frequencies. If you attach a signal generator to a loudspeaker you will get sound waves of different frequencies. The dial on the signal generator will tell you what the frequency is.

The oscilloscope displays the electrical signals as a graph on a screen. The graphs are called traces. The shape of the wave is called a **waveform**.

Figures 11.3 and 11.4 show the waveforms of some sound waves on an oscilloscope screen.

Each screen shows the same time period, so you can see how many waves have been made in a given time. All the pictures have the same scale.

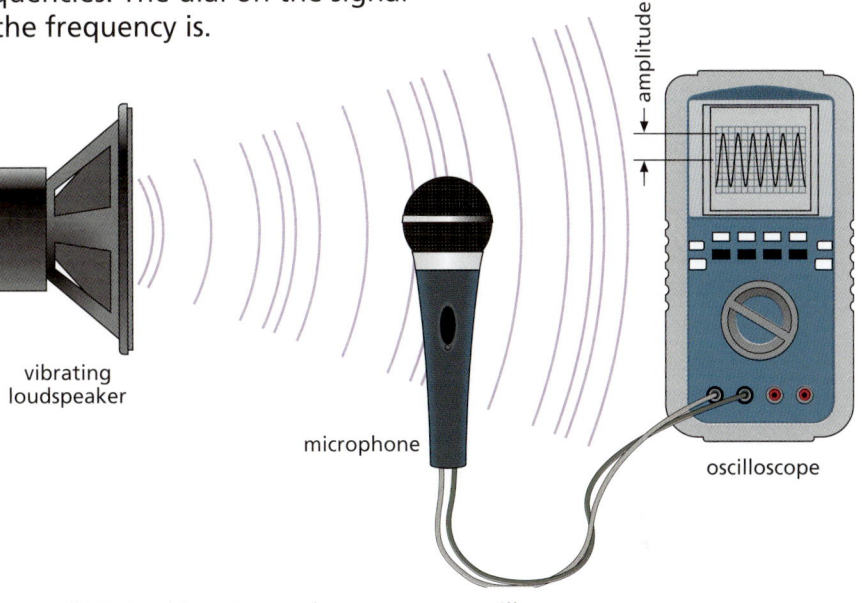

> **Key term**
>
> **waveform**: the shape of a wave.

11.2 *Looking at sound waves on an oscilloscope screen.*

- Volume
  - Sound A is quieter than sounds B and C. We know this because it has a smaller amplitude.

- Pitch
  - Sound A has the same pitch as sound B. We know this because they have the same wavelength and frequency. The same number of waves have been made in a given time.
  - Sound C has a higher pitch because it has a shorter wavelength and a higher frequency. More waves have been made in the same time.

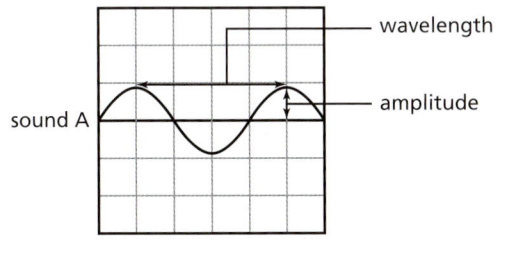

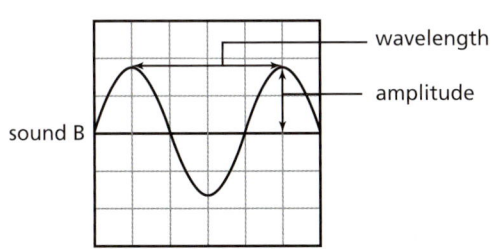

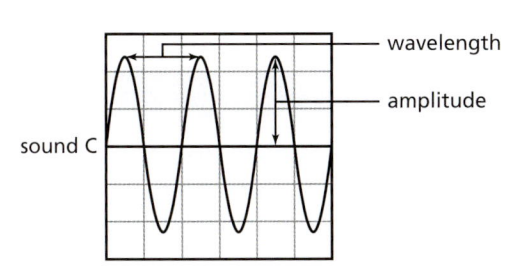

11.3 *Waveforms of sound waves shown on an oscilloscope screen.*

Loudness and pitch

Figure 11.4 shows the oscilloscope traces for sounds D, E and F. You should use these traces to answer questions 2 and 3.

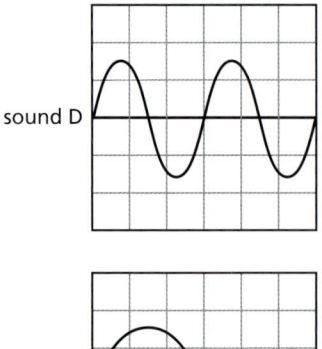

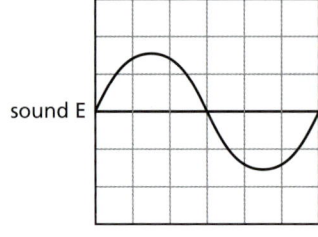

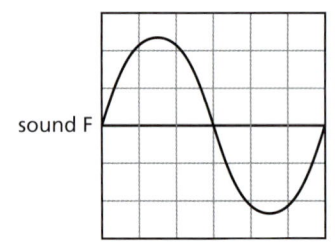

sound D

sound E

sound F

11.4 *Sounds D, E and F.*

2 Which of the sounds is the loudest? How do you know?

3 Which has the highest pitch? How do you know?

Usually, the bigger a musical instrument is, the lower the frequency of the notes it can make. This is because the size of the instrument sets the maximum wavelength of the sound waves it makes. The bigger the instrument, the longer the wavelength. This is why you can change the pitch of the note made by a stringed instrument like a guitar by shortening or lengthening the string.

4 Will shortening a guitar string make the pitch of the note higher or lower? Explain your answer.

Science in context: Your unique voiceprint

Voice recognition systems can be used to identify a person from their voice. You may be asked to speak a special password or passphrase. This is then stored electronically (as your 'voiceprint') and when you speak that password or passphrase again the electronic pattern made by your voice is compared to the pattern stored. This relies on the fact that your voice produces a waveform pattern that is different from anyone else's. The pitch, volume and speed of your speech, for example, are unique.

These systems are very effective and even a good imitation of your voice does not give the same waveform. This is because the way you say words depends on biological factors such as the size and shape of your vocal chords, nose and larynx and how they move when you speak. Criminals would find it very difficult to recreate your voiceprint artificially. However if they record your voice saying the special phrase they could use this to pretend to be you.

1. Give an example of where voice recognition systems could be useful.
2. Discuss the advantages and disadvantages of this technology.

Frequency range of human hearing

Extension When the ear detects sound, a thin layer of tissue called the eardrum is made to vibrate. These vibrations are passed on to tiny bones called ossicles and then on to the inner ear before being passed on to the brain in the form of electrical signals.

The human ear can hear frequencies as low as about 20 Hz and as high as about 20 000 Hz (20 kHz).

Anything lower than 20 Hz is called **infrasound**. We cannot hear this but the vibrations are still there.

Elephants can hear sound with frequencies as low as 5 Hz, but they cannot hear frequencies above 10 000 Hz.

Sounds waves with a frequency higher than 20 000 Hz are called **ultrasound**. We cannot hear these but some animals can.

Dogs have a hearing range of about 40 Hz to 60 000 Hz. Cats can hear even higher frequencies, up to 85 000 Hz. Dolphins can hear a very large range of frequencies, from less than 1 Hz to 200 000 Hz. Bats have a range of about 20 Hz to 120 000 Hz. Dolphins communicate with each other using ultrasound; bats do the same. Bats also judge distances using ultrasound echoes. This helps them to navigate.

Key terms

infrasound: sound waves with a frequency too low for humans to hear.

ultrasound: sound waves with a frequency too high for humans to hear.

5. Which of the animals dogs, cats, dolphins and bats:
   a) can hear the lowest frequency?
   b) can hear the highest frequency?
   c) can hear over the biggest range of frequencies?

6. Why can very high-pitched sounds hurt you and possibly damage your hearing? (Hint: think about what happens inside your ears when you hear sounds.)

Activity 11.1: Testing your hearing range

Extension Please note that this activity uses low-pitched and high-pitched sounds but it will not damage your hearing or cause you harm. If the results cause you concern about your hearing, please seek medical advice. This activity is not a medically approved hearing test so cannot be used to diagnose hearing issues.

If you already have hearing issues or are uncomfortable about doing this activity, please advise your teacher.

Set the signal generator at a very low frequency, too low to hear. Gradually increase the frequency and note when you can first hear a sound. Keep increasing the frequency (and the pitch of the sound) until you can no longer hear it. Note when this happens.

Activity 11.2: Changing the pitch

Get a glass beaker and a pencil. Tap the side of the beaker with a pencil. Listen to the note that this makes.

A1 What do you think will happen to the note produced if you add a little more water to the beaker?

A2 Why do you think this will happen?

Add a little more water to the beaker and repeat.

A3 Does the result match your prediction?

Add even more water and repeat again. Keep doing this until you can see a clear pattern to your results.

A4 What is the pattern? Is it what you expected?

A5 Explain whether your evidence is strong enough to support your conclusion.

Activity 11.3: Investigating musical bottles

You have discovered that adding more water to a glass beaker changes the pitch of the note it makes. Are there other ways to change the pitch?

A1 Write down a scientific question you would like to investigate about making music with bottles. For example, think about what else you could change and how this might affect the sound produced.

A2 Predict what will happen and use scientific ideas to explain your hypothesis.

A3 Describe how you will obtain evidence to test your hypothesis. Include what you will measure and how you will control any other variables.

A4 When you have collected your results, explain how well your evidence supports your hypothesis.

11.1

Key facts:

- ✔ The pitch of a sound depends on the frequency of the sound wave.
- ✔ The volume of a sound depends on the amplitude of the sound wave.
- ✔ The frequency of a wave is the number of waves per second and is measured in hertz (Hz).
- ✔ The shorter the wavelength of a sound wave, the higher its frequency is.
- ✔ The size of a musical instrument sets the maximum wavelength of the sound it can produce.

Check your skills progress:

- I can write a hypothesis based on scientific understanding, and say how it can be tested by investigating what will happen to a variable when a different variable is changed.
- I can write a plan of how to test my hypothesis including a description of how to make measurements and successfully control the remaining variables.
- I can use results to draw conclusions about a hypothesis.

Loudness and pitch

Chapter 11 . Topic 2
Interference

You will learn:
- To understand how to represent the interaction or reinforcement of sound waves using waveforms
- To use scientific knowledge to make predictions
- To describe the uses, strengths and limitations of models and analogies

Starting point

You should know that...	You should be able to...
Sound travels as a wave	Draw waveforms to compare waves of different amplitudes
The amplitude of a wave as shown on a waveform as the maximum height of the wave from the centre to the top or bottom	
The frequency of a wave is the number of waves per second	
The wavelength of a wave is the length of one complete wave	

What is interference?

When we look at a water wave or a waveform on an oscilloscope screen, we can use the amplitude of the wave to identify some key parts: **crests** and **troughs**. These are shown in figure 11.5.

Key terms

crest: the highest point of a wave.

trough: the lowest point of a wave.

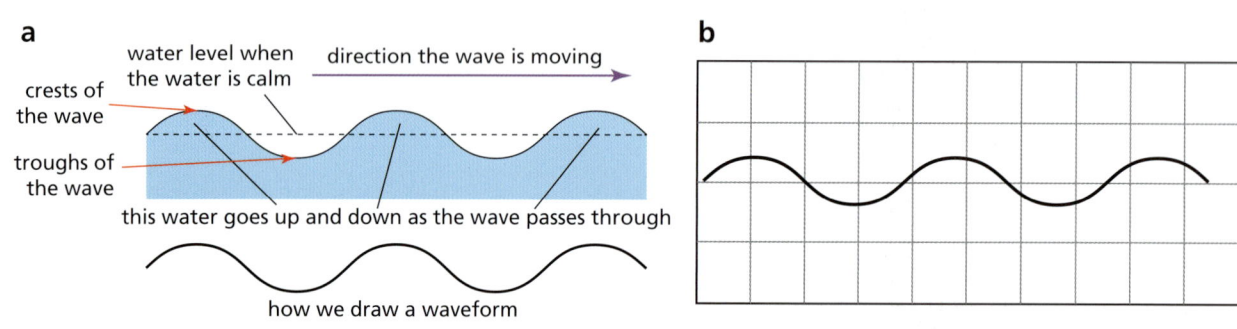

11.5 a Looking at crests and troughs on a water wave. **b** Looking at crests and troughs on a waveform shown on an oscilloscope screen.

Looking at the water wave in figure 11.5a, we can see that the crests are formed when the water particles move upwards to their highest point and the troughs are formed when the water particles move downwards to their lowest point.

200 Sound

For the waveform of a sound wave in figure 11.5b, the crests and troughs represent the positions where the particles in a sound wave are moving with their largest amplitude of vibration.

> **1** What would happen if the water particles were pushed upwards and downwards, using the same force, at the same time?

Sometimes two or more waves will meet each other. When two waves meet they combine rather like putting one wave on top of the other. This causes an effect called **interference**.

What happens as a result of interference depends on which parts of each wave meet.

The result of a trough meeting a crest will be different from the result when two crests meet.

The result of a wave meeting a wave with the opposite amplitude will be different from the result when two waves with the same amplitude meet.

Figure 11.6 shows what might happen when two identical water waves interfere.

> **Key terms**
>
> **constructive interference**: this happens when two or more waves are added together to make a bigger wave.
>
> **destructive interference**: this happens when two or more waves combine to make a smaller wave or to cancel each other out altogether.
>
> **interference**: what happens when two or more waves meet and their effects are added together.

a

b

Two identical waves may add together (reinforce) to make a double-height wave, or add together so as to cancel each other out.

11.6 Different effects of interference.

In figure 11.6a, where the two crests meet, the particles move upwards twice as far (because both waves are pushing the particles in the same direction at the same time). Where two troughs meet the particles move downwards twice as far (because both waves are pushing the particles downwards at the same time). This makes a wave with double the amplitude of the original waves. This type of interference is called **constructive interference**.

In figure 11.6b, at the crests of one wave the particles should be at their highest point, but where they meet at the troughs of the other wave the particles should be at their lowest point. The movements are equal size but in opposite directions so there is no overall movement up or down. This means the waves have cancelled each other out. This type of interference is called **destructive interference**.

- For two overlapping water waves, the waves can combine to give higher crests and deeper troughs, or the crests of one wave can fill in the troughs of the other wave, resulting in flat water.
- For two overlapping sound waves, the waves can combine to give a bigger particle disturbance and a louder area, or a smaller or no disturbance and a quieter area.

2 Two sound waves cancel each other out. Does this produce a loud or quiet area?

3 Two sound waves reinforce each other. Does this produce a loud or quiet area?

4 Use your understanding of particle movement to explain how two waves can cancel each other out.

5 a) Which pair of waves shown in figure 11.7 would combine to produce a wave with the biggest amplitude?

b) Which pair of waves shown in figure 11.7 would cancel each other out when they combined?

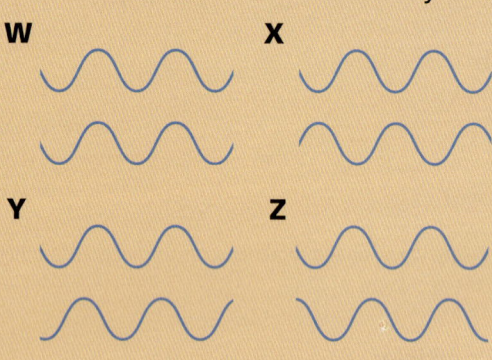

W   X

Y   Z

11.7 *Pairs of waves.*

6 Look at figure 11.7. Would you get the same results if one wave had twice the amplitude of the other?

7 Draw a pair of waves of the same frequency that would combine to produce a wave with half the amplitude of one of the original waves.

11.2 Noticing interference in everyday life

11.8 *This wave pattern was produced by a wave interfering with another wave reflected from the shore.*

Activity 11.4: Interference of sound waves

Your teacher may demonstrate this activity.

A Connect a signal generator to two identical loudspeakers, approximately 3–4 metres apart.

B Set the signal generator to produce a sound that can be heard easily. The speakers produce identical sound waves.

(Note, if you don't have a signal generator you can play a single note through two loudspeakers.)

C Connect a microphone to an oscilloscope.

D Starting at one loudspeaker, slowly move the microphone across to the other loudspeaker. Look at the amplitude of the waveform shown on the oscilloscope screen. This will show if there are any changes in the volume of the sound at different points between the loudspeakers.

A1 Would you expect the volume of the sound detected by the microphone to be the same at every point between the two loudspeakers?

A2 Explain your answer to A1.

A3 Do your results agree with your answer to A1?

A4 Are you confident that your results are good enough to be certain about your conclusion?

A5 You could do this experiment by just walking between the loudspeakers and listening to the volume. Why are you likely to get more useful results by using a microphone and oscilloscope instead?

Interference

8 Radio signals travel in the form of waves. Transmission masts send out these radio waves and they are then detected by an aerial connected to your radio. Sometimes, when you are travelling in a car on a road between two masts you notice that the radio signal gets stronger, then weaker and then stronger again. Explain why this happens.

Science in context: Shutting out the noise

Active noise-cancelling headphones let you listen to music through your headphones without also hearing all the noise in your surroundings that sometimes spoils your enjoyment.

The headphones work using the idea of destructive interference. There are tiny microphones which detect sounds around you. These sounds (the 'noise') are then processed and their waveforms reversed so that the parts that were crests become troughs and vice versa. These processed waveforms then combine with the waveforms of the noise and cancel them out.

There are possible problems caused by using this technology, for example, walking on the street using noise-cancelling headphones means you may not hear approaching traffic.

Use the information in the box above to answer questions 9 and 10.

9 a) Give *one* advantage of noise-cancelling technology.

b) Give *one* disadvantage of noise-cancelling technology.

10 Write a short report, 100–200 words on the subject of noise-cancelling headphones when used by workers in noisy factories, commenting on their advantages and disadvantages and including your opinion on whether or not they are a good thing.

Key facts:

✔ Interference occurs when two or more waves meet.

✔ The wave produced depends on the amplitude of the original waves and how they combine.

✔ Two sound waves can reinforce each other to produce a bigger disturbance. This gives a sound wave with a louder sound than the original waves.

✔ Two sound waves can cancel each other out to produce silence.

Check your skills progress:

- I can use the analogy with water waves to describe how two sound waves can combine to produce a louder sound or cancel each other out.

- I can use my knowledge and understanding to predict what will happen when two sound waves combine.

- I can draw conclusions from my results and discuss whether my results are good enough to be confident that my conclusion is right.

End of chapter review

Quick questions

1. What does pitch mean?

2. What feature of a sound wave determines its pitch?

3. What does volume mean?

4. What feature of a sound wave determines how loud it is?

5. Complete the sentence below. Use the correct word from the box.

   | bigger | smaller | longer | shorter |

   When two identical wave crests meet they make a wave with a _____ amplitude.

6. How do you lower the pitch of the note made by a stringed instrument like a guitar?

7. Why do large musical instruments usually make deeper sounds than small musical instruments?

8. When the crest of one water wave meets the trough of an identical water wave do you get a larger water wave or flat water?

Connect your understanding

9. How could you use a microphone and an oscilloscope to see what the sound waves made when you speak look like?

10. (a) How can you change the pitch of the sound a drum makes?

    (b) Explain your answer.

11. Copy the sound wave in figure 11.9.

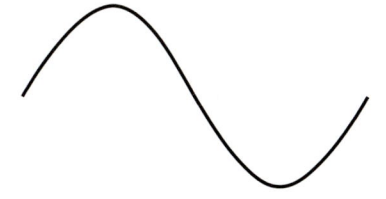

    11.9

    (a) Draw a sound wave that is louder but has the same pitch.

    (b) Draw a sound wave that has the same volume but a lower pitch than the first wave.

(c) Draw a sound wave that has a higher pitch and a lower volume than the first wave.

12. Draw accurate diagrams to show how two identical waves can interfere to produce a wave which has twice the amplitude of the original waves.

Challenge questions

13. A person makes a sound which starts at a very low pitch. The pitch then becomes higher and higher. At the same time, the sound gets quieter and quieter. Sketch a diagram to show what the sound wave would look like.

14. Explain why two waves which have different frequencies cannot cancel each other out completely.

15. (a) Describe how noise-cancelling headphones work.

    (b) Do you think noise-cancelling headphones are a good or bad thing? Explain your answer.

End of stage review

1. (a) What is the only method of heat transfer that can occur in a vacuum?

    A conduction

    B convection

    C radiation

   (b) Complete this sentence: Convection cannot happen in _____. This is because their particles cannot _____

   (c) Explain *two* ways that a vacuum flask prevents thermal transfers in or out.

2. Diante measured the weight of objects made of three different materials in air, then lowered them into water and measured the apparent weight in water. His results are shown in the table.

Object	Weight in air (N)	Apparent weight in water (N)	Upthrust (N)
A	3	1.6	
B	8	6.6	
C	1.3	0	

   (a) Complete the table to find the upthrust on each object.

   (b) What would you would notice about object **C** with an apparent weight of zero.

   (c) What can you conclude about the density of object **C**?

3. (a) In the circuit shown below, the current measured at ammeter 1 is 0.6 A. What will the current be at ammeter 2 and ammeter 3?

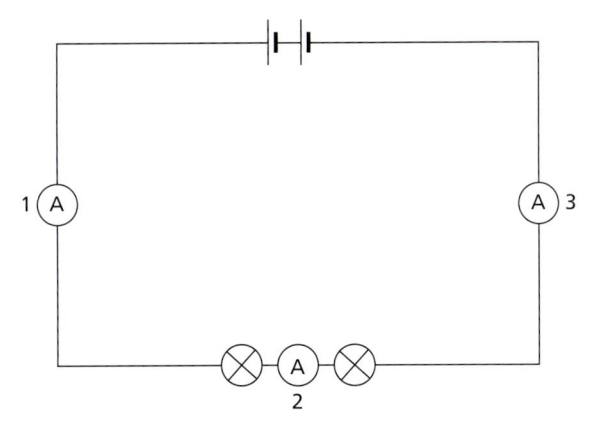

End of stage review

(b) Mihail wanted to measure the resistance of a lamp. Draw the circuit showing the position of the voltmeter.

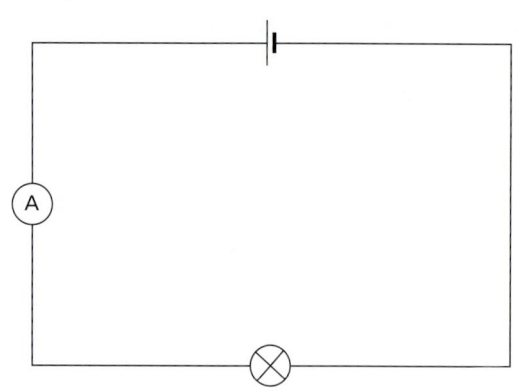

(c) Mihail connected his circuit. The ammeter reading was 0.2 A and the voltmeter reading was 1.2 V. Calculate the resistance of the lamp. Give the units.

4. (a) Mia uses an oscilloscope to record three sounds.

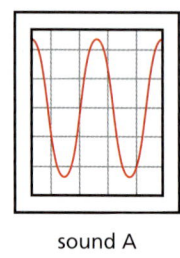

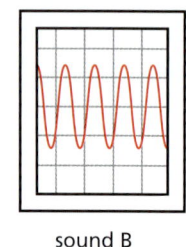

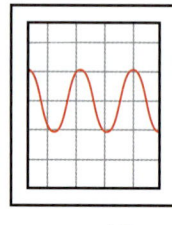

sound A   sound B   sound C

(i) Write the name of the sound that is the loudest.

(ii) Write the name of the sound that has the highest frequency.

(b) Kiran plucks a stretched elastic band and makes a sound identical to sound **C**.

(i) Draw a diagram to show how Kiran's sound wave could interfere with the waveform shown as sound **C** to make the smallest wave possible.

(ii) Is this an example of constructive or destructive interference?

Earth and space

Chapter 12: Plate tectonics

12.1:	Evidence for plate tectonics	211
12.2:	Explaining plate movement	224
End of chapter review		228

Chapter 13: Climate change

13.1:	The carbon cycle	232
13.2:	Impacts of climate change	240
End of chapter review		248

Chapter 14: Astronomy

14.1:	Collisions	252
14.2:	Observing the Universe	262
End of chapter review		266
End of stage review		270

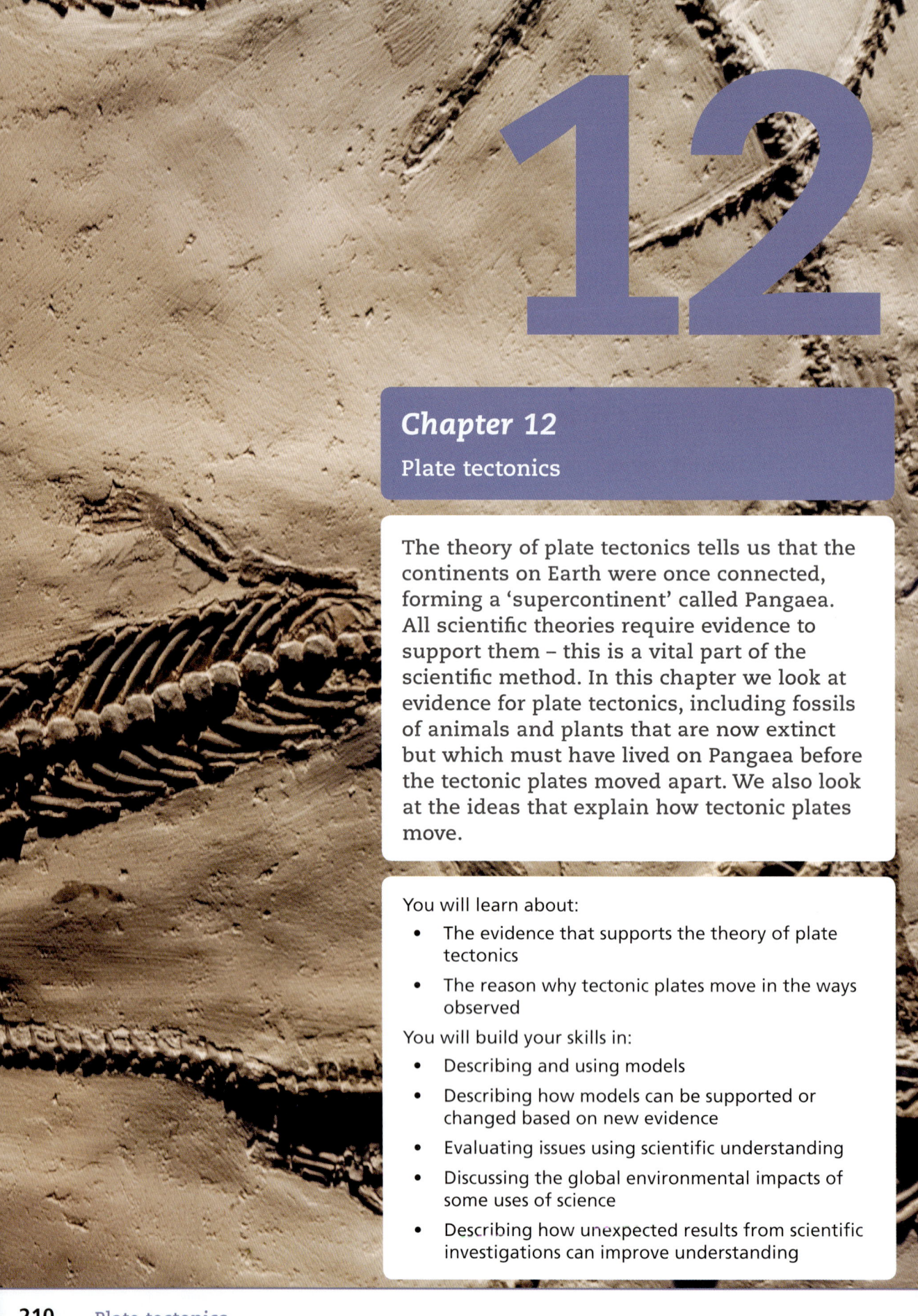

Chapter 12
Plate tectonics

The theory of plate tectonics tells us that the continents on Earth were once connected, forming a 'supercontinent' called Pangaea. All scientific theories require evidence to support them – this is a vital part of the scientific method. In this chapter we look at evidence for plate tectonics, including fossils of animals and plants that are now extinct but which must have lived on Pangaea before the tectonic plates moved apart. We also look at the ideas that explain how tectonic plates move.

You will learn about:
- The evidence that supports the theory of plate tectonics
- The reason why tectonic plates move in the ways observed

You will build your skills in:
- Describing and using models
- Describing how models can be supported or changed based on new evidence
- Evaluating issues using scientific understanding
- Discussing the global environmental impacts of some uses of science
- Describing how unexpected results from scientific investigations can improve understanding

Chapter 12 . Topic 1

Evidence for plate tectonics

You will learn:
- To explain the evidence for tectonic plate movement including coastal shapes, volcano and earthquakes, fossil records and the position of magnetic materials
- To understand that models and analogies can change according to scientific evidence
- To describe the uses, strengths and limitations of models and analogies
- To evaluate how the prediction is supported by the evidence collected
- To describe trends and patterns shown in a set of results, identifying, and explaining, any anomalous results present
- To describe examples where scientific understanding has been improved by the unexpected outcomes of scientific enquiries. To use scientific knowledge to make predictions

Starting point

You should know that...	You should be able to...
The Earth's crust is divided into a number of tectonic plates that 'float' on the mantle	Describe a model and its strengths and weaknesses
Wegener suggested that the Earth's continents are moving apart	Describe how scientific hypotheses can be supported or contradicted by evidence
Earthquakes and volcanoes occur most often at the boundaries between tectonic plates	Describe trends and patterns in results
Some rocks that form over long periods of time produce layers that help us determine when they formed	

Continental coasts

If you have ever completed a jigsaw puzzle, you will know that the shapes of two pieces have to match exactly for them to fit together neatly (figure 12.1). Two pieces that do not match will not fit together.

12.1 *Pieces in a jigsaw puzzle have to match exactly to fit together.*

Scientists observing the Earth's continents noticed that sometimes, the **coastlines** of two separate continents appear to match very well. This is particularly apparent when we look at South America and Africa (Figure 12.2).

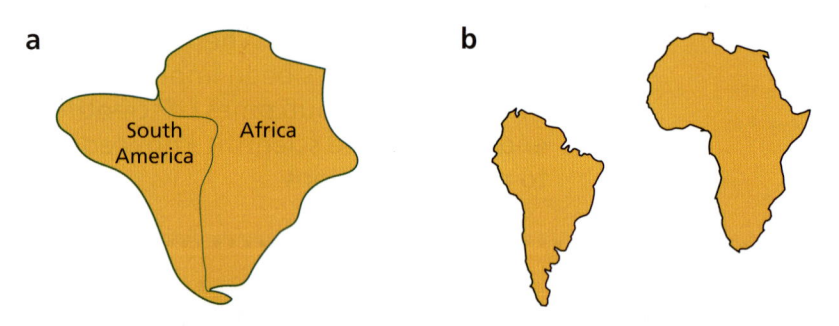

Key terms

coastline: outside edge of a continent, where rock meets the ocean.

Pangaea: supercontinent on Earth that broke apart about 175 million years ago.

supercontinent: area of land where a number of continents were joined together.

12.2 *a Map showing South America and Africa when joined.*
b The coastlines of modern-day continents of South America and Africa.

It is more than the shapes of continents that fit together. Over millions of years, rocks form in layers. At coasts, waves in the sea cause these rock layers to be exposed (figure 12.3). Scientists have compared the rock layers in coasts that are thousands of kilometres apart, such as on the eastern side of South America and the western side of Africa, and found that the layers match in many places.

12.3 *Layers of rock on a coastline.*

The 'jigsaw puzzle' shapes that match up and the rock layers that match up form strong evidence that the coasts of continents were once joined together, and that these continents must have moved apart. The joined continents formed what scientists call a **supercontinent**, which they have named **Pangaea**.

Making links

You should have learned about how different types of rocks and rock layers are formed.

a) Describe briefly how sedimentary rocks form.
b) Suggest how sedimentary rocks naturally form clear layers.

12.1

Activity 12.1: Making a model of Pangaea

Work in small groups. Your teacher will hand you an outline map of the world as it appears today.

1. Cut out the shapes of the main continents.
2. Experiment with arrangements of the continents to make pairs of continents fit together. Start with South America and Africa.
3. Investigate whether it is possible to make all the continents fit together to suggest what Pangaea looked like.

A1 Which continents appear to fit together well?

A2 Some coasts of continents fit together less well. Suggest what might have happened to the 'missing' land that linked these continents together.

A3 Compare your group's ideas with those of other groups. Have you all had the same ideas?

A4 By looking at the continents, which are where the Earth's crust rises above the surface of the oceans, we see that our model is not complete. Important areas of the Earth's crust are not included. Explain what areas of the Earth's crust are missing. Suggest where the rock that is missing from the model has come from.

---

1 Draw a diagram to show coastal rock layers, using different colours to shade the different layers, that shows how the coasts of two continents match up.

2 Sketch a map outline of the shapes of South America and Africa to show how they fit together.

3 The latest investigations suggest that Pangaea started to break apart about 175 million years ago. Explain why the rock layers found on the coasts of South America and Africa must be more than 175 million years old.

4 The eastern coast of South America and the western coast of Africa are not on plate boundaries.

   a) Where is the plate boundary found between South America and Africa?

   b) Describe what is happening at this plate boundary to cause the separation of South America and Africa.

Evidence for plate tectonics

Volcanoes and earthquakes

Stage 7 Chapter 10 described how earthquakes are sudden movements of the Earth's crust when forces build up over long periods of time, and that volcanoes appear at places where the Earth is thinner and weaker, which allows molten rock to break through the surface.

Over hundreds of years, scientists observed that earthquakes and volcanoes happen much more often in particular parts of the Earth's surface. For example, there are many volcanoes and frequent earthquakes along the western coast of South America. Figure 12.4 shows where volcanoes have been observed around the world.

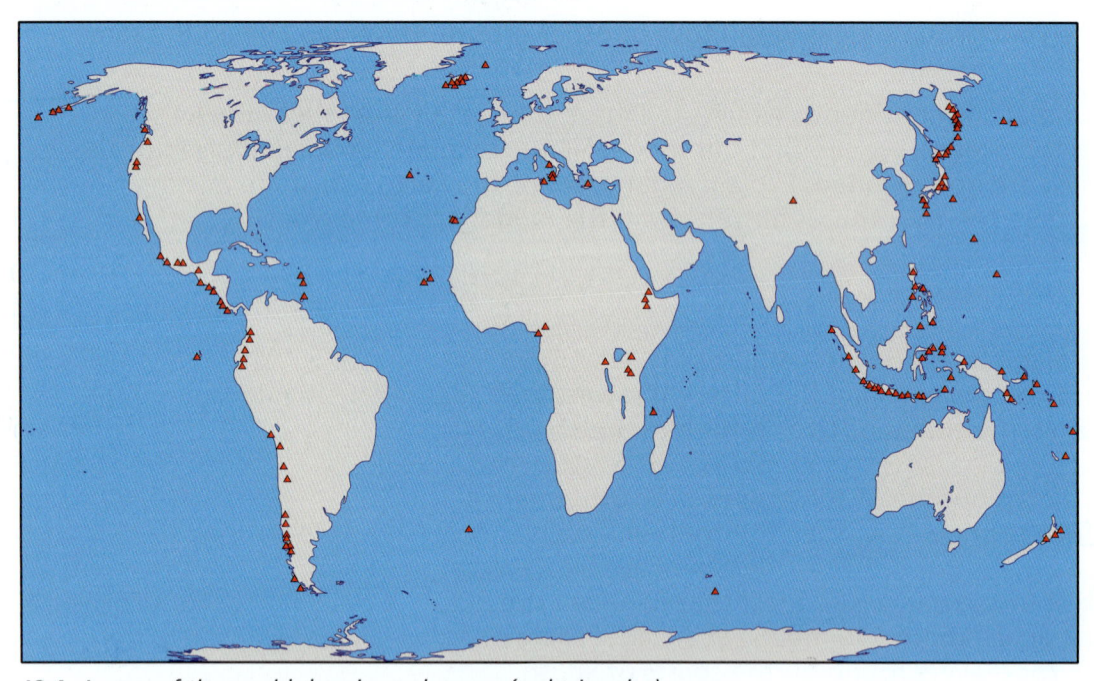

12.4 *A map of the world showing volcanoes (red triangles).*

Some of this evidence was produced unexpectedly. In the 1960s, a network of detectors that could record small vibrations in the Earth's crust was placed around the world. These detectors were intended to monitor the testing of nuclear bombs, which caused particular patterns of vibrations. But they also detected vibrations due to earthquakes and volcanoes. These detectors produced the first detailed map of regions where most earthquakes and volcanoes occurred naturally, and helped produce the first map of Earth's tectonic plate boundaries.

The western coast of South America forms the edge of a tectonic plate. This plate is moving towards and pushing against a tectonic plate under the Pacific Ocean, which is being pushed below the continent of South America. Large forces build up at these plate boundaries, causing earthquakes and volcanoes.

12.1

In fact nearly all volcanoes and most large earthquakes are found along plate boundaries. This provides strong evidence for the movement of tectonic plates.

> **Making links**
>
> In Stage 7, you may have learned about plate boundaries. They are important in linking the evidence of volcanoes and earthquakes to the theory of plate tectonics.
>
> a) Describe how fold mountains may also occur at a plate boundary.
> b) Explain why it is easy to predict the places on Earth where earthquakes are likely to occur, but not easy to predict when they will occur.

Activity 12.2: The Great Rift Valley

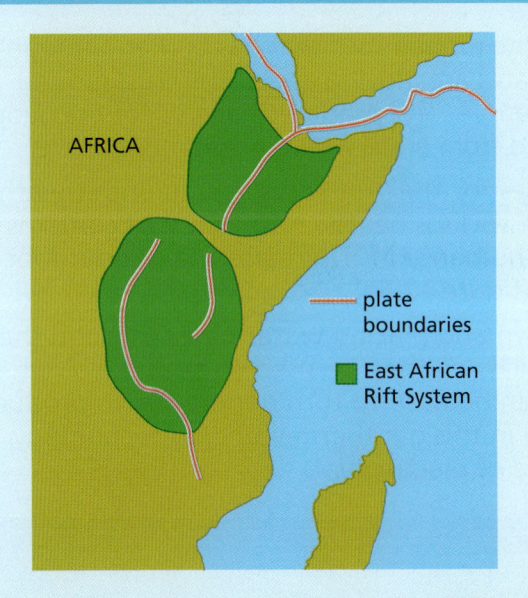

a   b

12.5 a *A map of East Africa with an area marked that is called the East African Rift System.* **b** *One part of this area.*

The East African Rift System is an area where scientists think that a tectonic plate is splitting into two new plates, forming a new plate boundary.

A1 The plate appears to be breaking into two pieces that are moving apart. Predict what types of observable events are likely to happen in this area.

A2 Suggest why deep valleys and lakes are forming along the plate boundary as it develops.

A3 Describe the timescale over which the new plates will move apart.

Evidence for plate tectonics   **215**

5 Look at figure 12.4.

  a) Describe *three* areas where large numbers of volcanoes are found.

  b) Suggest why these areas have large numbers of volcanoes.

6 Iceland is an island in the North Atlantic Ocean. Iceland sits on the boundary of two tectonic plates that are moving apart. Explain why there are a large number of volcanoes in Iceland.

7 If tectonic plates did not exist, and the whole of the Earth's crust was one solid piece, would there be no volcanoes, some volcanoes or many volcanoes? Explain your answer.

Science in context: Making use of plate tectonics

Iceland is an island that has formed as a result of the molten rock that has broken through the Earth's crust at a plate boundary where the plates are moving apart. The crust is quite thin under Iceland and there are many active volcanoes. This produces hazards for the people of Iceland; sometimes people have to be evacuated from areas where a volcano is active.

However, people in Iceland have found many uses for the 'hot rocks' found underneath the island. Water that circulates through the hot rocks is heated naturally and contains many minerals that are believed to be good for human skin. There are natural outdoor baths that people use, such as the Blue Lagoon (figure 12.6a).

Another use is to provide energy. By drilling down and placing water pipes through the hot rocks, energy is transferred to the water which can then be used to heat buildings. Water that is heated so that it becomes steam can be used to turn generators to produce electricity (figure 12.6b). Iceland leads the world in this geothermal energy technology, which is a renewable resource and a clean source of electricity.

12.6 **a** The Blue Lagoon, where people bathe in the hot, mineral-rich water. **b** A geothermal power plant.

1. Evaluate whether geothermal technology could be used to generate electricity all around the world instead of fossil fuels such as gas or oil.

   You should consider the advantages and disadvantages, and potential environmental impacts of the technology in your answer.

12.1

Fossils

Fossils form over many millions of years when the remains of dead animals and plants are preserved in layers of sedimentary rock. One very important fact to remember is that the fossil forms at the place the animal or plant died. When we find a fossil within layers of rock on a hillside, we can be fairly certain that the living thing was alive near the area where the fossil is found. Changes in rock layers, or earthquakes, or the action of glaciers may move rocks small distances, but not over hundreds of kilometres.

> **Making links**
>
> You may have learned about how fossils are formed.
>
> a) Describe the process that causes fossils to form.
>
> b) Explain why fossils are mostly found in sedimentary rocks.

Figure 12.7a shows the fossil of a plant, a tree fern called *Glossopteris*. Figure 12.7b is an image showing what scientists think *Glossopteris* looked like when it was alive. This plant is now extinct – there have been no living examples of it for many millions of years.

12.7 a *Glossopteris fern fossil.* **b** *What the tree fern looked like when it was alive*

> **Key terms**
>
> **fossils:** remains of dead organisms from many millions of years ago that have solidified due to the pressure of sedimentary rocks forming above them.
>
> ***Glossopteris***: plant that lived on Pangaea but became extinct over 175 million years ago; fossils found today provide evidence for plate movement.

Glossopteris is interesting because fossils of it have been found in South America, Africa, southern Asia, Antarctica and Australia. The only sensible explanation for this is that these places must have been joined together at the time *Glossopteris* ferns lived on Earth. Figure 12.8 is a map of how scientists think some of the Earth's tectonic plates were once joined together. The shaded bands show where fossils of different species of animals and plants have been found.

Evidence for plate tectonics

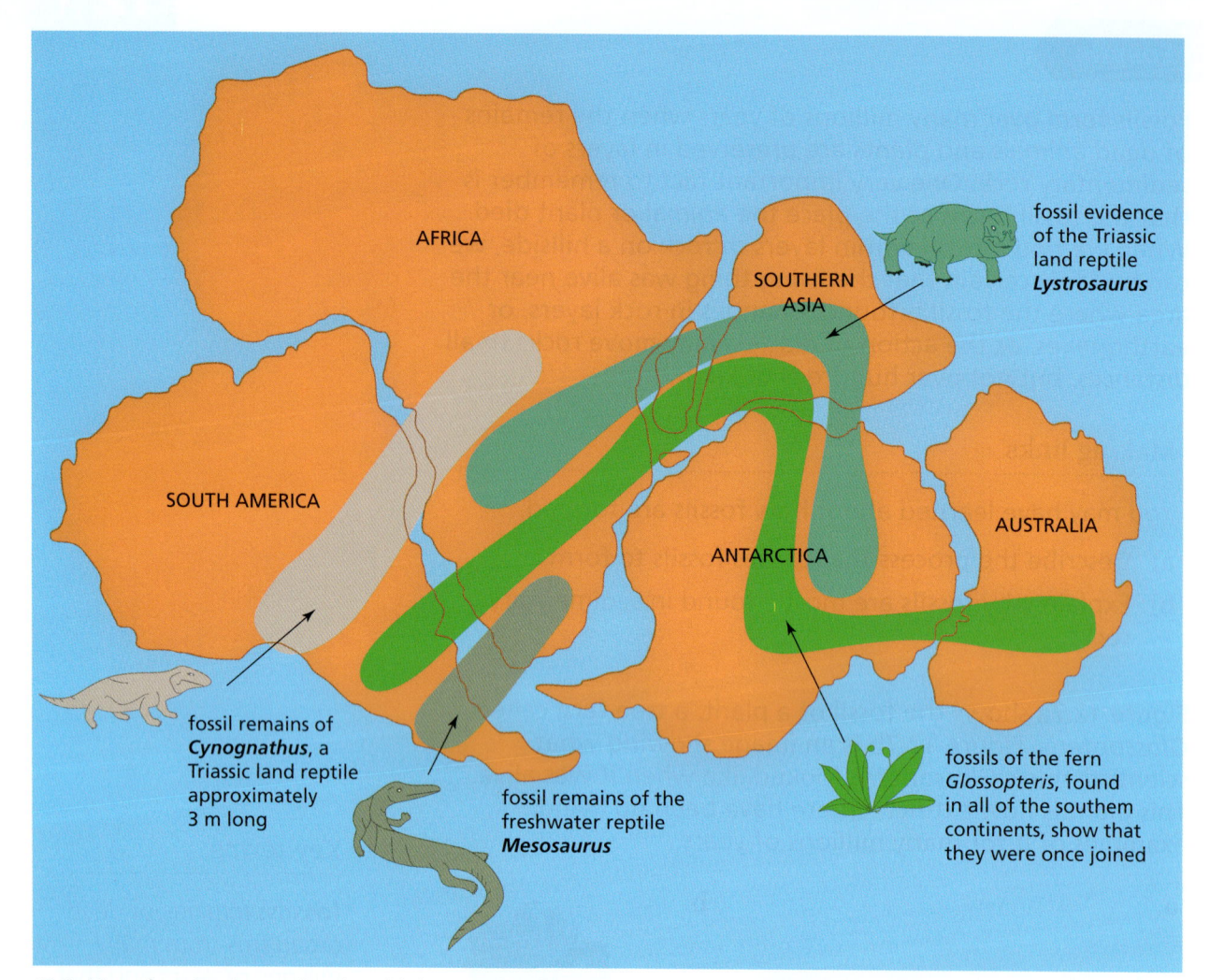

12.8 Map showing how scientists think tectonic plates were once joined together and the areas where fossils of different living things have been found.

> **Key terms**
>
> **Cynognathus**: reptile that lived on Pangaea but became extinct over 175 million years ago; fossils found today provide evidence for plate movement.
>
> **Lystrosaurus**: reptile that lived on Pangaea but became extinct over 175 million years ago; fossils found today provide evidence for plate movement.
>
> **Mesosaurus**: reptile that lived in fresh water on and near Pangaea but became extinct over 175 million years ago; fossils found today provide evidence for plate movement.

12.1

Activity 12.3: Investigating which fossils can provide evidence of plate tectonics

The table lists some species of animals and plants that have been found as fossils in at least two different continents.

Species	Habitat?	Found on which continent(s)?	When did it live?	Can it be used as evidence?	Reason
Fern *Glossopteris*	Land	South America, Africa, Asia, Antarctica and Australia	300 million years ago	Yes	It was a plant whose fossil has been found on different continents and could not move on its own or cross oceans
Reptile *Lystrosaurus*					
Blue whale					
Reptile *Cygnonathus*					
Bird-like dinosaur *Archaeopteryx*					

A1 Complete the table in Worksheet 12.1d by researching information and deciding whether each type of fossil can or cannot be used as evidence of plate tectonics. The table includes an empty row for you to use to insert your answer for question A3.

A2 Record your reason for each decision in the last column of the table.

A3 Research a different species of organism that has been found as a fossil and can be used to support plate tectonics. Add this to the final, empty row of the table and describe the reason you found for it, providing evidence.

8 List *three* living things other than *Glossopteris* that provide fossil evidence for the movement of tectonic plates.

9 Name the land-based animal in figure 12.8 that lived in what we now know as South America and Africa.

10 Suggest reasons why we can only use fossils of land animals, freshwater animals and plants as evidence for the movement of tectonic plates.

11 Suggest why it is important that we can only consider fossils of living things that are now extinct as evidence of plate tectonics.

Evidence for plate tectonics

Magnetic materials

> **Making links**
>
> You should have learned in Stage 8 Chapter 10 about magnetic fields and how the Earth produces a magnetic field.
>
> a) Describe briefly how you could show the magnetic field lines around a bar magnet using iron filings.
>
> b) Name the piece of equipment you could use to demonstrate that the Earth has a magnetic field.

Scientists investigating the seabed of the Atlantic Ocean discovered something quite unexpected. The rocks under the centre of the ocean displayed 'striped' magnetic patterns. The explanation for this provided more evidence for plate movement.

When molten rock breaks through a weak spot in the seabed, it rapidly cools to form a type of rock called **basalt**. Basalt contains quantities of minerals that can be magnetised. The core of the Earth acts as a strong magnet, causing the rapidly cooling rock under the ocean to produce a magnetic pattern that aligns with the magnetic field of Earth.

Scientists found that there were 'stripes' of rock in the seabed that ran parallel to the plate boundary under the Atlantic Ocean. One stripe would have a **magnetic alignment** in one direction, and the next stripe would have a magnetic alignment in the opposite direction. The explanation for this is that the Earth's magnetic field reverses direction from time to time, so that a layer of rock that forms after a **magnetic field reversal** contains atoms that line up in the opposite direction. By investigating the stripes of rock on the seabed, scientists determined that there had to be a plate boundary under the ocean, where the plates were moving apart. Fresh molten rock rises into the gap between the plates and cools. The solid rock moves away from the boundary as the tectonic plate moves. When the Earth's magnetic field reverses, the next stripe of rock forms at the plate boundary. Figure 12.9 illustrates this process.

> **Key terms**
>
> **basalt**: a type of rock that contains quantities of minerals that can be magnetised.
>
> **deduce**: arrive at a logical conclusion based on available information.
>
> **magnetic alignment**: occurs where rocks that are magnetised produce magnetic fields that line up with the Earth's magnetic field.
>
> **magnetic field reversal**: process where the direction of Earth's magnetic field changes to be in the opposite direction.

Plate tectonics

12.1

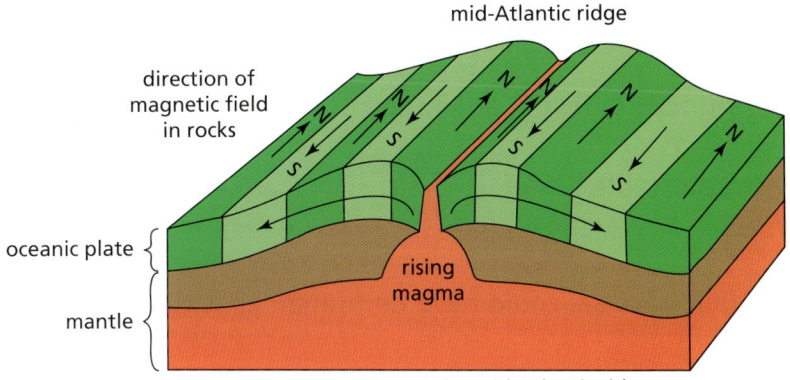

12.9 *Magnetic stripes in rocks produced at a plate boundary.*

Scientists can estimate the ages of rock layers by investigating the direction in which different layers of rock align magnetically. By estimating the amount of time that passes between reversals of the Earth's magnetic field, scientists can count the stripes between the plate boundary and the coastline of a continent and **deduce** how long ago the continents were linked.

We do not understand fully what happens during a magnetic field reversal, as the process of changing can take thousands of years and the time interval between changes varies from a few thousand years to over a million years. Scientists have used a wide range of evidence to conclude that the Earth's magnetic field has reversed 182 times in the last 83 million years. The average time between reversals is about 450 000 years.

Activity 12.4: Magnetic field reversals

In this activity you will investigate how to model Earth's magnetic field and predict how humans and animals may be affected by the next reversal in the direction of the field.

1. Use a compass to observe the direction of the Earth's magnetic field.
2. Use a bar magnet with the compass to model the Earth's magnetic field. Check that the bar magnet is placed so that the compass points in the same direction as in step 1.
3. In your group, decide how you could model a full reversal in the Earth's magnetic field. Predict how you need to move the bar magnet to model this.
4. Test your prediction by making the move. Has it produced the correct result? If not, how do you need to change the placement of the bar magnet to make the field reversed?
5. There is more than one way to move the bar magnet to model a field reversal. Suggest a second way to do this and test the outcome.

A1 Which pole of the magnet did you need to bring closer to the compass to make it model the Earth's magnetic field?

A2 Suggest what magnetic pole is near Earth's geographic north pole. Explain your answer.

Evidence for plate tectonics

A3 Write down your method for modelling a field reversal. Did this produce the planned effect?

A4 Write down an alternative method for modelling a field reversal. Did this produce the planned effect?

A5 A number of animals are known to be able to detect the Earth's magnetic field and use it to navigate. Research these animals and suggest the effect a magnetic field reversal would have on them.

A6 Describe the effects a magnetic field reversal could have on human activities.

12 Name *two* metals that can be magnetised and are found in the Earth's core.

13 A student suspends a bar magnet in a freely moving cradle and allows it to align to the Earth's magnetic field. The magnet's north pole points towards the Arctic region of Earth. What is the polarity (north or south) of the Earth's magnetic field in the Arctic?

14 If the magnetic field of Earth changes on average once every 450 000 years, and observations of rocks on the seabed show that there have been 120 reversals of magnetic field since two continents started to separate, how long ago were the continents still joined together?

15 Explain why using the number of magnetic field reversals to calculate the time when continents were joined together is not an accurate piece of evidence. Suggest what other types of evidence could be investigated and used to support the calculations.

12.1

Key facts:

- ✔ The scientific theory of plate tectonics is supported by a number of types of evidence.
- ✔ The shapes of the coastlines of continents that are far apart suggest that these continents were once joined together.
- ✔ Rock layers in coastlines that are now thousands of kilometres apart match up, suggesting these coastlines were once joined together.
- ✔ Earthquakes and volcanoes occur much more frequently in areas that are boundaries between two tectonic plates, suggesting that the plates are moving.
- ✔ Fossils of particular species of extinct animals and plants that could not cross oceans have been found in different continents, suggesting that the continents were once joined together.
- ✔ The Earth's magnetic field reverses from time to time, causing different arrangements of magnetic materials in stripes moving outwards from plate boundaries.

Check your skills progress:

- I can describe the evidence for plate tectonics including matching coastlines and rock layers, patterns of earthquakes and volcanoes, fossils and magnetic alignment of rocks moving outwards from a plate boundary.
- I can describe how some of this evidence was found unexpectedly.
- I can use models and analogies such as jigsaw puzzles to describe how matching coastlines provide evidence for plate tectonics.

Evidence for plate tectonics

Chapter 12 . Topic 2
Explaining plate movement

You will learn:
- To explain how convection currents cause tectonic plate movement
- To describe the model of plate tectonics and some of its strengths and weaknesses

Starting point

You should know that...	You should be able to...
The Earth's crust is divided into a number of tectonic plates that 'float' on the mantle	Use models and analogies to describe the theory of plate tectonics
The theory of plate tectonics is supported by evidence including matching coastlines, earthquakes and volcanoes, fossils and magnetic patterns in rock	Describe patterns in results

Convection currents

Particles in liquids that are heated rise upwards, and particles that are cooling fall downwards. These movements are called convection currents and are best observed in an experiment.

The diagram you will draw at the end of Activity 12.5 shows how particles in a liquid move due to the heating and cooling in convection currents.

Key term

mantle: deep layer of molten rock underneath the Earth's crust.

The effect of convection currents on tectonic plates

Scientists believe that under the Earth's crust is a very deep layer called the **mantle**. The rock in the mantle is not a runny liquid like water, it is more like a sticky, stretchy substance that can flow, but only very slowly.

At the centre of Earth is a hot, metal core containing iron and nickel. This is a powerful source of heat that causes convection currents to form in the mantle outside the core. This results in the surface of the mantle moving. We can think of tectonic plates in the Earth's crust as 'floating' on the surface of the mantle (figure 12.10). As the mantle moves, it pulls the tectonic plates with it.

Plate tectonics

12.2

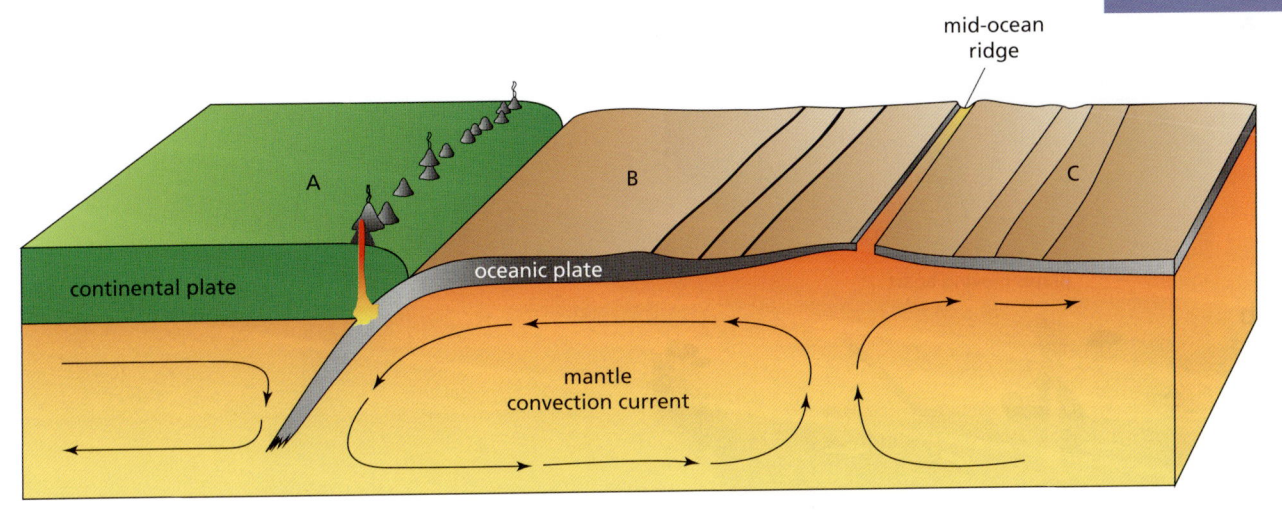

12.10 *Convection currents move tectonic plates.*

There are nine major tectonic plates that form most of the crust of Earth. There is a plate boundary between each pair of plates. You will remember from Stage 7 Chapter 10 that there are different types of plate boundary (figure 12.11):

- Where two plates are moving apart, molten rock rises to fill the gap between the plates, which cools to form new rock attached to the plates (figure 12.11a).

- Where two plates push together, they can either both push upwards to form fold mountains, or one plate rises above the other, forming volcanoes and causing earthquakes (figures 12.11b, c).

- Where two plates slide past each other, earthquakes occur as a result of the friction forces between the rock layers as they rub together (figure 12.11d).

Explaining plate movement 225

a

ridge

plates moving apart

b

one plate pushes towards and rises above another plate

c

crust   mantle

d

earthquakes

plates sliding along each other

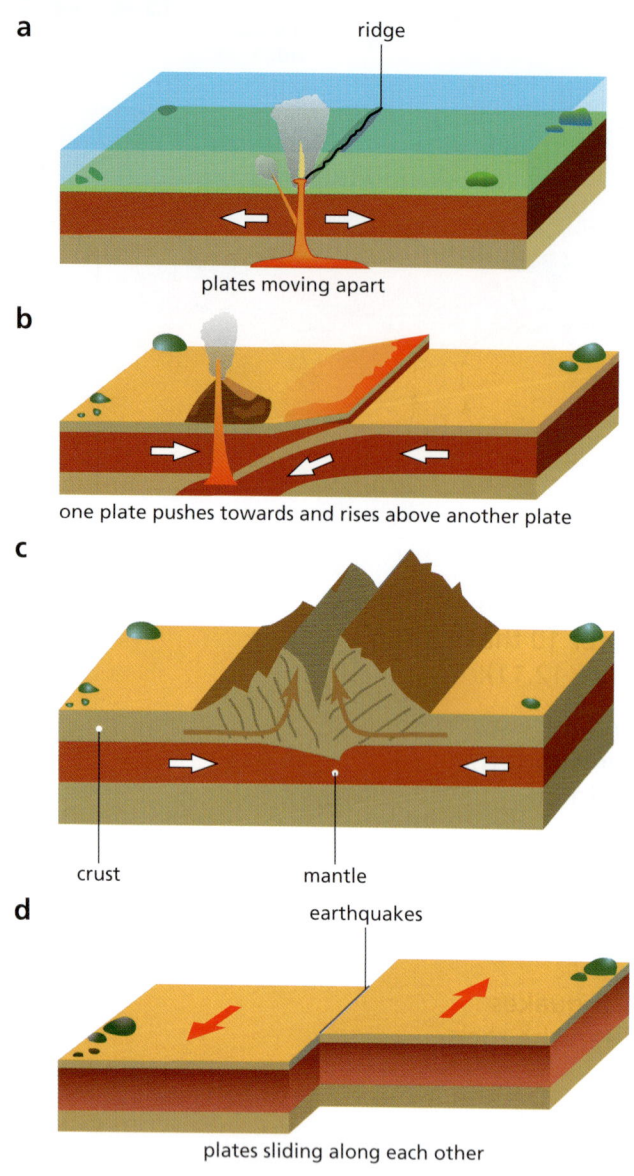

12.11 *Types of boundaries between tectonic plates.*

> **1** Figure 12.10 shows three tectonic plates and two different kinds of plate boundary. Describe the direction of movement of plates **A** and **B**.
>
> **2** Describe the direction of movement of plates **B** and **C**.
>
> **3** Suggest why it is difficult to find direct evidence that there are convection currents in the Earth's mantle.
>
> **4** The Earth is shaped like a ball. At some plate boundaries, two plates push towards each other. Describe how the Earth's shape means that if there are plates that push together, there must also be plates that are moving apart.

226   Plate tectonics

12.2

Key facts:

✔ Heating a liquid in one area causes particles of the liquid to rise upwards, spread outwards and then fall back down in an area where the liquid cools.

✔ This movement due to heating is called a convection current.

✔ The Earth's core causes heating in parts of the mantle, creating convection currents.

✔ These convection currents are responsible for the movement of tectonic plates.

Check your skills progress:

- I can make predictions based on my knowledge of convection currents and plate tectonics.
- I can carry out practical work safely.

Explaining plate movement

End of chapter review

Quick questions

1. Which of the following can be used as evidence for plate tectonics?
   (a) fossils
   (b) rock layers on coastlines
   (c) magnetic materials in rocks
   (d) all three of the above

2. There are several ways in which thermal energy can be moved in and between substances. Which of the following explains how tectonic plates move?
   (a) radiation
   (b) conduction
   (c) convection
   (d) all three of the above

3. Which of the following types of animals have fossils that can provide evidence of the movement of tectonic plates?
   (a) sea fish
   (b) birds
   (c) freshwater fish
   (d) mammals that swim in the sea

4. Which type of plate boundary is usually found under oceans?
   (a) where two plates push together so that one goes beneath the other
   (b) where two plates push together so that both rise upwards
   (c) where two plates move sideways past each other
   (d) where two plates move apart

5. Name the supercontinent from which the continents we see today formed.
   (a) Pangaea
   (b) Oceania
   (c) Antarctica
   (d) Africa

6. (a) Name *two* extinct species of living things that provide evidence for plate tectonics.

   (b) Outline briefly how these living things provide evidence for plate tectonics.

7. Scientists can explain how tectonic plates move because of heat produced from inside the Earth.

   (a) Describe how heat rising from the Earth's core through the mantle causes molten rock to move.

   (b) Figure 12.12 shows two plates that are moving apart. Draw arrows to show how the mantle moves under these plates.

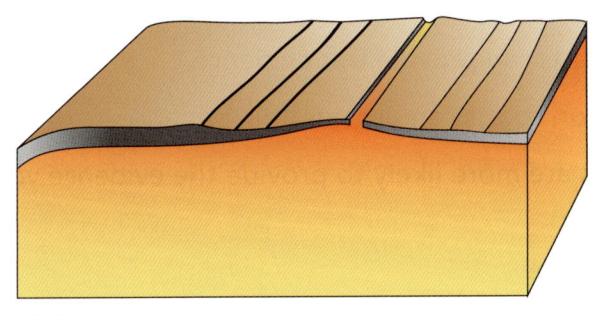

   12.12

Connect your understanding

8. Iceland is located on a plate boundary.

   (a) Describe evidence that shows how we can be sure that Iceland is on a plate boundary.

   (b) Is Iceland likely to be a good location to find fossil evidence for plate tectonics?

   (c) Give *two* reasons for your answer to part (b).

9. A scientist suggests that the continent containing Australia was once joined to Antarctica as part of a supercontinent.

   (a) Examine the shapes of Australia and Antarctica and say whether you agree with this suggestion.

   (b) Explain your answer.

   (c) Describe *three* other types of evidence you would look for to support your answer.

10. Magnetic fields can provide evidence for plate tectonics.

    (a) Describe how you could show that the Earth has a magnetic field.

    (b) We know that the direction of the Earth's magnetic field reverses once every 400 000 to 500 000 years. Explain how we know this.

    (c) Describe how the Earth's magnetic field affects basalt rocks that form from molten rock.

    (d) Use your answers to (a), (b) and (c) to explain how magnetic fields can provide evidence for plate tectonics.

11. The coasts of continents can provide evidence for plate tectonics.

    (a) Describe how the shapes of coasts can provide this evidence.

    (b) Describe how the rocks found on coasts can provide this evidence.

    (c) Suggest why sedimentary rocks are more likely to provide the evidence you described in (b).

Challenge question

    (d) Explain how sedimentary rocks on coasts may contain another type of evidence for plate tectonics.

Chapter 13
Climate change

Different places on Earth experience frequent extreme weather events such as very high winds, high rainfall in a short space of time, or long spells of extreme heat with no rainfall. With little or no warning, people can have their homes destroyed or their own lives threatened. Scientists predict that as the Earth's climate warms, there will be more of these events and they will get more extreme. In this chapter we look at a natural cycle, the carbon cycle, and how it has been affected by human activities, and consider some of the effects of climate change.

You will learn about:
- The carbon cycle, including the natural parts of the cycle and the parts affected by human activities
- The measured and predicted effects of climate change

You will build your skills in:
- Planning investigations
- Making risk assessments
- Deciding what equipment to use for investigations
- Describing the use of science in society, industry and research
- Evaluating issues using scientific understanding
- Discussing the global environmental impacts of some uses of science

Chapter 13 . Topic 1
The carbon cycle

You will learn:
- To describe how photosynthesis, respiration, feeding, decomposition and combustion make up the carbon cycle

Starting point

You should know that...	You should be able to...
The Earth's climate can change due to a change in the mixture of gases in the atmosphere	Plan an investigation while considering independent, dependent and control variables
Carbohydrates including glucose are stores of energy for animals and plants	Make risk assessments for practical work
	Make a conclusion from results

Photosynthesis and feeding

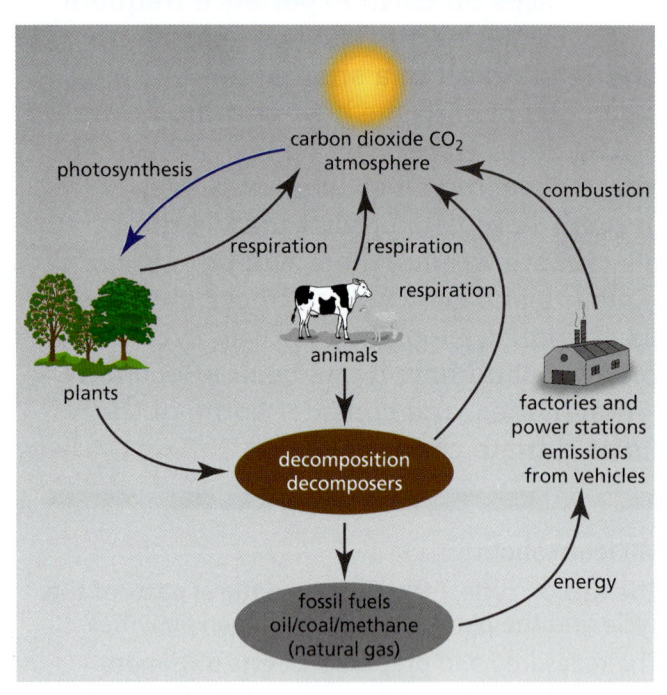

13.1 *Photosynthesis forms part of the carbon cycle.*

232   Climate change

13.1

In photosynthesis, plants use energy from sunlight to create food in the form of sugars from carbon dioxide taken from the air and water.

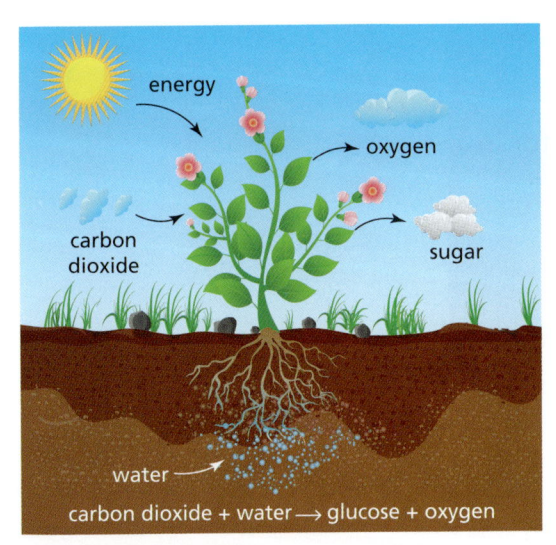

13.2 *Photosynthesis.*

The overall reaction involved is

carbon dioxide + water → glucose + oxygen

Note two very important aspects of this chemical reaction:

1. Plants make their own food in this way in parts of cells (organelles) called chloroplasts. Other organisms including animals and bacteria lack chloroplasts and so do not make their own food. They have to find food from other sources to provide the energy they need to live. This is why so many animals eat plants. Some animals eat other animals, but those other animals will have eaten plants, so the energy all animals need comes mainly from plants. One way or another, plants and animals get the energy they need to live from **nutrition**.

2. Photosynthesis is a very important reaction when considering climate change. In photosynthesis, carbon dioxide is taken out of the atmosphere and replaced by oxygen. Plants therefore act as a natural way of storing carbon dioxide, also called a **sink**.

Making links

In Stage 9 Biology, you learnt that photosynthesis occurs in plant cells called chloroplasts.

a) Name the substance present in chloroplasts that has to be present for photosynthesis to occur.

b) Describe the source of energy needed for photosynthesis.

Key terms

nutrition: life process by which plants and animals take in and break down substances and use them to get the nutrients needed for other life processes.

sink: something that takes in and stores significant quantities of a particular substance (for example, plants act as a sink for carbon dioxide).

The carbon cycle   233

1. Name the gas that is a reactant in photosynthesis.

2. Describe how the carbon atoms are present in photosynthesis. Which reactant contains carbon and which product contains carbon?

3. Explain why photosynthesis is an important factor in climate change.

4. Suggest why strategies to reduce the effects of climate change usually include plans to grow more plants.

Respiration

Respiration is a general name given to the process by which living organisms release energy through the conversion of glucose and oxygen to carbon dioxide and water. In eukaryotic organisms respiration takes place in parts of cells called **mitochondria**.

In plants, the respiration is usually aerobic respiration, meaning that oxygen and sugars are the reactants. The overall chemical reaction involved is

glucose + oxygen → carbon dioxide + water

Plants respire at all times, as they need the energy from sugars to stay alive. No sunlight is needed for respiration, so plants respire at night as well as during the day. This process releases carbon dioxide into the air.

Animals also respire at all times, and mostly use aerobic respiration, just like plants:

glucose + oxygen → carbon dioxide + water

This reaction releases carbon dioxide into the air.

In most bacteria, aerobic respiration also occurs, producing carbon dioxide and water just as in plants and animals.

Many forms of bacteria and other organisms use dead plants and animals as sources of energy for respiration. The plant or animal's body is **decomposed** by bacteria and other organisms, releasing carbon dioxide to the atmosphere.

Note how aerobic respiration by all types of organisms results in carbon dioxide being added to the air. We say that respiration is a **source** of carbon dioxide, just as photosynthesis is a sink of carbon dioxide.

We can build up our knowledge of photosynthesis and respiration to create a core part of the carbon cycle:

Key terms

decomposition: process in which bacteria and fungi feed on dead animals and plants.

mitochondria: organelles (parts) in cells where respiration occurs.

respiration: process by which organisms release energy through the conversion of glucose and oxygen to carbon dioxide and water.

source: something that produces significant quantities of a particular substance (for example, animals and plants act as a source for carbon dioxide).

13.1

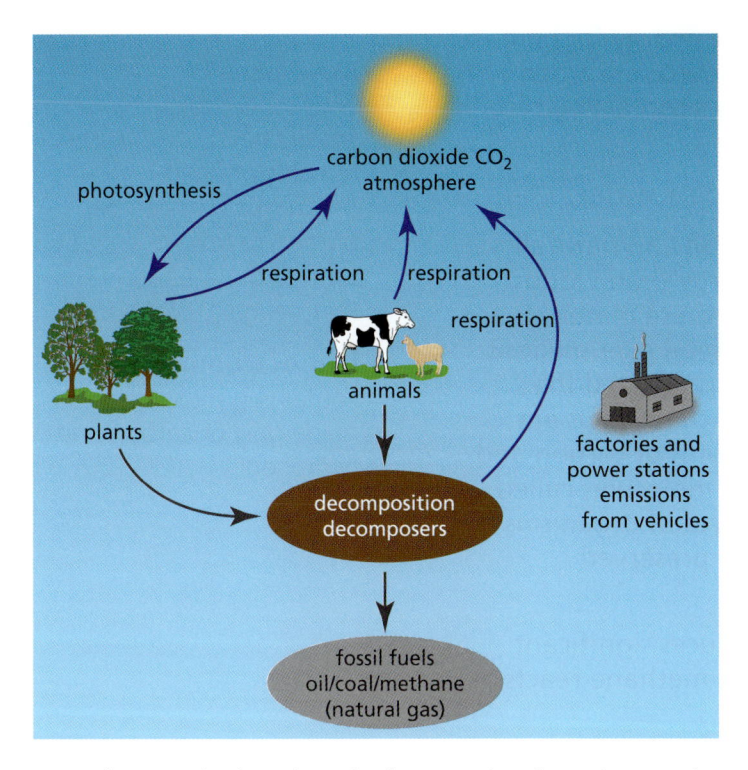

13.3 Photosynthesis and respiration together form the most important natural parts of the carbon cycle.

Each arrow represents a movement or transfer of carbon. Photosynthesis takes in carbon dioxide and acts as a sink. The different organisms that use respiration produce carbon dioxide and act as sources.

> **5** Describe how animals are sources of carbon dioxide both when they are alive, and after they have died.
>
> **6** During the daytime, plants produce both carbon dioxide and oxygen. During the night, plants produce carbon dioxide but not oxygen. Explain why this occurs.
>
> **7** 'Although plants produce carbon dioxide through respiration, they are still a very useful sink of carbon dioxide because they take in twice as much carbon dioxide as they produce.' What does this statement tell you about the reactions of photosynthesis and respiration in plants?

Making links

In Stage 8 Biology you may have learned that aerobic respiration is an essential reaction for living things.

a) In which organelles (parts) of cells does aerobic respiration take place?

b) Are these organelles present in plant cells, animal cells or both plant and animal cells?

Combustion

When considering climate change, we also need to understand the effects of human activities on the atmosphere. The history of human effects on the atmosphere goes back to the discovery of combustion, when early humans burned wood

The carbon cycle 235

and other materials from plants to produce energy for heat and for cooking food. Wood burning is a source of carbon dioxide, because wood is made of molecules containing carbon that react with oxygen:

wood + oxygen → carbon dioxide + water

Over time, humans discovered that coal, oil and natural gas (methane) produced much more energy than wood when they were combusted. All three of these materials are called **fossil fuels**, because they were formed over millions of years when layers of sedimentary rock squeezed the bodies of dead plants and animals. All of these fuels are made from molecules containing only atoms of carbon and hydrogen, so they are part of a family of molecules called **hydrocarbons**. Some skeletons or structures of organisms were preserved in this process, and these preserved organisms are what we call fossils.

The combustion of these fossil fuels produces significant amounts of carbon dioxide. For example, methane reacts as follows:

methane + oxygen → carbon dioxide + water

Coal and oil contain hydrocarbon molecules with more carbon atoms than methane, so burning coal and oil produces more carbon dioxide.

This process gives rise to another part of the carbon cycle.

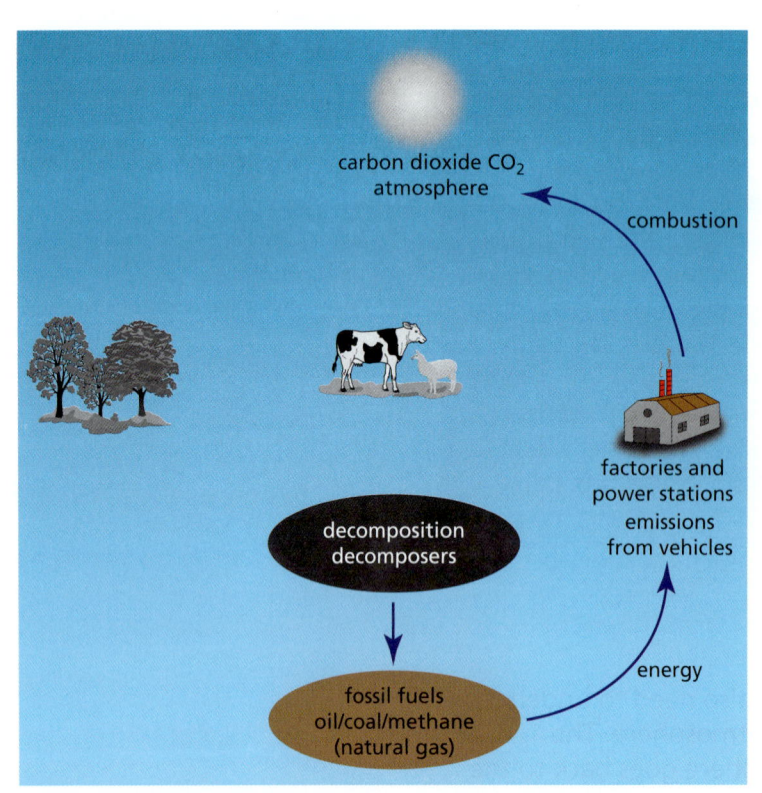

13.4 *Human activities also contribute to the carbon cycle.*

Key terms

fossil fuels: compressed remains of dead organisms that can be burned to release energy, including methane (natural gas), coal and oil.

hydrocarbon: substance containing molecules made only of carbon and hydrogen.

Making links

In Stage 8 and 9 Chemistry you may have learned that combustion is a chemical reaction that involves the transfer of energy.

a) Write a word equation that describes the combustion of coal (assume that coal is pure carbon).

b) Does this reaction take in or give out energy? Explain your answer.

Climate change

8. Which reaction, photosynthesis or respiration, is combustion most similar to? Explain the similarities and differences.

9. If an experiment catches fire in a school laboratory, there are different ways of stopping the fire. A class of students suggests the following methods. Analyse each suggested method, say whether it is a useful method and, if it is useful, explain how it would work.

   a) Spray water on the fire.
   b) Spray carbon dioxide gas on the fire.
   c) Spray oxygen on the fire.
   d) Place a thick blanket over the fire.

10. Scientists have proposed that companies which operate fossil-fuel burning power stations or factories could help to reduce their impact on climate change by planting large areas of new trees. Decide whether this is a good idea and explain your decision.

The complete carbon cycle

Figure 13.5 brings together the natural parts of the carbon cycle and the parts more recently created by human activities. Note that the substances involved in the cycle are mostly compounds containing carbon, not carbon as an element.

This diagram does not show a complete carbon cycle. There are other processes that you will study in the years ahead which also affect the amounts of carbon-containing substances. For example, some carbon dioxide in the atmosphere dissolves into the oceans. This means that the oceans are an important sink of carbon dioxide.

Climate scientists make predictions about how the Earth's climate will change by estimating the amounts of carbon dioxide produced or taken in by each of the processes shown in the carbon cycle. They can check these predictions by measuring the amount of carbon dioxide in the atmosphere at locations all around the world, and by using weather satellites to monitor temperatures in the different regions of Earth.

Over 97% of scientists agree that:
- The amount of carbon dioxide in the atmosphere is increasing.
- Much of this increase is due to human activities.
- This has already caused the average temperature to rise, and it will continue to rise until more carbon dioxide is taken out of the atmosphere than is put in.

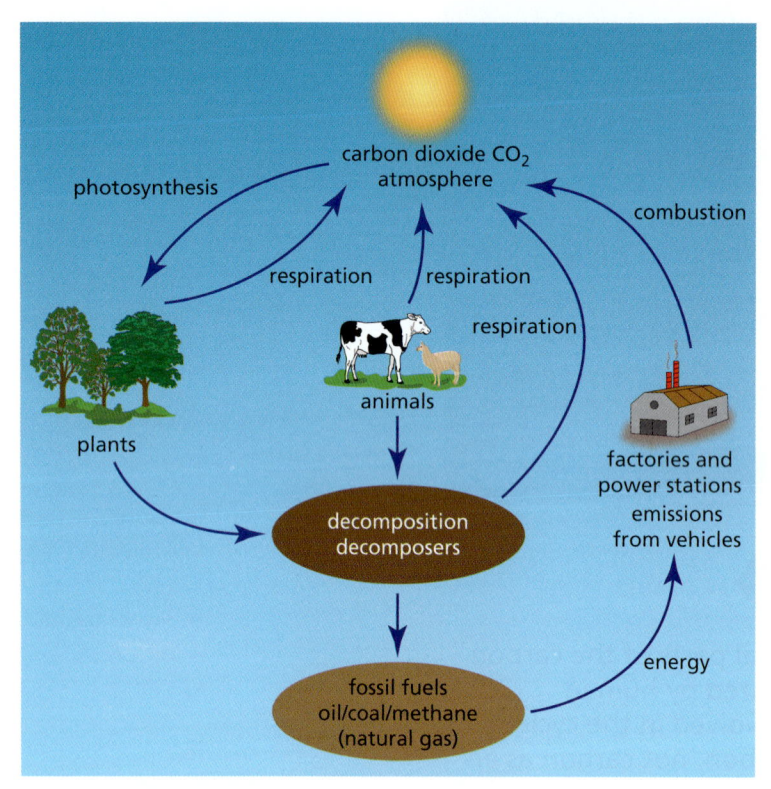

13.5 *The carbon cycle.*

> **11** Name the part of the diagram that is most affected by sunlight.
>
> **12** Name the parts of the carbon cycle that reduce the amount of carbon in the atmosphere.
>
> **13** Comment on the direction of the arrows that indicate human activities.
>
> **14** You know already about the effects of global warming on sea levels, due to the melting of polar ice sheets and glaciers. This melting also directly releases carbon dioxide into the atmosphere. Suggest where this released carbon dioxide comes from.

13.1

Key facts:

- ✔ Carbon-containing substances are important to all life on Earth.
- ✔ Photosynthesis in plants takes in carbon dioxide, water and sunlight and produces oxygen and energy-storing sugars such as glucose.
- ✔ Respiration is the process by which organisms release energy through the conversion of glucose and oxygen to carbon dioxide and water.
- ✔ Bacteria and fungi feed on dead animals and plants in the process called decomposition, which also releases carbon-containing substances.
- ✔ Combustion is the reaction of substances with oxygen, releasing energy.
- ✔ Combustion of carbon-containing substances produces carbon dioxide.
- ✔ Photosynthesis, respiration, decomposition and combustion all form parts of the carbon cycle.

Check your skills progress:

- I can plan investigations to test reactions in the carbon cycle including photosynthesis and respiration.
- I can decide what equipment is required to carry out an investigation and use it appropriately.
- I can carry out practical work safely and identify risks.

The carbon cycle

Chapter 13 . Topic 2

Impacts of climate change

You will learn:
- To describe the impacts of climate change, including sea level change, flooding, drought and extreme weather events
- To predict and test the outcome of a scientific enquiry
- To plan investigations
- To decide what equipment is needed for an investigation and use it correctly
- To evaluate the reliability of secondary information

Starting point

You should know that...	You should be able to...
Earth's climate is changing due to changes in the mixture of gases in the atmosphere	Use a range of secondary information sources to research and select relevant evidence to answer questions
Climate describes averages in atmospheric conditions over large areas and long periods of time, but weather describes atmospheric conditions in local areas over short periods of time	Make predictions based on scientific knowledge
The Earth's climate goes through a cycle, from warm periods to ice ages and back again, over many thousands of years	

Droughts

A **drought** occurs when there is very low rainfall in an area for a long period of time. This can affect plant and animal life in the area. It can also affect humans if the water that is stored in reservoirs or wells runs out.

As the Earth's average temperature rises due to increasing levels of greenhouse gases, particularly carbon dioxide, long-term patterns in weather are changing. This means that some areas of the Earth have greatly reduced levels of rainfall in the hottest months of the year, leading to droughts that are longer and more severe.

In some areas these droughts lead to large areas of dead or dry vegetation, which may catch fire. You may have seen coverage of these **wild fires** in places such as California, in the US, and Australia. These fires appear to be growing in intensity and are occurring more often.

Key terms

drought: unusually long period with low or no rainfall, causing water shortages.

wild fires: large fires in natural areas, which spread quickly due to dry and dead plants, often made worse in a drought.

Climate change

13.2

Science in context: Droughts in Malawi

Malawi is an African country that is affected regularly by drought. The land in Malawi varies greatly in height (between 0 m and 3000 m) and about one-fifth of the area of the country contains lakes. Lake Malawi extends for two-thirds of the length of the country. These factors together affect how much rainfall Malawi receives.

About 75% of the population in Malawi work on farms, so a year of very low rainfall that results in drought causes severe problems – there is less work for workers to do (so less income), and less food produced. A scientific study found that over a period of 55 years, there were four serious droughts and two severe droughts. A severe drought is where the government has to ask for help from other countries.

Science has an important role in analysing the effects of droughts and determining the causes. By analysing data from previous years, scientists can predict when changes in weather patterns may lead to drought before its effects take hold. This can help governments and people prepare so that the worst effects of drought can be reduced.

For example, the United Nations Food and Agriculture Organization has developed a project that aims to help 22 000 people in at-risk areas of Malawi. The project reacts to scientific forecasts of drought to distribute fast-growing and drought-tolerant crop seeds, and to vaccinate farm animals to prevent outbreaks of disease. The project also sets up small-scale irrigation (watering) systems and education to help reduce water wastage.

13.6 *In periods of drought, rivers run dry and the ground dries out.*

13.7 *Long, hot periods of drought lead to wild fires.*

13.8 *Lack of rain stunts the growth of maize plants in Malawi.*

Making links

You may have learned that plants and animals can be affected severely by drought.

a) In areas affected by drought, some wild plants continue to grow but crops are usually quite badly affected. Suggest why drought affects some plants and not others.

b) Suggest *two* ways in which animals living in areas affected by droughts can cope with the extreme conditions.

1 Many places have some years where there is less rainfall than average. Explain why experiencing low amounts of rainfall does not have to result in drought.

2 Explain why climate change caused by human activities can lead to more, longer droughts.

Impacts of climate change 241

3 Some areas of farmland that are more likely to experience droughts are supported by irrigation systems. These systems collect rainwater in areas that are generally wetter, and divert it by pipes, pumps and aqueducts (structures/bridges which carry water over areas of land) to the farmland. Suggest why this may not be a practical system to set up in some places.

Activity 13.1: Investigating the effects of drought

Your teacher will give you four plastic or waxed paper cups containing soil and a packet of bean seeds.

1 Your task is to demonstrate the effects of drought on plants by comparing the growth of bean seedlings that are given different amounts of water. Decide how you will set up the four pots to show the differences in growth. Think about how much water each pot should get and how often.
2 One of the cups should be regularly watered with normal amounts of water, so that you can compare the other pots to this one.
3 Decide what you will measure each day to show the differences in plant growth, if any are found.
4 Predict how each cup of seedlings will develop.
5 Observe the seedlings for up to 10 days. Record your measurements and observations each day. Include diagrams or photos in your observations.
6 Write a conclusion that describes the effects on seedling growth of different amounts of water.

A1 Which variables were controlled to make it a fair test? How were they controlled?
A2 What did you decide to measure and observe?
A3 Did any seedlings show very little or no growth? Suggest why this happened.
A4 Explain what effects drought can have on the growth of crops.

Floods

It is easy to see how a warmer average temperature can lead to hotter, drier spells of weather. What is not so obvious is that rising temperatures can also lead to more periods of heavier rainfall in some places. Longer spells of higher temperatures over oceans cause more water to be evaporated to form clouds. When these clouds pass over land, there is more water to fall as rain. Many countries around the world are finding that intense periods of heavy rainfall causes rivers to overflow and break through defences, causing flooding in built-up areas more often.

13.9 Towns near rivers can flood rapidly after periods of extreme rainfall.

13.2

Building **flood defences** such as higher river banks and using pumps to channel water away from built-up areas are expensive activities. Governments across the world will have to set aside more money to defend against floods as climate change continues.

> **4** Explain why increasing average temperatures can lead to flooding happening more often.
>
> **5** Some cities have spent large amounts of money on building higher river banks and walls to stop rivers causing flooding. This can protect the city but may also cause problems for places further down the river that have not flooded before. Suggest what problems may be caused and why.

Sea level change and sea flooding

You should remember from Stages 7 and 8 that increasing levels of carbon dioxide and other greenhouse gases in the atmosphere causes ice at the poles and in glaciers to melt faster. In turn this leads to rising sea levels. Countries with long coastlines and island countries are already experiencing these rising sea levels.

Examples where governments are already planning for rising sea levels:

* City of Osaka in Japan, where it is estimated that 5.2 million people may have to move to other places to live, because where they currently live will be under water as sea levels rise
* Shanghai, China, which is one of the cities most vulnerable to flooding due to a rising sea level
* Alexandria in Egypt, where 3 million people could be affected, as well as large areas of farming land in the Nile river delta

Key term

flood defences: walls, banks and other constructions designed to prevent flooding.

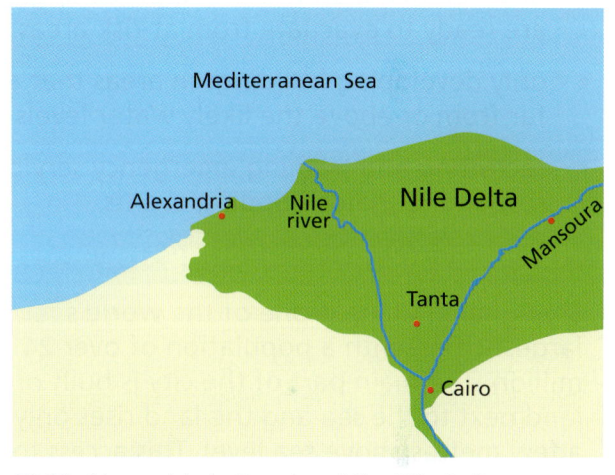

13.10 Alexandria in Egypt and the Nile Delta.

Figure 13.10 shows a map of the area around Alexandria. The city stands at the edge of the Nile Delta, a very large area of low-lying land. The Nile is Africa's longest river and it carries large amounts of soil, sand and organic matter along its length. As it approaches the Mediterranean Sea, the river spreads out and flows more slowly. The soil, sand and organic matter are deposited over a wide area, creating land that is rich in nutrients and ideal for farming.

Impacts of climate change 243

Because the land is low-lying, even small rises in sea levels will flood large areas. The shaded areas in figure 13.10 show the land that will be permanently flooded by 2070 if no flood defences are developed.

Because it takes time for the climate to change after the amount of carbon dioxide in the atmosphere changes, even if all countries now stopped producing more carbon dioxide, it would still take many years before the sea level reached a peak. This is because the effect of increased carbon dioxide on temperature takes time, often several years.

Governments of major coastal cities can prepare for sea level changes in a number of ways, including:

- building flood defences such as sea walls, moveable barriers, major new drainage channels and areas of land outside the city that flood water can be diverted towards
- developing warning systems that alert people at times the city is at increased risk (such as during spring tides or when major storms are approaching), so that people are ready to evacuate from at-risk areas
- only developing buildings in areas that are sufficiently far from or above the likely water levels
- recruiting and training emergency services ready to respond to major flooding events

Making links

In Stage 8 Chapter 11 you may have learned about the effects of climate change on island nations. Rising sea levels are of great concern to countries that contain groups of small islands, such as the Maldives and the Seychelles.

a) Suggest why these island nations are particularly worried about the effects of climate change.

b) Explain the difference between changing sea levels due to ice age cycles and the present changing sea levels.

Activity 13.2: Investigating the effects of climate change on Shanghai

Shanghai in China is one of the world's largest cities, with a population of over 24 million. The main part of the city is built on land next to the sea and the land rises only a few metres above sea level. This access to the sea has allowed Shanghai to become the world's busiest container port. It is also a global financial hub for major banks and investors.

13.11 *City skyline of Shanghai.*

A1 International teams of scientists have rated Shanghai as the world's most vulnerable city to the effects of climate change. Suggest how Shanghai could be affected by climate change.

A2 If the Earth's average temperature rises by 3°C then three-quarters of the population of Shanghai would need to move to avoid being flooded. Suggest *three* things that could be done to prevent this happening.

A3 Explain why governments need to plan many years ahead when working out how to respond to climate change.

A4 Find a map of Shanghai and investigate online how much of the city could be flooded if no defences were being built.

6 Explain why it is more difficult for less wealthy countries to prepare for the effects of climate change.

7 It has been suggested that if all countries stopped producing greenhouse gases in the next few years, then cities would not need to build defences against sea flooding. Explain why, even if this did happen, some flood defences would still need to be built.

8 Many cities around the world have developed near coastlines. Will all these cities be at risk from the effects of climate change? Explain your answer.

Other extreme weather events

The general effect of a rising average temperature is that the Earth's atmosphere acts as a store of more energy. Although the detail of what types and times of events are very difficult to predict, scientists are confident that the raised energy will mean there will be more extreme weather events.

What is an extreme weather event? This is something where one or more weather conditions are significantly different to the average or expected peak values. Examples we have already described include:

- drought
- floods

Other examples include:

- hurricanes, where wind speeds are over 33 m/s and can go as high as 70 m/s, accompanied by intense rainfall
- heat waves, where temperatures might be so high they threaten life
- cold spells, where temperatures are so low they threaten life

Some of these events can occur in most places around the world, such as flooding, but hurricanes tend to occur only in certain parts of the world due to the patterns of air circulation in the atmosphere and because of local conditions.

> **Making links**
>
> Remember the difference between climate and weather.
>
> Classify the following events or patterns as changes in climate or as weather events.
>
> a) hurricanes
>
> b) a rise in average temperature
>
> c) a heat wave
>
> d) a rise in sea level
>
> e) one day of flooding due to recent heavy rainfall

Activity 13.3: Investigating Hurricane Katrina

In August 2005, a powerful hurricane moved from the sea onto land along the south coast of the United States. Although many areas along the coast had walls designed to protect against sea flooding, these defences were broken by the power of Hurricane Katrina. Many people were evacuated from their homes before the storm reached the shore, but despite this, over 1800 people were killed. The cost of repairing the damage caused made it the costliest natural disaster in the history of the US.

13.12 *Thousands of homes were damaged by high winds, heavy rain and sea flooding.*

A1 Use internet research to find out facts about Hurricane Katrina. Make sure to record which websites you used for each fact and comment on whether you think each website is a reliable source of information. Include in your findings:

a) the estimated maximum strength of the winds produced by Katrina

b) why New Orleans was flooded when it had flood defences

c) the meaning of the term 'storm surge' and how it is connected with hurricanes

d) the estimated total cost of damage caused by the hurricane

A2 Some people have suggested that the power of Hurricane Katrina was worse because of global warming. Do you agree? Explain your answer.

A3 Decide whether you think there will be more or fewer storms like Katrina in the next 50 years. Explain your answer.

13.2

9 Not all coastal cities around the world need to prepare for hurricanes. Explain why.

10 Suggest some of the effects of a long spell of much higher temperatures than usual (a heat wave).

11 Give *two* reasons why the effects of a hurricane reaching land could be worse because of climate change.

12 Is it possible to say whether any one weather event was definitely caused by climate change? Justify your answer.

Key facts:
- ✔ Climate change is already having measurable effects on sea level and the frequency of extreme weather events.
- ✔ Extreme weather events include hurricanes, long spells of very heavy rainfall leading to flooding and long spells of low rainfall leading to droughts.
- ✔ Sea levels are rising and will continue to rise as a result of changes in climate.

Check your skills progress:
- I can make and test predictions about the effects of lack of water on plants.
- I can choose and use equipment for a scientific investigation.
- I can evaluate the reliability of secondary sources of information.

End of chapter review

Quick questions

1. What diagram shows the connections between photosynthesis, respiration, decomposition and combustion?

   a the nitrogen cycle

   b an energy level diagram

   c the carbon cycle

   d a pie chart showing the percentages of gases in the atmosphere

2. Name the process that involves cells in living organisms taking in oxygen and producing carbon dioxide.

   a photosynthesis   b respiration

   c combustion   d decomposition

3. Name the process that takes in carbon dioxide and produces oxygen.

   a photosynthesis   b respiration

   c combustion   d decomposition

4. Name the process that contributes significant amounts of carbon dioxide to the atmosphere due to human activities.

   a photosynthesis   b respiration

   c combustion   d decomposition

5. (a) Describe *two* effects that drought can have on plants.

   (b) Explain why droughts have a much greater effect on countries that raise most of their income from farming.

6. A local council is planning to build flood defences. To estimate the height of wall they need to build, they look at the local records and plan a wall that would just have prevented the highest flood on record in that area.

   (a) Explain why this height may not be enough.

   (b) Prepare an argument to present to the council to explain why climate change means they may need to build higher defences.

Connect your understanding

7. **(a)** Suggest *two* reasons why people often build cities near to coastlines.

   (b) Describe *two* effects of climate change that will most affect cities near to coastlines.

   (c) Suggest *three* ways in which people in cities can prepare for these effects.

8. **(a)** Look at the carbon cycle in figure 13.5. The parts of the cycle that have downwards-pointing arrows show carbon dioxide sinks. Explain what the term 'carbon dioxide sinks' means

   (b) What do the upwards-pointing arrows represent?

   (c) Describe the trend in the arrows that represent human activities.

   (d) Explain why this trend is important for the Earth's climate.

9. The table shows the average rainfall for a year for four different locations, taken over a 50-year time span. The second row shows the total rainfall for each region in 2018.

Location	1	2	3	4
Average rainfall per year (mm)	1200	600	200	2100
Total rainfall in 2018 (mm)	120	400	160	1900

   (a) Suggest which region or regions is/are most likely to have suffered a drought in 2018. Give a reason for your answer.

   (b) Give *two* effects of drought that affect people.

   (c) Explain why continuing climate change means people should expect more frequent and more severe droughts.

10. A student says that respiration is the reverse of photosynthesis.

    (a) Write the word equation for photosynthesis.

    (b) Write the word equation for respiration that the student is referring to.

    (c) Explain why the student is wrong. (Hint: think about other substances involved in the reactions.)

    (d) Which reaction helps to reduce the amount of carbon dioxide in the atmosphere?

    (e) Explain why the reaction described in part d may be important for our survival.

11. **Figure 13.13** shows an incomplete carbon cycle.

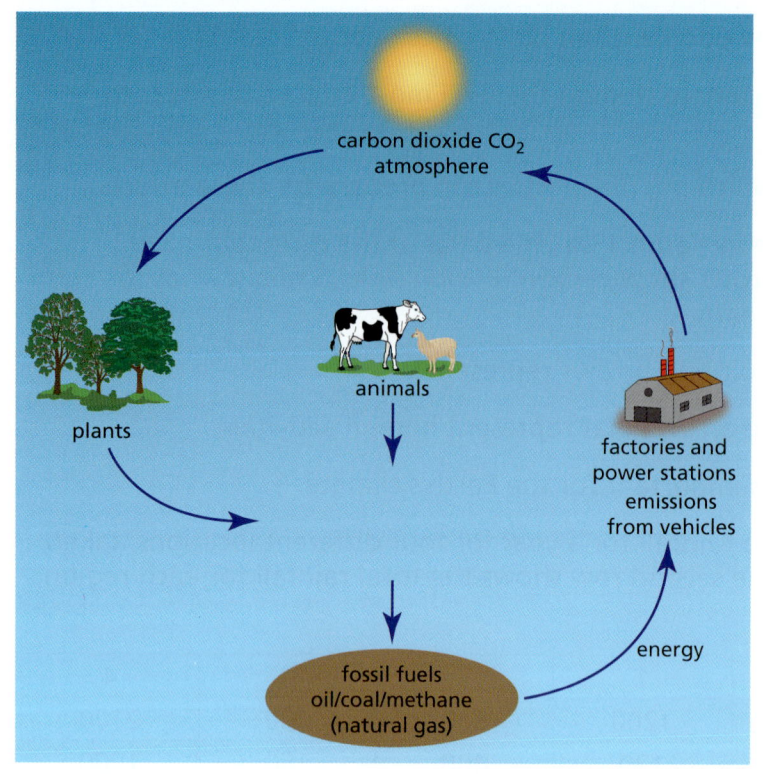

13.13 *The carbon cycle.*

(a) *Three* labels are missing from arrows or ovals. Complete these labels.

(b) *Three* arrows and their labels are missing. Draw in these arrows and label them with the name of the process involved.

(c) Use this diagram to explain why human activities are contributing to climate change.

Challenge question

12. Some scientists are working on methods of capturing the gases produced by human activities and reacting the carbon dioxide with substances so that it can be stored underground.

    (a) Suggest where this would appear on the carbon cycle diagram.

    (b) Predict the effect of this process on the rate of climate change.

14

Chapter 14
Astronomy

One of the reasons this scientific method developed was because, for thousands of years, humans have looked up at the night sky and wondered 'What is out there? Where have we come from?' With modern instruments, we are able to look across billions of light-years and find that we are all made of stars. The atoms that make up our bodies have come from the dust and gas that make stars and are made by stars. In this chapter we look at the clouds of dust and gas that form stars, and at some of the ideas scientists have to explain how the Moon formed and why the dinosaurs became extinct.

You will learn about:
- Ideas for how the Moon formed
- Ideas about how asteroids colliding with Earth could cause major changes in climate and lead to mass extinctions
- The clouds of dust and gas we call nebulae
- How stars form in some nebulae

You will build your skills in:
- Sorting, grouping and classifying information
- Describing how models reflect current scientific evidence and can change
- Evaluating the strength of evidence and how it supports, or contradicts, a prediction

Chapter 14 . Topic 1

Collisions

You will learn:
- To describe the theory for the Moon formation known as collision theory and its evidence
- To describe how an asteroid colliding with the Earth could cause climate change and mass extinction events
- To understand that models and analogies can change according to scientific evidence
- To describe the uses, strengths and limitations of models and analogies
- To use observations, measurements, secondary sources of information and keys, to organise and classify organisms, objects, materials, or phenomena

Starting point

You should know that...	You should be able to...
Our Solar System formed from a cloud of gas and dust, which clumped together as a result of the force of gravity	Describe the strengths and limitations of a model
Asteroids are made from rock thought to have formed at the same time as the rest of the Solar System	Describe how scientific hypotheses can be supported or contradicted by evidence
The tides on Earth are due to the Moon and the force of gravity	Sort, group and classify information

Ideas about how the Moon formed

After the Sun and planets started to form in our Solar System, it took at least 100 million years for the Moon to form. We know this because samples of rock from the Moon have been analysed and their age determined.

Scientists produced three main ideas for how the Moon formed.

- Idea 1: A rocky object, such as an asteroid, was pulled into orbit around the Earth because of the gravitational force of the Earth. This is called the **capture hypothesis**.

- Idea 2: The Moon formed at about the same time as the Earth, from the dust and gas of the solar nebula, and was pulled by gravity into orbit around the Earth. This is called the **co-formation hypothesis**.

- Idea 3: A large object roughly the same size and mass as the planet Mars, that had formed at about the same time as Earth, crashed into the early Earth and split the

Key terms

capture hypothesis: the idea that the Moon is a large asteroid that has been pulled into orbit around the Earth.

co-formation hypothesis: the idea that the Moon and Earth formed together, close to each other, at the same time.

collision hypothesis: the idea that a large object roughly the same size and mass as the planet Mars collided with the Earth, releasing rocks that were pulled together to form the Moon.

252 Astronomy

mass of rock into two objects – the Earth and the Moon. This is called the **collision hypothesis**.

As with all scientific ideas, scientists have looked for evidence to support or disprove each of these hypotheses. Some evidence for and against each idea is given in table 14.1.

Hypothesis	Evidence for	Evidence against
1 – Capture	• Some rocks that make up the Earth and Moon are similar, but there are some differences too. This would make sense if the Moon formed separately to the Earth.	• There are more similarities than differences between the rocks found on Earth and on the Moon. • When we look at asteroids that have been captured by other planets, they have unusual shapes and are not usually very round, but the Moon is very round. • The Moon is much bigger compared to Earth than the moons around other planets in the Solar System, so it is less likely for such a relatively large object to be captured by the Earth.
2 – Co-formation	• Some rocks that make up the Earth and Moon are very similar, and an object that formed close to the Earth at about the same time would mostly contain rocks that are similar. • The Moon is much bigger compared to Earth than the moons around other planets in the solar system, which may mean they formed at the same time.	• Some rocks on the Moon are different to Earth, but if they formed at the same time we would expect them to be exactly the same. • The Moon is less dense than the Earth, meaning both probably formed in different ways or places.
3 – Collision	• From studies of the other planets and moons in the Solar System, scientists think the early Solar System was a violent place, with many collisions between objects. A large object colliding with Earth is quite a likely thing to have happened then. • The colliding object would have caused the outer layers of Earth to move away until they were gradually gathered back together by the force of gravity. This would mean a large part of the Moon would have formed from rocks in the crust of the early Earth, producing some similar rocks, but also differences too (such as the Moon's lower density).	• Most models based on the collision theory predict that more than 60% of the Moon should be made up of the material that came from the colliding object. However, rock samples taken from the Moon suggest much less than 60% of the Moon is different in this way.

Table 14.1 *Ideas for how the Moon formed.*

1 Describe the evidence scientists can collect to support or contradict the different theories for the formation of the Moon.

2 Suggest why we may never know for certain how the Moon formed.

Activity 14.1: Evaluating different hypotheses

When more than one hypothesis for a process is supported by evidence, scientists evaluate each hypothesis and its evidence to decide which they think is the most likely. They also suggest how more investigations could be made to find more evidence that may support or contradict each hypothesis.

A1 Work in pairs. Your teacher will give you a worksheet containing a number of different statements. Cut these statements out so they can be sorted into groups.

A2 On a large sheet of paper, draw a table with four rows and three columns. Leave enough space in each cell of the table so that you can write a number of statements in each cell. The top row is for headings: Hypothesis, Evidence for, Evidence against.

A3 Identify which *three* statements are hypotheses. Arrange these in the first column.

A4 The remaining statements describe evidence that has been collected from scientific investigations. Discuss each statement with your partner. Sort the statements into two piles depending on whether the statement is useful evidence for any of the hypotheses. If a statement is not useful for any hypothesis, put it in a discard pile. When you have finished sorting the statements, put the discard pile to one side – for the next stage you will need only the useful statements.

A5 Now discuss the first hypothesis in your table. Arrange the useful evidence statements to show which of them support the hypothesis, and which contradict it. Make a written note for each statement in the correct row and column of the table.

A6 Repeat step 5 for each of the other hypotheses.

A7 Agree with your partner which hypothesis you think is most likely to be correct, based on the supporting and contradicting evidence.

A8 Identify one further investigation you think could help support or contradict your chosen hypothesis.

Making links

Stage 7 Topic 10.1 also evaluates a hypothesis (Wegener's hypothesis of continental drift).

a) What is the definition of a hypothesis?

b) Did Wegener have enough evidence to convince all scientists that his hypothesis was correct? Explain your answer.

c) Name the theory that was developed following Wegener's hypothesis.

14.1

The Moon and its evidence

So far, the evidence collected most strongly supports the collision hypothesis. A hypothesis that is supported by enough evidence to be accepted as the most likely explanation is developed further by scientists into a theory. We will discuss this collision theory in more detail, as well as what we know about the Moon and how the supporting evidence was collected.

Figure 14.1 shows a picture of the Moon as we see it from Earth.

> **Key term**
>
> **crater**: a roughly circular hole in the surface rock of a moon or planet caused by the impact of a large rock or asteroid.

14.1 *The Moon.*

Even simple photographs like these tell us a number of things about the Moon.

- It is very evenly round.
- The surface is grey and rocky.
- Some areas of the surface appear smooth, and other areas are covered by circular dips called **craters**.
- From Earth, we can only see one half of the surface – the same half points towards us at all times.

What do these facts tell us and what do they suggest?

- The roundness suggests the Moon has formed and been made stable mainly due to its own gravity.
- There appears to be no surface water and no life of any kind.
- There is no atmosphere.
- There are no volcanoes and no tectonic plates.
- The craters show that many smaller objects have collided with the surface of the Moon.

Collisions 255

- The Moon must rotate around its own axis at exactly the same speed as the Moon orbits the Earth. This suggests the orbit of the Moon around the Earth has been stable for a very long time – many hundreds of millions of years.

There have been many probes sent to the Moon to take photographs, measure its properties and sometimes collect samples of Moon rock and return them to Earth to be analysed. The most famous visits are those of the six Apollo missions that landed humans on the Moon in the late 1960s and early 1970s (figure 14.2).

14.2 *The Apollo 15 mission to the Moon was the first to take a powered 'car', the 'Lunar Rover'.*

Most of the probes sent to the Moon have been **robotic**, so they operate by themselves without a person needing to control them.

> **Key term**
>
> **robotic**: describes a device that works by itself, without a human needing to control its movements.

Activity 14.2: Explaining the collision theory

Work in pairs. You will need a large sheet of plain paper, a ruler and suitable pens and pencils to complete this activity.

- **A1** Use a pencil and ruler to divide the paper into four equally sized rectangles.
- **A2** In the final rectangle, sketch a diagram of the Earth and Moon as they are now.
- **A3** Use the other rectangles to draw the stages of the formation of the Moon according to the collision theory. Add arrows to show how the stages are ordered.
- **A4** Write a short description of what happens at each of your stages.
- **A5** Add descriptions of the evidence for each stage of the process.

3 Describe how the Moon is thought to have formed, using the collision theory.

4 Identify *one* strength and *one* limitation of the collision theory model for the formation of the Moon.

5 In the future, it is expected that humans will build places to live on the Moon. Suggest *three* problems that humans will have to overcome to do this.

6 Earth has one large moon. Jupiter has at least 67 moons.

   a) Suggest a reason why Jupiter has so many more moons.

   b) Scientists think the capture hypothesis is the most likely explanation for the existence of Jupiter's moons. Explain why this is a more likely explanation than the collision hypothesis.

Asteroid collisions

Figure 14.3 shows a place in Arizona, United States, called 'Meteor Crater'. It is 1200 m wide and 170 m deep, with raised ground around its edges that rises to 45 m above the surrounding land. Scientists have used computer modelling to determine what caused this wide, deep hole in the ground.

14.3 *Meteor Crater in Arizona, United States.*

The modelling suggests that a solid piece of rock, containing nickel and iron and about 50 m across, hit the surface of the Earth. It was travelling at about 13 000 metres per second, and the force of the collision caused the moving rock and a large area of Earth's crust to explode and turn to gas and dust.

The piece of rock came from an asteroid that was pulled into the Earth's atmosphere by the force of gravity. An asteroid that enters the atmosphere in this way is called a **meteor**. Most of this meteor would have been burnt away due to friction between the fast-moving rock and the air. Only a small part of the meteor was left when it reached the ground, yet it still caused a very large crater.

Some of the original meteor can be left behind after the collision, as a piece of rock called a **meteorite**. In the case of Meteor Crater in Arizona, the meteorite was destroyed in the explosion.

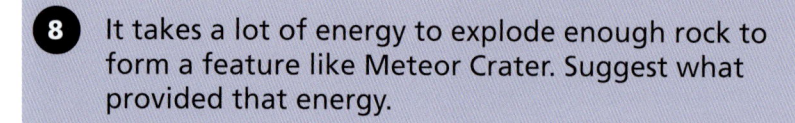

14.4 *Meteorite sample.*

> **7** Explain why a meteorite is much smaller than the meteor it came from.
>
> **8** It takes a lot of energy to explode enough rock to form a feature like Meteor Crater. Suggest what provided that energy.
>
> **9** Why can we see so many craters on the Moon caused by collisions, but very few on Earth?

Key terms

meteor: an asteroid that enters the Earth's atmosphere.

meteorite: the piece of rock that is left behind after a meteor collides with the Earth's surface.

shock wave: the squeezing of a volume of air caused by an explosion, resulting in a wave of high pressure that spreads out from the explosion.

The effects of asteroid collisions

Scientists have found evidence that much larger asteroids collided with Earth in the past. By comparing the energy released in these collisions with other major events such as earthquakes and volcanoes, scientists suggest that effects of these collisions would include:

- melting or exploding rocks thrown large distances from the point of impact
- blasts of intense heat radiating outwards from the impact
- **shock waves**, in which air around the impact is squeezed into a smaller volume, causing rings of very high pressure that expand outwards at high speed
- sudden gusts of wind at extreme speeds
- tsunamis, if the impact is in or near an ocean
- shaking of the Earth's crust
- clouds of dust and gas thrown high into Earth's atmosphere

All these effects can cause significant damage to the ground, plants and animals over large areas of Earth's surface.

14.1

Evidence from fossils shows that around 230 million years ago, the Earth was home to hundreds of species of dinosaurs. Yet around 65 million years ago, nearly all these species had become extinct. There were other significant changes too:

- The fossil records suggest that huge areas of forest were destroyed at around the same time, possibly as a result of massive fires.
- Many other species of animals also became extinct around this time; in fact, around 75% of the animal species on Earth died out, leaving only smaller mammals, birds, reptiles, fish and amphibians.

The most likely explanation for this **mass extinction** is called the Alvarez hypothesis, named after Luis and Walter Alvarez, who proposed in 1980 that an asteroid about the size of a large mountain collided with Earth around 66 million years ago.

The effects of an asteroid impact on this scale would have been enormous. In particular, gas, dust and rock fragments would have been thrown high into the atmosphere. The amounts produced would have caused the Earth's climate to change significantly.

Science in context: Making models of asteroid impacts

We know that asteroids have collided with Earth in the past, and we know that there are thousands of asteroids in the Solar System. Therefore teams of scientists find as much evidence as they can of past asteroid collisions, and use this to build a mathematical model that can predict what the effects would be of different sized asteroids colliding with Earth. They also measure the movements of known asteroids to predict when each asteroid might come close to Earth.

Since the Alvarez hypothesis was proposed, teams of scientists have looked for evidence to support it. The key evidence supporting the hypothesis includes:

1. Unusually large amounts of the element iridium in rock layers from around 66 million years ago. Iridium is normally rare on Earth but has been found in higher percentages within meteorites.
2. Images from satellites and from the work of geologists show there is a large impact crater centred on the town of Chicxulub, near the coast of Mexico. This crater is almost 150 km in diameter, and rock samples from its edges show it was formed about 66 million years ago.
3. Fossils discovered in North Dakota, in the United States, in 2019 showed that there was an entire ecosystem of plants and animals that died out around 65 million years ago. The rock layers containing these fossils also contained large numbers of pieces of glassy rock, formed when rocks were melted rapidly and then cooled.

Key term

mass extinction: when a very large number of species of living things become extinct over a short time.

It is fortunate that asteroids of this size rarely come close to Earth. Scientists estimate an impact of this size would happen on Earth only once every few hundred million years.

Activity 14.3: Predicting the effects of collisions with different sizes of asteroids

Scientists around the world record the sizes and movements of thousands of asteroids to predict which asteroids are most likely to collide with Earth, and which would have the largest effects on Earth if they did collide.

Table 14.2 shows a set of data about four different asteroids observed in our Solar System.

Asteroid	Diameter	Estimated average chance that an asteroid of this size will collide with Earth
A	4 m	1 every 1.3 years
B	20 m	1 every 60 years
C	500 m	1 in every 500 000 years
D	over 10 km	1 in every 250 million years

Table 14.2

Table 14.3 lists the effects of the asteroids thought to have caused the Meteor Crater in Arizona and the Chicxulub Crater in Mexico.

Asteroid	Diameter	Effects
Produced Meteor Crater, Arizona	50 m	• Crater 1200 m wide • Area of crust the size of the crater exploded and turned to gas and dust • Large explosion and local fires • Death of animals and plants within several km of impact • No mass extinction • Dust and gas in atmosphere but no long-lasting climate change • Minor shaking of the crust
Produced Chicxulub Crater, Mexico	between 10 km and 80 km	• Crater 150 000 m wide • Area of crust the size of the crater exploded and turned to gas and dust • Huge explosion and fires for hundreds of km • Death of animals and plants within hundreds of km of impact • Permanent climate change • Mass extinction of 75% of species of living things • Major shaking of the crust

Table 14.3

Compare the size of each asteroid in table 14.2 with the two asteroids in table 14.3.

Astronomy

14.1

A1 Why are the diameters in table 14.3 listed as 'estimated'? Include in your answer a suggestion for how these diameters can be estimated.

A2 Predict which asteroids would have less of an effect on Earth than the one which caused Meteor Crater, Arizona. Explain your answer.

A3 Predict which asteroids would have a similar effect on Earth to the one which caused Chicxulub Crater, Mexico.

A4 Why is there no 'estimated chance that it will collide with Earth' column in table 14.3?

A5 Suggest which asteroids in table 14.2 appear most likely to collide with Earth.

A6 Asteroids below 20 m in diameter usually do not reach the ground. Explain why not.

A7 Compare your answers to questions A2 and A3. Suggest how concerned we should be about the chances of a mass extinction due to an asteroid collision.

10 The Chicxulub crater is likely to have been formed by the impact of an asteroid. Describe *three* other effects of such an impact.

11 Suggest how changes in the amounts of dust and gas present in the atmosphere could cause climate change.

12 Explain why the impact of a smaller asteroid, such as that which caused Meteor Crater in Arizona, is unlikely to have caused the mass extinction of animal and plant species.

13 Some scientists suggest that many of the effects used as evidence for the impact of an asteroid could also be produced by huge volcanoes. Describe which pieces of evidence could be produced in this way.

Key facts:
- The collision theory suggests that an asteroid colliding with the Earth caused the formation of the Moon.
- The impact of an asteroid on Earth can cause many effects, including an explosion, shock waves, tsunami, extremely high winds, ground shaking and clouds of dust and gas.
- Around 65 million years ago, about 75% of the species on Earth became extinct, including the dinosaurs.
- The best hypothesis to explain this extinction is that an asteroid collided with Earth.

Check your skills progress:
- I can describe the evidence for the collision theory of the formation of the Moon.
- I can describe the evidence for the impact of an asteroid causing mass extinctions.
- I can explain how models are developed and used to understand past asteroid collisions and predict future collisions.

Chapter 14. Topic 2

Observing the Universe

You will learn:
- To understand how stars can form from the clouds of dust and gas known as nebulae
- To understand that models and analogies can change according to scientific evidence
- To describe the uses, strengths and limitations of models and analogies
- To use scientific knowledge and understanding to suggest a testable hypothesis
- To plan investigations used to test hypotheses
- To use observations, measurements, secondary sources of information and keys, to organise and classify organisms, objects, materials, or phenomena
- To interpret results and form conclusions using scientific knowledge and understanding
- To use scientific knowledge to make predictions
- To evaluate how well the prediction is supported by the evidence collected
- To carry out practical work in a safe manner to minimise risks
- To identify hazards and minimise risks
- To evaluate experimental method, explaining any improvements suggested

Starting point

You should know that...	You should be able to...
The Solar System formed from a cloud of dust and gas	Identify the stages of a cycle
The force of gravity causes areas of dust and gas to pull together forming stars, gaseous planets and rocky planets	Describe how scientific hypotheses can be supported or contradicted by evidence

Nebulae

When we look up into the night sky, we can see thousands of stars because they produce their own light. We can also see the light from the Sun as it reflects off the Moon and the other planets in our Solar System. However, the stars and planets only account for a small percentage of all the **matter** in the Universe. Much more matter is found in the form of dust and gas.

Most of the gas we can observe between stars contains just two elements: hydrogen and helium. There is about three times as much hydrogen as helium. A much smaller amount of the matter between stars forms dust, containing mainly the elements carbon, silicon and oxygen. Some of this gas and dust is gathered together in clouds that we call **nebulae**.

Key terms

matter: any substance that has mass, which is usually made up of atoms or molecules containing protons, neutrons and electrons.

nebula (plural nebulae): a cloud of interstellar gas and dust.

Some nebulae are produced when a very large star explodes at the end of its life. Other nebulae are produced when the force due to gravity causes interstellar gas and dust to gather together.

We can observe a nebula when the light from nearby stars reflects off it or is blocked by it. Sometimes radiation that passes through the nebula causes atoms of gas to gain energy, which then re-emit the energy as light that we can see. Figure 14.5a shows the Orion Nebula – the pink colour is produced by light emitted by hydrogen gas. Figure 14.5b shows the Horsehead Nebula, which looks dark because dust blocks the light from the stars and gas behind it.

14.5a *Orion Nebula.*

14.5b *Horsehead Nebula.*

Activity 14.4: Classifying nebulae

Some nebulae have been forming because a star has exploded. Other nebulae are places where stars are forming. This activity investigates how our observations of nebulae can help us tell the difference between them.

Figure 14.6 shows images of two nebulae: 14.6a shows a nebula formed recently after a star exploded and 14.6b shows a nebula where stars are forming.

14.6a *The Crab Nebula, which is expanding outwards from a star that exploded at its centre.*

14.6b *The Omega Nebula, showing a number of newly formed stars.*

Observing the Universe

A1 Compare the two pictures and describe the differences you can see between the nebulae.

A2 Suggest a hypothesis to explain your observations. This should take the form 'Nebulae formed by stars exploding show … because …, but nebulae where stars are forming show … because …'.

A3 Describe how you could find more evidence to support or contradict your hypothesis.

A4 Describe how computer modelling could be used to make predictions using your hypothesis.

A5 Evidence might be found in future that contradicts your hypothesis. Describe the correct scientific approach to using this evidence.

Star formation

When a nebula is formed by the force due to gravity, the dust and gas are slowly pulled together. Some parts of the nebula become denser, and atoms of hydrogen are pulled closer to each other. Eventually the forces of attraction become so strong that the nuclei of pairs of hydrogen atoms merge in a process called **nuclear fusion**. This process releases huge amounts of energy, in the form of electromagnetic waves including visible light and infra-red radiation. A star has been formed. The dense parts of a nebula in which new stars are formed is known as a **stellar nursery**.

There are many star-forming nebulae that we can observe in our galaxy, the Milky Way. Figure 14.7 shows one.

There is a wide range of sizes of stars. Some are much larger than our Sun. A massive star of that type expands at the end of its life to form a huge stars called a **red supergiant** before collapsing suddenly, creating a massive explosion called a **supernova**. After the explosion, layers of gas and dust are thrown off at huge speeds. This gas and dust forms a nebula centred on the position of the original star.

14.7 *The Eagle Nebula contains gas and dust in which new stars are forming.*

Key terms

nuclear fusion: process in which the nuclei of two atoms are merged together, releasing large amounts of energy.

red supergiant: a huge, red-coloured star that is formed when a massive star expands towards the end of its life.

stellar nursery: the dense part of a nebula in which new stars are formed.

supernova: the explosion of a massive star at the end of its life, which produces a nebula.

Making links

Stage 7 Topic 11.1 describes how the Sun and planets formed from a solar nebula.

a) Compare this process to the formation of stars in nebulae outside our Solar System.

b) Predict whether you would expect planets to form around these other stars. Justify your answer.

14.2

Activity 14.5: Building a life cycle of very large stars

Astronomers think that most of the matter that forms stars goes through a life cycle. This hypothesis depends on linking the nebulae that are formed by exploding stars to the nebulae that are forming stars.

Work in pairs. You will need a large sheet of plain paper, a ruler and suitable pens and pencils to complete this activity.

A1 Use a pencil and ruler to divide the paper into four roughly equally sized areas, arranged in a circle.

A2 In the area nearest the top, draw or describe a nebula. List the gases and materials that form the dust in a nebula.

A3 Use the other areas to draw the stages in a life cycle of a massive star. Add arrows to show how the stages are ordered.

A4 Write a short description of what happens at each of your stages.

A5 Suggest how astronomers could look for evidence for each stage of the process.

Key facts:

✔ Nebulae are clouds of interstellar dust and gas.

✔ Nebulae mostly contain the gases hydrogen and helium.

✔ Nebulae can be formed by exploding massive stars at the end of their lives.

✔ Dust and gas in some nebulae are slowly being pulled together by the force of gravity, eventually forming new stars powered by nuclear fusion of hydrogen.

Check your skills progress:

- I can organise the processes of a star's life into a cycle.

- I can describe how to observe nebulae to determine whether they are star-forming areas or have been produced by exploding stars.

- I can describe how evidence supports or contradicts a hypothesis, and how to amend a hypothesis when new evidence appears.

Observing the Universe

End of chapter review

Quick questions

1. Name the theory that is the most likely explanation for the formation of the Moon.

    a capture

    b collision

    c co-formation

    d combustion

2. Name the type of force that causes most of the rock in a meteor to burn away before it collides with the Earth.

    a gravity

    b magnetism

    c combustion

    d friction

3. Which of the following can be caused by an asteroid colliding with Earth?

    a tsunami

    b climate change

    c high winds

    d all of the above

4. Name the element that forms the biggest proportion of the Universe.

    a oxygen

    b hydrogen

    c helium

    d carbon

5. Name the process that takes place within a star to produce light and infra-red radiation.

    a ionisation

    b nuclear fission

    c nuclear fusion

    d radioactivity

6. (a) Describe *two* effects of an asteroid impact on the Moon.

   (b) Describe *two* effects of an asteroid impact that could occur on Earth but could not occur on the Moon.

7. (a) Describe *one* process that produces a nebula.

   (b) Describe how observing a nebula could provide evidence to support ideas about the formation of our Solar System.

8. (a) Describe the difference between a theory and a hypothesis.

   (b) Describe *three* methods that have been used to obtain evidence for the formation of the Moon.

Connect your understanding

9. Use the words from the box to complete the following sentences. Some words may not be used.

meteor	asteroid	gravity	crater	rock

   Asteroids are objects in space which are made out of ....

   Some asteroids can be pulled towards the Earth by the force of ....

   Once an asteroid enters the Earth's atmosphere it becomes a ....

   which may collide with the Earth's surface to make a hole in the ground known as a ....

10. Figure 14.8 shows a meteorite.

    14.8

    (a) Suggest what type of object in the Solar System the meteorite came from.

    (b) Describe when and how objects like these formed.

    (c) Scientists believe that by analysing the contents of a meteorite, we can find evidence of what the early Solar System contained. Explain why this is.

    (d) Comment on the size of the meteorite compared to the object it came from, and explain any differences.

11. Figure 14.9 shows a nebula.

    14.9

    (a) Describe what a nebula contains.

    (b) Explain *three* different reasons why we can see light from a nebula.

    (c) Explain why large parts of this nebula appear pink or red.

    (d) Explain the importance of the substance that causes the nebula to appear pink or red.

12. (a) State the *two* main types of nebulae.

    (b) Some nebulae are called 'nurseries for stars'. Suggest what you think this means.

    (c) Describe the differences we can observe between the two main types of nebulae.

    (d) Explain the connection between the two main types of nebulae.

13. Figure 14.10 shows the life cycle of a massive star.

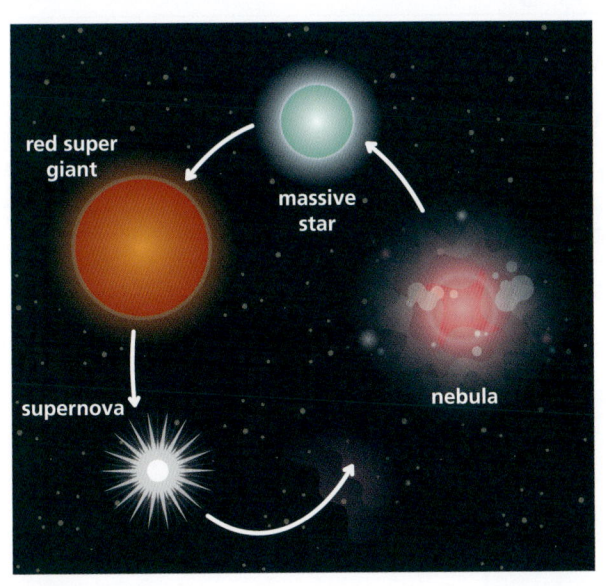

14.10

(a) State *two* ways that the formation of stars within a nebula is a similar process to the formation of our Solar System.

(b) Astronomers have observed hundreds of planets orbiting stars other than our Sun. Explain how observing these stars and planets can help us understand more about our own Solar System.

(c) Explain why the life cycle of the star is shown as a circle.

(d) A scientist called Carl Sagan said that 'we are made of star-stuff'. Explain what you think he meant.

14. A large area of the Earth's crust appears to form what is called the Chicxulub crater. This is used as evidence in support of the Alvarez hypothesis.

(a) State the Alvarez hypothesis.

(b) Explain how the Chicxulub crater provides evidence in support of the Alvarez hypothesis.

(c) Describe *two* other types of evidence found further away from the crater that suggest an asteroid impact occurred at this time.

Challenge question

(d) It is not certain that the Alvarez hypothesis is correct. Explain how the evidence could be interpreted in a different way to support a different hypothesis.

End of stage review

1. Select the *two* items that provide evidence for the theory of plate tectonics.
   a the distribution of glaciers around the world
   b matching rock layers in the coastlines of separate continents
   c matching fossils of land-based animals in separate continents
   d matching fossils of flying animals in separate continents

2. The diagram shows a set of linked processes.

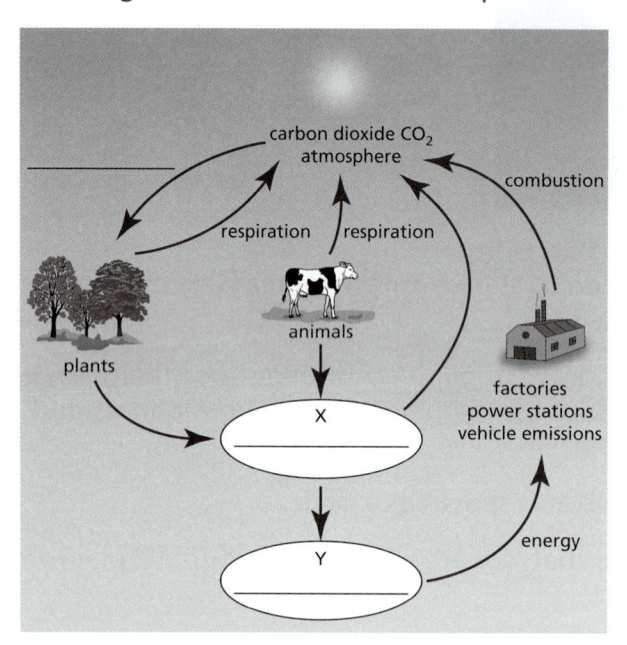

   (a) State what this diagram represents.
   (b) Name the missing text labelled **X** and **Y**.

   X = _____

   Y = _____

   (c) State the correct label for the process linking carbon dioxide to plants.
   (d) Write a word equation for the process labelled 'respiration'.

3. (a) State what is meant by the term 'drought'.
   (b) Predict *two* effects on droughts of the widespread use of fossil fuels. Justify your answers.

4. Describe *three* possible effects of an asteroid impact on Earth.

5. The image shows two nebulae.

   (a) State what materials a nebula contains.

   (b) Explain *two* processes that mean a nebula can be seen.

   (c) Describe how new stars form in some nebulae.

Periodic Table

1	2											3	4	5	6	7	0
																	4 **He** helium 2
7 **Li** lithium 3	9 **Be** beryllium 4											11 **B** boron 5	12 **C** carbon 6	14 **N** nitrogen 7	16 **O** oxygen 8	19 **F** fluorine 9	20 **Ne** neon 10
23 **Na** sodium 11	24 **Mg** magnesium 12											27 **Al** aluminium 13	28 **Si** silicon 14	31 **P** phosphorus 15	32 **S** sulfur 16	35.5 **Cl** chlorine 17	40 **Ar** argon 18
39 **K** potassium 19	40 **Ca** calcium 20	45 **Sc** scandium 21	48 **Ti** titanium 22	51 **V** vanadium 23	52 **Cr** chromium 24	55 **Mn** manganese 25	56 **Fe** iron 26	59 **Co** cobalt 27	59 **Ni** nickel 28	63.5 **Cu** copper 29	65 **Zn** zinc 30	70 **Ga** gallium 31	73 **Ge** germanium 32	75 **As** arsenic 33	79 **Se** selenium 34	80 **Br** bromine 35	84 **Kr** krypton 36
85 **Rb** rubidium 37	88 **Sr** strontium 38	89 **Y** yttrium 39	91 **Zr** zirconium 40	93 **Nb** niobium 41	96 **Mo** molybdenum 42	[98] **Tc** technetium 43	101 **Ru** ruthenium 44	103 **Rh** rhodium 45	106 **Pd** palladium 46	108 **Ag** silver 47	112 **Cd** cadmium 48	115 **In** indium 49	119 **Sn** tin 50	122 **Sb** antimony 51	128 **Te** tellurium 52	127 **I** iodine 53	131 **Xe** xenon 54
133 **Cs** caesium 55	137 **Ba** barium 56	139 **La*** lanthanum 57	178 **Hf** hafnium 72	181 **Ta** tantalum 73	184 **W** tungsten 74	186 **Re** rhenium 75	190 **Os** osmium 76	192 **Ir** iridium 77	195 **Pt** platinum 78	197 **Au** gold 79	201 **Hg** mercury 80	204 **Tl** thallium 81	207 **Pb** lead 82	209 **Bi** bismuth 83	**Po** polonium 84	**At** astatine 85	**Rn** radon 86
Fr francium 87	**Ra** radium 88	**Ac**** actinium 89	**Rf** rutherfordium 104	**Db** dubnium 105	**Sg** seaborgium 106	**Bh** bohrium 107	**Hs** hassium 108	**Mt** meitnerium 109	**Ds** darmstadtium 110	**Rg** roentgenium 111							

1
H
hydrogen
1

Key

relative atomic mass
atomic symbol
name
atomic (proton) number

La lathanoids

Ac actinoids

Elements 1 to 92 are naturally occurring elements on Earth. Elements 93 and above are man-made.

Glossary

absorb: to take in or soak up; to take in energy.

adaptation: characteristic of an organism that helps it to survive in a certain ecosystem.

aerobic respiration: respiration that requires oxygen to release energy from glucose.

alkali: a base that is soluble.

alkaline solution: a solution formed when a base dissolves in water.

amplitude: the maximum height of the wave, from the centre to the top or bottom.

anomalous: result that is very different from what you expect based on other results, perhaps because you made a mistake while recording it or something unexpected happened.

balanced forces: when the resultant force is zero.

basalt: a type of rock that contains quantities of minerals that can be magnetised.

base: a compound that can react with an acid and neutralise it.

bladder: organ that stores urine.

blood vessels: tube-shaped organs that carry blood around the body.

capture hypothesis: the idea that the Moon is a large asteroid that has been pulled into orbit around the Earth.

carbohydrate: nutrient needed for energy. Examples include starch and sugars (such as glucose).

chemical property: a property that is seen when a substance takes part in a chemical change.

chemical reaction: change in which new substances are produced.

chlorophyll: green substance that absorbs light, to get energy for photosynthesis.

chloroplast: green part of a cell that contains chlorophyll.

chromosome: structure containing a molecule of DNA, which carries genetic information in genes.

coastline: outside edge of a continent, where rock meets the ocean.

co-formation hypothesis: the idea that the Moon and Earth formed together, close to each other, at the same time.

collision hypothesis: the idea that a large object roughly the same size and mass as the planet Mars collided with the Earth, releasing rocks that were pulled together to form the Moon.

combustion: chemical reaction between a substance and oxygen, which transfers energy as heat and light.

compound: substance made from elements.

concentration: a measurement of how many particles of a certain type there are in a volume of liquid or gas.

conduction: form of heat transfer in which thermal energy passes through a substance from particle to particle. Conduction occurs mainly in solids.

conservation of energy: energy cannot be created or destroyed. The total amount of energy is constant.

constructive interference: this happens when two or more waves are added together to make a bigger wave.

continuous variation: variation that can have any value within a range.

convection: form of thermal transfer in which thermal energy causes a substance to expand and rise. This then cools and sinks. Convection only occurs in gases and liquids.

convection current: the movement of particles in a fluid due to convection.

covalent bond: a bond made when a pair of electrons is shared by two atoms.

Glossary

crater: a roughly circular hole in the surface rock of a moon or planet caused by the impact of a large rock or asteroid.

crest: the highest point of a wave.

crystallisation: the formation of crystals from their solution.

Cynognathus: reptile that lived on Pangaea but became extinct over 175 million years ago; fossils found today provide evidence for plate movement.

data: numbers and words that can be organised to give information.

decomposition: process in which bacteria and fungi feed on dead animals and plants.

deduce: arrive at a logical conclusion based on available information.

density: the mass of an object divided by its volume.

destructive interference: this happens when two or more waves combine to make a smaller wave or to cancel each other out altogether.

diffusion: the spreading out of particles from where there are many (high concentration) to where there are fewer (lower concentration).

discontinuous variation: variation that has a distinct set of options or categories.

displacement reaction: chemical reaction in which a more reactive metal displaces (takes the place of) a less reactive metal from a compound, to form a new compound.

DNA: the substance that carries genetic information.

dot-and-cross diagram: a diagram used to show a covalent bond between atoms in a molecule. Electrons are represented by dots or crosses.

drought: unusually long period with low or no rainfall, causing water shortages.

drug: any substance that changes something about the way your body works.

ecosystem: all the organisms and the physical factors in an area.

egg cell: female gamete.

electrons: very small negatively charged particles in an atom.

element: substance that contains only one type of atom.

embryo: small ball of cells that develops from a fertilised egg cell. It becomes attached to the uterus lining and develops into a fetus.

emit: give out energy in the form of radiation.

endangered: a species is endangered if there are not many individuals left alive.

environment: the other organisms and physical factors around a certain organism.

environmental variation: variation in characteristics caused by an organism's surroundings.

evaporation: when a liquid turns into a gas, at a temperature lower than the boiling point. An evaporating liquid takes energy with it and so it cools the surface it was evaporating on; separating technique used to remove water from a solution.

evolution: a gradual change in something over time.

excretion: getting rid of wastes that are made inside an organism.

excretory system: organ system that removes wastes from the blood and produces urine.

extinction: when a species dies out completely.

fertilisation: when an egg cell nucleus and a sperm cell nucleus fuse (join) and form a fertilised egg cell.

fertilised egg cell: cell produced when a sperm and egg cell fuse.

Glossary

filtration: separating technique used to remove an insoluble solid from a solution.

flood defences: walls, banks and other constructions designed to prevent flooding.

fluid: a substance that can flow from one place to another – a gas or a liquid.

formula: shows the chemical symbols of elements in a compound, and how many of each type of atom there are.

fossil fuels: remains of dead organisms that can be burned to release energy, including methane (natural gas), coal and oil.

fossils: remains of dead organisms from many millions of years ago that have solidified due to the pressure of sedimentary rocks forming above them.

frequency: the number of times an event occurs; the number of waves per second.

frequency diagram: any diagram showing the frequency of something.

gamete: specialised cell needed for sexual reproduction.

gene: section of DNA that controls the development of a specific characteristic.

genetic material: substance found in a cell that controls how the cell develops and what it does. The genetic material of most organisms is DNA.

giant structure: an element or compound that is made up of atoms or ions joined together by strong bonds.

Glossopteris: plant that lived on Pangaea but became extinct over 175 million years ago; fossils found today provide evidence for plate movement.

glucose: sugar made by digesting carbohydrates (in animals) and by photosynthesis (in plants).

group: column in the Periodic Table.

guard cell: cell that helps form a stoma in a leaf, to allow gases in and out.

hazard: harm that something may cause.

hertz: the unit of frequency. 1 Hz = one complete wave every second.

hydrocarbon: substance containing molecules made only of carbon and hydrogen.

inert: unable to take part in a chemical reaction.

infrasound: sound waves with a frequency too low for humans to hear.

inheritance: passing of features from parents to children.

inherited variation: variation in characteristics caused by an organism's parents.

insulator: a material which is a poor thermal conductor.

interference: what happens when two or more waves meet and their effects are added together.

invasive species: a non-native species that damages an ecosystem.

iodine solution: liquid that turns from orange to blue-black when added to starch.

ion: an atom which has gained at least one electron to be negatively charged or lost at least one electron to be positively charged.

ionic bond: an attraction between a positively charged ion and a negatively charged ion.

joule: the scientific unit for energy. Its abbreviation is J. 1000 J = 1 kilojoule (kJ); 1 000 000 J = 1 megajoule (MJ).

kidney: an organ that removes waste substances from the blood.

kinetic energy: energy stored by an object because it is moving.

Lystrosaurus: reptile that lived on Pangaea but became extinct over 175 million years ago; fossils found today provide evidence for plate movement.

Glossary

magnetic alignment: occurs where rocks that are magnetised produce magnetic fields that line up with the Earth's magnetic field.

magnetic field reversal: process where the direction of Earth's magnetic field changes to be in the opposite direction.

mantle: deep layer of molten rock underneath the Earth's crust.

mass: the amount of matter in an object – it is measured in grams or kilograms.

mass extinction: when a very large number of species of living things become extinct over a short time.

matter: any substance that has mass, which is usually made up of atoms or molecules containing protons, neutrons and electrons.

Mesosaurus: reptile that lived in fresh water on and near Pangaea but became extinct over 175 million years ago; fossils found today provide evidence for plate movement.

meteor: an asteroid that enters the Earth's atmosphere.

meteorite: the piece of rock that is left behind after a meteor collides with the Earth's surface.

minerals: nutrients that living organisms need in small amounts for health, growth and repair. Also called mineral salts.

mitochondria: organelles (parts) in cells where respiration occurs.

molecule: a group of two or more atoms joined together.

natural selection: the process by which organisms have (by chance) better adaptations for new environmental conditions, making them more likely to survive and reproduce than other individuals of that species.

nebula (plural nebulae): a cloud of interstellar gas and dust.

neutrons: particles with no charge in the nucleus of an atom.

nuclear fusion: process in which the nuclei of two atoms are merged together, releasing large amounts of energy.

nucleus: the central part of an atom – contains protons and neutrons.

nutrition: life process by which plants and animals take in and break down substances and use them to get the nutrients needed for other life processes.

organ system: group of organs working together.

Pangaea: supercontinent on Earth that broke apart about 175 million years ago.

parallel circuit: a circuit made up of more than one loop.

period: row in the Periodic Table.

Periodic Table: how the elements are arranged, in order of their atomic number.

photosynthesis: a series of chemical reactions in which carbon dioxide and water are converted to glucose and oxygen.

physical property: the property that can be observed or measured without changing the basic nature of the substance.

pitch: how high or low a sound is.

pollutant: a substance in an ecosystem that can cause harm to organisms.

pollution: when a substance in an ecosystem causes harm to organisms.

population: the total number of individual organisms of one species living in a certain area.

potential energy: the amount of stored energy an object has because of its position.

Glossary

predator: animal that hunts and eats other animals (called prey).

prey: animal that is hunted and eaten by other animals (called predators).

product: substance made during a chemical reaction.

protons: positively charged particles in the nucleus of an atom.

radiation: form of energy transfer in which thermal energy is released as infra-red radiation. There is no change in matter for energy to transfer in this way.

range: the highest and lowest values in a set of data.

rate of reaction: how fast a chemical reaction happens.

raw material: another term for reactant.

reactant: substance that changes in a chemical reaction to form products.

reactivity: how likely it is that a substance will undergo a chemical reaction.

reactivity series: series of metals written in order from the most reactive to the least reactive.

red supergiant: a huge, red-coloured star that is formed when a massive star expands towards the end of its life.

reliable: measurements are reliable when repeated measurements give results that are very similar.

renal system: another name for the excretory system.

repeatable: results that are the same each time they are taken, when the same method and equipment are used.

resistance: a measure of how difficult it is for current to flow. Measured in ohms.

resistor: a device which resists the flow of current.

respiration: process by which organisms release energy through the conversion of glucose and oxygen to carbon dioxide and water.

resultant force: shows the single total force acting on an object when all the forces acting on it are added up.

risk: chance of a hazard causing harm.

robotic: describes a device that works by itself, without a human needing to control its movements.

root hair cell: plant cell found in roots that is adapted for taking in water quickly.

salt: a type of compound that consists of metal atoms joined to non-metal atoms, e.g. sodium chloride.

series circuit: a circuit made up of a single loop.

sex cell: another term for a gamete.

sex chromosome: chromosome that comes in two types, X and Y. Sex chromosomes control whether someone is male (XY) or female (XX).

sex determination: how a person's sex (whether they are male or female) is controlled.

sexual reproduction: the type of reproduction involving male and female gametes coming together.

shells: the paths or orbits that electrons move along in an atom.

shock wave: the squeezing of a volume of air caused by an explosion, resulting in a wave of high pressure that spreads out from the explosion.

simple structure: an element or compound that is made up of molecules.

sink: something that takes in and stores significant quantities of a particular substance (for example, plants act as a sink for carbon dioxide).

Glossary

source: something that produces significant quantities of a particular substance (for example, animals and plants act as a source for carbon dioxide).

sperm cell: male gamete.

starch: large, insoluble carbohydrate made by plants to store energy and an important energy source in human diets.

stellar nursery: the dense part of a nebula in which new stars are formed.

stillborn: the term used to describe a baby that is dead when it is born.

stoma (plural stomata): hole in a leaf, formed between two guard cells.

sugar: soluble carbohydrate, which exists as small molecules. Glucose is an example.

supercontinent: area of land where a number of continents were joined together.

supernova: the explosion of a massive star at the end of its life, which produces a nebula.

surface area: the area of a surface, measured in squared units such as square centimetres (cm^2).

symbol equation: way of showing a chemical reaction using formulae – a balanced symbol equation has equal numbers of each type of atom on both sides of the equation.

tally chart: a table used to help count things.

temperature: a measure of how hot or cold something is. It is the average amount of thermal energy in a substance.

theory: idea or set of ideas that explains an observation.

theory: a hypothesis with enough supporting evidence that it is thought to be the most likely explanation for a process.

thermal energy: energy stored in an object due to its temperature.

transpiration: the loss of water vapour through the stomata on the surface of the leaves.

trough: the lowest point of a wave.

ultrasound: sound waves with a frequency too high for humans to hear.

unbalanced forces: when there is a resultant force.

upthrust: the upwards force on an object from the liquid or gas in which it is floating.

urea: main waste substance removed from the blood by the kidneys.

ureter: tube-shaped organ that carries urine from a kidney to the bladder.

urethra: tube-shaped organ that carries urine from the bladder to outside of the body.

urinate: to release urine from the bladder.

urine: liquid containing urea and other wastes.

variation: differences between characteristics.

voltage: a measure of energy in a circuit.

voltmeter: device for measuring voltage.

volume: the amount of space an object takes up, measured in cm^3.

waveform: the shape of a wave.

wavelength: the length of one complete wave.

whole number: number without fractions or a decimal point.

wild fires: large fires in natural areas, which spread quickly due to dry and dead plants, often made worse in a drought.

wilting: when a plant becomes floppy due to lack of water.

word equation: model showing what happens in a chemical reaction, with reactants on the left of an arrow and products on the right.

xylem cell: plant cell that is adapted to form hollow tubes to transport water.

xylem vessel: tube formed by the joining of many dead xylem cells.

Index

A
absorption 273
    of energy 157–158
    of water 13
acids 118–123
adaptations 55–57, 67–69, 273
    leaves 6–7
aerobic respiration 7, 234–235, 238, 273
aerographite 106
air 171–172
all-electric vehicles (EVs) 146
Alvarez hypothesis 259
amplitude 193–195, 198, 273
anomalous results 2, 3, 273
artificial photosynthesis 5
asteroid collisions 257–261
atomic number 83–86
atomic structure 82–86

B
balanced forces 165–168, 273
basalt 220, 273
bases 119, 273
bird adaptations 56
bladder 27, 273
blood vessels 27, 29, 273
boiling 158–160
bonding 93–97

C
capture hypothesis 252–253, 273
carbohydrates 7–8, 273
carbon capture 111
carbon cycle 231, 232–239
carbon dioxide 110–111, 232–239
carbonates 118–120
chemical bonds 93–97
chemical properties 87, 88, 273
chemical reactions 3–4, 108–139, 273
    changes in 109–113
    displacement reactions 124–127, 274
    equations and formulae 114–117
    methods for making salts 118–123
    rates of reaction 128–134, 277
chlorophyll 4–5, 9, 273
chloroplasts 4, 233, 273
chromosomes 41–43, 47, 48–49, 273
climate change 111, 231, 240
    impacts 240–247
coastlines 211–213, 273
co-formation hypothesis 252–253, 273
collision hypothesis 252–253, 255–256, 273
collisions 252–261
combustion 110–111, 112, 232, 235–237, 273
compounds 7, 93, 116–117, 273
concentration 131–132, 273
conduction 152–154, 273
conservation
    of energy 113, 143–147, 273
    of mass 110–112
constructive interference 201, 273
continental coasts 211–213
continuous variation 35–38, 273
convection 154–156, 273
convection currents 154–156, 224–227, 273
    effect on tectonic plates 224–227
cooling by evaporation 159
coral reef bleaching 40
covalent bonds 94–95, 98, 99–100, 273
craters 255, 258, 274
crests 200–202, 274
crystallisation 121–123, 274
current 175–183
    series and parallel circuits 184–189, 276, 277
Cynognathus 218, 274

D
Darwin, Charles 33, 58–61
data 36, 274
decomposition 232, 234, 235, 236, 274
density 103–106, 274
    floating and 169–172
deserts 68–69
destructive interference 201–202, 204, 274
dialysis 29
diamonds 98, 102
diet during pregnancy 51
diffusion 6, 274
discontinuous variation 34–35, 274
diseases 54, 70–71
displacement reactions 124–127, 274
dissipation of energy 144, 150
DNA 41–43, 274
dot-and-cross diagrams 94, 274
droughts 240–242, 245, 274
drugs 52, 54, 274

E
earthquakes 214–216, 225
Earth's magnetic field 220–222
East African Rift System 215
ecosystems 55, 67–71, 274
egg cells 44–49, 54, 274
electricity 175–189
    series and parallel circuits 184–189
    voltage and resistance 175–183

Index

electrons 83, 84, 274
    arrangement 84–85
elements 7, 274
embryo 46, 50–51, 274
endangered species 72, 274
energy 141–163
    conservation 113, 142–147, 273
    heating and cooling 148–151
    measuring energy changes 145–146
    thermal *see* thermal energy
environment 68–70, 274
environmental variation 38–40, 274
evaporation 121–123, 158–160, 274
evolution 33, 57–59, 72, 274
excretion 26, 274
excretory system 25–33, 274
extinction 71–73, 274
    mass extinction 252, 259–261, 276
extreme weather events 245–247

F
feeding 232–234, 281
fertilisation 45–49, 274
fertilisers 18–19, 127
fetal growth and development 50–54
filtration 121, 122, 275
floating 165–174
flood defences 245, 246, 275
flooding 242–245, 247
    sea flooding 245–247
formulae 115–117, 275
fossil fuels 235–237, 275
fossils 217–219, 236, 237, 259, 275
frequency (events) 37, 275

frequency (waves) 194, 197–198, 275
    range of human hearing 197–198
frequency diagrams 37, 275

G
gametes (sex cells) 44–49, 275
gases 153–154, 156, 171
genes 41–43, 59, 68, 275
genetic material 41–42, 47, 275
giant structures 98–99, 101, 275
Glossopteris 217–219, 275
glucose 3–4, 7, 234–235, 275
Group 1 (alkali metals) 85, 88–89
groups 85–86, 88–89, 275
guard cells 6, 275

H
hazards 8–9, 275
hearing, range of 197–198
heat *see* thermal energy
hertz 194, 275
hurricanes 245, 246
hydrocarbons 236, 275

I
Iceland 216
implantation 50, 275
in vitro fertilisation (IVF) 46
inert substances 125, 275
infrasound 197, 275
inheritance 47–48, 275
inherited variation 39, 41–43, 68, 275
insulators 152–154, 157, 275
interference 200–204, 275
invasive species 71, 275
iodine solution 7, 8, 275
ionic bonds 96, 98, 275
ions 98–99, 116, 275
iron 124–127

J
joules 145–146, 275

K
kidneys 26–30, 275
    problems 28–29
kinetic energy 142–145, 275

L
leaves 6–7
light 9, 10–11
light-dependent resistors (LDRs) 179, 180
lighting 188
loudness 193–199
Lystrosaurus 218, 275

M
magnetic alignment 220, 276
magnetic field reversals 220–222, 276
magnetic materials 220–222
Malawi 241
mantle 224, 276
mass 103–106, 128–129, 169, 276
    conservation of 110–113
    measuring 104–105
mass extinction 72, 259–260, 276
mass number 83–84
matter 262, 276
Mesosaurus 218, 276
metals 88, 95, 99
    reactivity 124–127
Meteor Crater 257–258, 262
meteorites 258, 276
meteors 258, 276
minerals (mineral salts) 3, 276
    and healthy plant growth 16–18
    transport in plants 12–20
mitochondria 234, 276
models of the atom 82–83

Index

molecules 93–97, 99–100, 276
Moon 251–257
    hypotheses about its formation 252–254

N

natural selection 33, 55–61, 72, 276
nebulae 262–264, 276
neutrons 83, 84, 276
noise-cancelling headphones 204
nuclear fusion 264, 276
nucleus 83, 84, 276

O

oscilloscope screen 195–196
oxygen 3–5, 233, 234–236

P

palisade cells 6
Pangaea 212–213, 276
parallel circuits 185–189, 276
particle theory 105–106, 132–133, 153
pendulum 142–144
peppered moths 60
Periodic Table 81–89, 272, 276
    and atomic structure 82–86
    trends 87–89
periods 85–86, 276
photosynthesis 2, 3–11, 275, 276
    and feeding 232–234
physical properties 87, 89, 99, 100, 276
pitch 193–199, 276
placenta 52–53
plant veins 6
plants
    growth 16–18
    photosynthesis *see* photosynthesis
    transport in 12–20

plate boundaries 214–215, 220–221, 225–227
plate tectonics 210–230
    evidence for 211–223
    explaining plate movement 224–227
polar regions 69
pollutants 73–74, 276
pollution 73–74, 276
populations 57, 276
    changes and extinction 67–76
    factors affecting size of 69–71
potential energy 142–145, 276
predators 70–71, 277
pregnancy 50–54
prey 70–71, 277
products 3–4, 114–115, 277
protons 83–84, 277
purification of salts 121

R

radiation 156–158, 277
range 36, 277
rates of reaction 128–134, 277
    factors affecting 131–134
reactants 3–4, 114–115, 277
reactivity 87–88, 125–127, 277
reactivity series 125, 277
red supergiants 264, 277
refrigeration 134
reliability 10, 277
repeatability 10, 277
resistance 178–183, 277
    voltage, current and 181–183
resistors 179–181, 277
resources 3, 67–68
respiration 232, 234–237, 277
    aerobic 7, 234–235, 236, 273
resultant force 167, 277
risks 8–9, 277

robotic devices 256, 277
root hair cells 13, 277

S

salts 125, 277
    making 118–123
sea flooding 243–245, 246
sea level change 243–245
series circuits 184–189, 277
sex chromosomes 47, 277
sex determination 47, 277
sexual reproduction 44–49, 277
Shanghai 243, 244
shells 83, 84, 85, 277
shock waves 258, 259, 277
simple structures 99, 100–101, 277
sinking 165–172
sinks 233, 237, 277
smoking 52–53
solar energy 158
soluble salts 121
sound 193–199, 200–203
    interference of sound waves 200–204
    loudness and pitch 193–199
sources 234, 235, 278
sperm cells 44–49, 278
spongy cells 6
star formation 264–265
starch 7–8, 278
stillborn babies 53, 278
stomata 6, 278
sugars 7, 278
supercontinent 212–213, 278
supernovae 264, 278
surface area 131, 133–134, 278
symbol equations 115, 278

T

tally charts 36–37, 278
temperature 131–132, 278
    and thermal energy 148–149

Index

theories 109, 255, 256, 278
thermal energy 148–151, 278
    movement of 149–150
    transfer mechanisms 152–160
thermistors 179, 180
tobacco smoking 52–53
transpiration 14–16, 278
trends 87–89
troughs 200–202, 278
twins 48

U
ultrasound 197, 278
    fetal scanning 50–51
unbalanced forces 167–168, 278
Universe 262–265
upthrust 165–169, 278
urea 25, 27–29, 278
ureters 27, 278
urethra 27, 278
urination 27, 278
urine 25, 26–30, 278
uterus 46, 50

V
variation 33–40, 274, 278
    causes of 38–40
    inherited 39, 41–43, 68, 275
voice recognition systems 196–197
volcanoes 214–216, 225
voltage 176–178, 278
    resistance, current and 181–183
    series and parallel circuits 188–189
voltmeters 176–178, 188, 278
volume 103–106, 169, 278
    measuring 104–106

W
water 99, 100, 234–235
    reactions with Group 1 elements 88
    transport in plants 12–20
waveforms 195–197, 200, 201, 278
wavelength 194, 195–196, 278
waves
    interference 200–204
    sound *see* sound
weather balloons 172
wild fires 240, 241, 278
wilting 12, 278
word equations 114–115, 279

X
xylem cells 6, 13, 279
xylem vessels 13, 14, 15, 279

Acknowledgements

The publishers wish to thank the following for permission to reproduce photographs and artworks. Every effort has been made to trace copyright holders and to obtain their permission for the use of copyright materials. The publishers will gladly receive any information enabling them to rectify any error or omission at the first opportunity.

(t = top, c = centre, b = bottom, r = right, l = left)

This textbook includes images that are licensed under the Attribution-ShareAlike 3.0 Unported (CC BY-SA 3.0) where indicated.

p 2 Stephen Moehle/Shutterstock, p 3 Elly Godfroy / Alamy Stock Photo, p 4 Frantisek Staud/Shutterstock, p 5 National Geographic Image Collection / Alamy Stock Photo, p 8 Science Photo Library, p 9 Le Do/Shutterstock, p 12 Stephen VanHorn/Shutterstock, p 13bl Aldona Griskeviciene/Shutterstock, p 15 & p 23 D. Kucharski K. Kucharska/Shutterstock, p 18 Editorial Image, LLC/Alamy Stock Photo, p 25 Alvaro German Vilela/Shutterstock, p 27 La Gorda/Shutterstock, p 29 gopixa/Shutterstock, p 33 Aldona Griskeviciene/Shutterstock, p 34t Don Mammoser/Shutterstock, p 34b Joule Sorubou/Shutterstock, p 35 Red Images, LLC / Alamy Stock Photo, p 36 ESB Professional/Shutterstock, p 38 R Kristoffersen/Shutterstock, p 39t Vichaiyut Tongmak/Shutterstock, p 39b ton koene / Alamy Stock Photo, p 40 Ethan Daniels/Shutterstock, p 41 blickwinkel / Alamy Stock Photo, p 42t Science Picture Co / Alamy Stock Photo, p 42bl A. BARRINGTON BROWN, © GONVILLE & CAIUS COLLEGE / SCIENCE PHOTO LIBRARY, p 42bc Heritage Image Partnership Ltd / Alamy Stock Photo, p 42br Science History Images / Alamy Stock Photo, p 45 EYE OF SCIENCE / SCIENCE PHOTO LIBRARY, p 47t ZouZou/Shutterstock, p 47b Kateryna Kon/Shutterstock, p 50 Roman Zaiets/Shutterstock, p 51t Igor Normann/Shutterstock, p 51b Evan Lorne/Shutterstock, p 52t Odua Images/shutterstock, p 52b Everett Collection Inc / Alamy Stock Photo, p 54 SamaraHeisz5/Shutterstock, p 55 Vaclav Sebek/Shutterstock, p 56 Vecton/Shutterstock, p 57t Universal Images Group North America LLC / Alamy Stock Photo, p 57b aleks1949/Shutterstock, p 58 Everett Historical/Shutterstock, p 60 IanRedding/Shutterstock, p 64 cgwp.co.uk / Alamy Stock Photo, p 65 Marco Maggesi/Shutterstock, p 66 sirtravelalot/Shutterstock, p 68 Cat Downie/Shutterstock, p 69t Tommy Lee Walker/Shutterstock, p 69b Jim Cumming/Shutterstock, p 71t WildMedia/Shutterstock, p 71b Brenda Smith DVM/Shutterstock, p 72 2630ben/Shutterstock, p 73 Rich Carey/Shutterstock, p 76t ANDREI RASPUTIN/Shutterstock, p 76b Sophia Granchinho/Shutterstock, p 81 Phil Degginger / Alamy Stock Photo, p 86 ITAR-TASS News Agency / Alamy Stock Photo, p 88t ANDREW LAMBERT PHOTOGRAPHY/SCIENCE PHOTO LIBRARY, p 88b sciencephotos / Alamy Stock Photo, p 89 Srg Gushchin/Shutterstock, p 92 Dario Lo Presti/Shutterstock, p 96 adapted from VectorMine/Shutterstock, p 98r Andris Torms/Shutterstock, p 99t Emre Terim/Shutterstock, p 102 ElRoi/Shutterstock, p 103 stockcreations/Shutterstock, p 105 trekandshoot/Shuterstock, p 106 Free2KnowFree2Think reprinted under Attribution-ShareAlike 3.0 Unported (CC BY-SA 3.0) https://creativecommons.org/licenses/by-sa/3.0/, p 108 Fahroni/Shutterstock, p 109 Mazur Travel/Shutterstock, p 110t Vic Lab/Shutterstock, p 110b usk75/Shutterstock, p 111t ANDREW LAMBERT PHOTOGRAPHY / SCIENCE PHOTO LIBRARY, p 111b Asianet-Pakistan/Shutterstock, p 114 adapted from Inna Bigun/Shutterstock, p 115 pupunkkop/Shutterstock, p 118 GIPHOTOSTOCK / SCIENCE PHOTO LIBRARY, p 119 GIPHOTOSTOCK / SCIENCE PHOTO LIBRARY, p 120 Paolo Gallo/Shutterstock, p 122t Swapan Photography/Shutterstock, p 122b Joerg Boethling / Alamy Stock Photo, p 127 ABCDstock/Shutterstock, p 134 frantic00/Shutterstock, p 141 StockPhotosArt/Shutterstock, p 146 petovarga/Shutterstock, p 152 Pises Tungittipokai/Shutterstock, p 158 Iosif Gromadko/Shutterstock, p 160 Agarianna76/Shutterstock, p 163 ARENA Creative/Shutterstock, p 164 Ethan Daniels/Shutterstock, p 166 NicoElNino/Shutterstock, p 170 Elenarts/Shutterstock,

Acknowledgements

p 172 Edward Haylan/Shutterstock, p 175 daniilphotos/Shutterstock, p 177tl skaljac/Shutterstock, p 177tr Nor Gal/Shutterstock, p 178b sciencephotos / Alamy Stock Photo, p 179t StockPhotosLV/Shutterstock, p 179c Sea Strong/Shutterstock, p 179b charistoone-images / Alamy Stock Photo, p 180l Cristian Storto/Shutterstock, p 180r cunaplus/Shutterstock, p 188l Pushish Images/Shutterstock, p 188r Alexander Gubernatorov/Shutterstock, p 192 Igor Bulgarin/Shutterstock, p 203 ljleoville/Shutterstock, p 210 Joaquin Corbalan P/Shutterstock, p 212t tadamichi/Shutterstock, p 212br chattanongzen/Shutterstock, p 215l adapted from NASA Space Shuttle radar topography image, p 215r Joanna Rigby-Jones/Shutterstock, p 216l Puripat Lertpunyaroj/Shutterstock, p 216r Desintegrator / Alamy Stock Photo, p 217l Breck P. Kent/Shutterstock, p 217r Catmando/Shutterstock, p 218 U.S. Geological Survey Department of the Interior/USGS, p 226 Designua/Shutterstock, p 231 Leonard Zhukovsky/Shutterstock, p 241t Quintanilla/Shutterstock, p 241c Morphius Film/Shutterstock, p 241b JULIAN LOTT/Shutterstock, p 242 Christian Wilkinson/Shutterstock, p 244 Iakov Kalinin/Shutterstock, p 246 Robert A. Mansker/Shutterstock, p 251 NASA images/Shutterstock, p 255 Cristian Cestaro/Shutterstock, p 256 Izan Maqbool/Shutterstock, p 257 Gioele Mottarlini/Shutterstock, p 258 Bjoern Wylezich/Shutterstock, p 263tl Antares_StarExplorer/Shutterstock, p 263tr Tragoolchitr Jittasaiyapan/Shutterstock, p 263bl Allexxandar/Shutterstock, p 263br NASA images/Shutterstock, p 264 Mohamed Elkhamisy/Shutterstock, p 267 abriendomundo/Shutterstock, p 268 Lukasz Pawel Szczepanski/Shutterstock, p 269 adapted from VectorMine/Shutterstock, p 271 Lukasz Pawel Szczepanski/Shutterstock.